Shaping History

Shaping History

Ordinary People in European Politics
1500–1700

Wayne te Brake

UNIVERSITY OF CALIFORNIA PRESS

Berkeley / Los Angeles / London

University of California Press
Berkeley and Los Angeles, California

University of California Press
London, England

Library of Congress Cataloging-in-Publication Data

Te Brake, Wayne Philip.
   Shaping history: ordinary people in European politics, 1500–1700 /
Wayne te Brake.
     p.   cm.
   Includes bibliographical references and index.
   ISBN 0-520-21170-7 (cloth: alk. paper). —ISBN 0-520-21318-1
(ppk.: alk. paper)
     1. Europe—Politics and government—1492–1648. 2. Europe—
Politics and governement—1648–1715. I. Title.
D231.B73   1998
940.2—dc21
                                                                97-36930
                                                                CIP

Printed in the United States of America

1 2 3 4 5 6 7 8 9

The paper used in this publication meets the minimum requirements of
American National Standard for Information Sciences—Permanence of
Paper for Printed Library Materials. ANSI Z39.48-1984

For Nelva,
Martin, Maria, and Nicholas

Contents

Figures

Preface

This work has been longer in the making than I imagined, and I would like to think that it is much the better for that fact. This apparent tardiness, I should add immediately, is not entirely my fault, as an impressively large number of people and institutions have emboldened and enabled me to write this small book about this enormous topic. The enormity of the topic is what I originally underestimated, and as a consequence the scope of my ambitions has changed dramatically even though my purpose has, I think, remained constant: to describe and account for the variety of ways in which ordinary people have shaped their own political histories. Thus I am especially pleased to acknowledge the generosity of those who have continued to support my work when it might have seemed that I had lost my bearings.

Indirectly, this book has its origins in my graduate work at the University of Michigan where a very special cohort of students and faculty introduced me to the interdisciplinary challenges of social history, contentious politics, and historical comparison. But more directly, it originated in a memorable conversation, over lunch at a favorite haunt in Greenwich Village, with two friends whose academic lives have intersected with mine in countless ways both before and since. In the summer of 1990, as I anticipated a whole year of research and writing at the Netherlands Institute for Advanced Studies in the Humanities and Social Sciences (NIAS), Michael Hanagan and Charles Tilly urged me to spend at least some portion of that year sketching out what I imagined to be the larger comparative context in which a dynamic, social, and internally comparative history of popular politics in the Dutch Republic, which I had proposed to write, would be as salient to our understanding of the course of European history as I claimed it would be. I readily agreed, but I have been wrestling with the implications of that agreement ever since. Now, if all the wrestling has been fruitful, I imagine Mike and Chuck deserve some of the credit; if not, I'll take all the blame.

One of the genuine privileges of a year at NIAS is that with the support of its excellent staff and the encouragement of one's colleagues, one can indeed wrestle with the implications of an apparently simple commitment to explore the larger comparative dimensions of an otherwise parochial research project. To be sure, I continued to lecture, write, and organize a conference on the history of contentious politics in the Dutch Republic, but by the end of that year, it was clear that I was merely at the beginning of a much larger project that has taken me far beyond the familiar boundaries of the Dutch confederation and back in time, not to the middle of the seventeenth century, but to the beginning of the sixteenth.

Since then, a number of institutions have helped to keep this project going and to bring it to its conclusion. In the summer of 1992, the Maison des Science de l'Homme, under the direction of Maurice Aymard, generously supported six weeks of very productive work in Paris, and in the summer of 1993, Professor Harry S. Stout, Master of Berkeley College at Yale University, provided both a place to work and access to the wonderful resources of the Sterling Memorial Library. Though a bicycling accident interrupted my work in the summer and fall of 1993, I was able to make up for some of the lost time during a sabbatical leave from Purchase College in the fall of 1994, during which time the Maryknoll School of Theology in Ossining provided a haven for work away from home. Then, in the winter of 1995, the Harry Frank Guggenheim Foundation awarded me a very generous two-year research grant that promised initially to interrupt my work on the social history of popular politics by focusing my attention on the "cultural politics" of religious war in early modern Europe. Much to my delight, however, this new research proved to be a substantial enrichment of my by then "old" research, and in the end gave a mighty stimulus to the completion of this work. For all of this tangible faith in the promise of my work, I am deeply grateful.

Various versions of the chapters that follow have benefited from the critical suggestions of a number of colleagues as well as numerous seminar and lecture audiences in both Europe and North America. On several occasions over many years, the Center for Studies of Social Change at the

New School for Social Research, and especially the proseminar on state formation and collective action, provided a stimulating context for the discussion and development of my work. I would also like to thank especially Anton Blok, Jeff Goodwin, Lise Grande, Michael Hanagan, Marjolein 't Hart, Dan Kryder, Kelly Moore, Olaf Mörke, Henk van Nierop, Maarten Prak, Michelle Stoddard, John Theibault, David Underdown and Dale Van Kley, all of whom read and commented on at least one piece of the manuscript without seeing the whole. Risto Alapuro, Robert M. Stein, and Charles Tilly gave me the great benefit of careful and very constructive readings of the entire manuscript. As always, Bill te Brake helped me think it all through from the very beginning.

At the University of California Press, Stanley Holwitz gave me invaluable support and encouragement from a very early date, and I am very grateful for his constancy throughout this long project. Meanwhile, my students in European history courses at Purchase College were the first audience for most of the ideas contained in this work; to those who were subjected to the half-baked versions, I offer my apologies. My graduate students at Yale University in the spring of 1997 encouraged me to do one last revision of several of the figures, and their influence should be readily visible to them. Finally, at the very last moment, Fausta Navardo and Eric Nicholson very generously helped me to acquire the cover illustration.

In more ways than they will ever know, my family—Nelva, Martin, Maria, and Nicholas—has helped me keep both my bearings and my sense of humor. They are always willing to celebrate the good times, but in this case they literally had to nurse me through the bad. This work is dedicated to them; I hope it is a worthy offering.

Ossining, New York
April 1997

Breaking and Entering

[In the pre-industrial era,] those engaging in popular disturbances are sometimes peasants. . . , but more often a mixed population of what in England were termed "lower orders" and in France menu peuple. . . ; *they appear frequently in itinerant bands, "captained" or "generaled" by men whose personality, style of dress or speech, and momentary assumption of authority mark them out as leaders; they are fired as much by memories of customary rights or a nostalgia for past utopias as by present grievances or hopes of material improvement; they dispense a rough-and-ready kind of "natural justice" by breaking windows, wrecking machinery, storming markets, burning their enemies of the moment in effigy, firing hayricks, and "pulling down" their houses, farms, fences, mills or pubs, but rarely by taking lives.* George Rudé, *The Crowd in History*

Thus, in sixteenth-century France, we have seen crowds taking on the role of priest, pastor, or magistrate to defend doctrine or purify the religious community—either to maintain its Catholic boundaries and structure, or to re-form relations within it. We have seen that popular religious violence could receive legitimation from different features of political and religious life, as well as from the group identity of the people in the crowds. The targets and character of crowd violence differed somewhat between Catholics and Protestants, depending on their sense of the source of the danger and on their religious sensibility. But in both cases, religious violence had a connection in time, place, and form with the life of worship, and the

1

violent actions themselves were drawn from a store of punitive or
purificatory traditions. . . . Even in the extreme case of religious vio-
lence, crowds do not act in a mindless way.

Natalie Zemon Davis,
Society and Culture in Early Modern France

All of these [seventeenth-century French] risings involved significant
numbers of peasants, or at least of rural people. Their frequency, and
the relative unimportance of land and landlords as direct objects of
contention within them, require some rethinking of peasant rebel-
lion. The universal orientation of these rebellions to agents of the
state, and their nearly universal inception with reaction to the efforts
of authorities to assemble the means of warmaking, underscore the
impact of statemaking on the interests of peasants. . . . In the seven-
teenth century the dominant influences driving French peasants into
revolt were the efforts of authorities to seize peasant labor, commodi-
ties, and capital.   Charles Tilly, *As Sociology Meets History*

One of the most significant developments in European
historical studies in the last four decades has been the explosion of
research that allows us to take ordinary people seriously as political
actors long before the creation of stable parliamentary democracies.
Inspired variously by such well-known examples as George Rudé's project of identifying the "faces in the crowd," Natalie Zemon Davis's careful
elucidation of the "meaning" of riots and popular protests, and Charles
Tilly's account of the changing patterns of "popular collective action," literally hundreds of scholars have set off to the archives to discover the particulars of what we might label the history of popular politics. Over the
years their research has not only enriched our sense of the variety of
actors but also revealed the diversity of their political messages and the
range of their actions. Never before have ordinary people—which is to
say, those who were excluded from the realm of officialdom; subjects as
opposed to rulers—seemed so active and noisy, so eminently capable of
shaping their own history.

So what kind of history did these ordinary Europeans make? In what
concrete ways did ordinary people influence and shape their political des-
tinies? To what extent can ordinary Europeans be said to have created
their own political futures rather than being condemned merely to suffer
the impositions of their more powerful superiors? Given the richness and
diversity of the accumulated research, it may be somewhat surprising that
there have been very few attempts to synthesize the results, but on the
face of it, most historians will find questions like these to be hopelessly

broad and impractical. To date, those authors who have sought to reassemble the myriad pieces of popular microhistory into larger packages have either limited their work to a certain category of events—such as urban riots or peasant rebellions—or focused on a relatively bounded territory—typically the domain, or some subunit, of a modern national state. Given the large and linguistically diverse literature, such limiting strategies are obviously practical, but the history of popular politics surely transcends the territorial boundaries of provinces, national states, and linguistic groups and defies the categorical limits that separate "riots" from "rebellions," "revolts" from "revolutions," and the whole lot of such events from merely nonviolent action. Indeed, unless we intentionally ask questions that transcend the categorical limits and the territorial boundaries of the current literature, we will never find the answers and thus squander the excellent opportunity we now have to replace the old elite-centered histories of European politics with something significantly new.

Building on the accumulated studies of popular collective action, then, this book attempts to synthesize what might usefully be called the social history of European politics during the particularly tumultuous era that began with the Protestant Reformation and ended with the so-called Crisis of the Seventeenth Century. If social history is concerned with how ordinary people actively "lived the big changes" in history (Tilly 1985:11), then the "early modern" period is an especially valuable laboratory, not only because of the voluminous literature on popular political behavior, but because it is replete with "big changes." Besides the disintegration of the Roman Catholic church and the consequent reshaping of the European cultural and political landscape, this period also witnessed both the rise of a European world economy and a military revolution that inaugurated the era of European domination on a global scale (see Wallerstein 1974, 1980; Parker 1988). In highlighting the political action of ordinary people in relation to the transformation of the cultural and political landscape of Europe, this study naturally takes issue with a number of scholarly interpretations of these big changes. It explicitly undermines elite-centered accounts of both the Reformation and the consolidation of a peculiarly European system of states, but it also questions more implicitly the direct correlation of capitalist development and changes in warfare with the emergent patterns of state formation in early modern Europe. In a far more constructive sense, however, my primary goal is to describe and account for the variety of ways in which ordinary people, by breaking their rulers' exclusive claims to political and cultural sovereignty and boldly entering political arenas that were legally closed to them, helped to shape the cultural and political landscape of modern Europe.

Toward a Social History of European Politics

Before we set off on this synthetic quest, it is important to recognize just how far we have already come and to clarify some of the concepts that are essential to the book's argument. Let us begin in the realm of political history by underscoring how far we are now removed from the days when historians were primarily concerned with recording or glorifying the deeds of (monarchical) rulers and their principal (military) agents. Even when elite patronage of historical writing gave way in the nineteenth century to professionalization in university departments, (political) historians still focused on war making, diplomacy, and courtly intrigue during eras characterized by "feudalism," the "new monarchies," or "absolutism"; they magisterially assigned praise or blame to the leading actors depending on their apparent success or failure in the story being told. More recently, however, historians who are directly concerned with politics have, on the whole, become much more critical of the "official story" embedded in the archives and annals of those who claimed authority over the lives of ordinary people. Focusing on the routine practice as opposed to the theoretical claims of early modern government, we now realize, for example, just how indirect and limited the authority of even "absolute" monarchs actually was; indeed, one very thoughtful analysis has recently described the "myth of absolutism" as the now-moribund product of sixteenth-century anti-French propaganda filtered through the distorting lens of nineteenth-century nationalism (Henshall 1992; see also Collins 1995). At the same time, closer attention to the differences among European states has undermined the notion of a singular, normative path of European political development and yielded instead to a more broadly comparative understanding of divergent paths of early modern state consolidation in relation both to the economic geography of preindustrial Europe and the changing fortunes and technology of war (see Rokkan 1975; Blockmans 1989; Tilly 1990; Downing 1992; Ertman 1997).

The research agendas of social historians have also changed dramatically. George Trevelyan, combating the hegemony of political history, asserted for better or worse that social history was history with the politics left out; in a similar vein the French Annales school defiantly distinguished between the *longue durée* of social, economic, and even geological processes and the mere events of political history. Not surprisingly, the social history that first gained a toehold within history curricula often emphasized the enduring social and demographic structures of premodern societies and the conservatism or even the immutability of "traditional" cultures. Still, a few pioneers like Natalie Davis, George Rudé, and Edward Thompson doggedly explored the interfaces between social and political history, identifying the faces of individual actors within riotous "crowds" and interpreting the often symbolic meaning of politically contentious action by ordinary people. Others, such as Barrington Moore, put macrohistorical questions on the research agenda—questions that linked the political actions or alignments of ordinary people with macrohistorical processes like state formation and the rise of capitalism. Still others, such as Charles Tilly and Yves-Marie Bercé, proposed that violent conflict and rebellion provided especially valuable clues to popular political aspirations and capacities because authorities usually documented them with care. Each of these strands proved to be valuable in itself, yet a healthy eclecticism and cross-fertilization have served to retard the growth of mutually antagonistic schools or camps. Gradually, then, the study of "collective action" or "collective violence" in general and "crowds," "riots," and "popular protest" in particular became quite respectable as a specialized field of inquiry within social history.

The problem is that in explicating collective behavior or reconstructing the microhistory of particular events—that is, by focusing on ordinary people as intentional actors—the current social-historical literature separates popular politics from the main line of political history. Indeed, the political actions of ordinary people are typically the *explicandum*—that which needs to be explained by independent variables outside the realm of popular politics—rather than a part of the explanation of large-scale historical change. The unfortunate result is that popular political actors are more often than not portrayed as the noble, if largely ineffectual, victims of larger historical processes far beyond their control. The challenge for the next generation of research is, as I see it, to move beyond the study of intentional action to the exploration of consequential action—to link the more fragmented histories of popular political action with the newer accounts of varied political development within Europe in ways that allow us to see the extent to which ordinary people were fully fledged political actors, capable of shaping their own history.

In other words, the specific task of the social historian of European politics is to explore the ways in which ordinary people were directly implicated in larger causal sequences that can be said to account for the different paths of political-historical change.

To envision this kind of comparative social history of politics, it is essential to define "politics" in sufficiently broad and inclusive terms—in terms that diminish the salience of such hoary questions as *whether* ordinary people were political or *when* they finally became political and highlight instead the variety of ways in which they *actually were* political prior to or outside the institutionalization of some form of popular sovereignty. To this end, it is useful to regard politics as an ongoing bargaining process between those who claim governmental authority in a given territory (rulers) and those over whom that authority is said to extend (subjects).[1] As unconventionally vague as it may seem at first blush, this is a relatively restrictive conception of politics in the sense that it singles out the interactions between rulers and their subjects or citizens.[2] It is thus not concerned with relations of power as such; nor does it focus directly on the "politics" of the bedroom or the "politics" of the workplace. This is nevertheless an expansive notion of politics in the sense that it includes within the scope of the political bargaining process, for example, popular protests that fall short of demands for the direct exercise of political authority and political movements that develop outside the realm of electoral or directly representational political systems. What makes "ordinary" people ordinary in this strictly political sense is their status as political subjects. Thus in situations in which power is concentrated in a very few hands, it is quite possible that people who in a social,

1. Cf. Reddy 1977: 89, who notes the shortcomings of bargaining theories of popular politics; he argues, in particular, that "the idea of political bargaining short circuits the question of political legitimacy." Here the idea of an ongoing political bargaining process will not be taken to exclude popular challenges to claims of political legitimacy made by or on behalf of their rulers. My argument is simply that such challenges are not different in kind from more routine political interactions where the legitimacy of established or putative rulers is not immediately or overtly at stake; indeed, all forms of extralegal or extraconstitutional political action can be said to strain at the boundaries of political legitimacy. See also Tilly 1978; Scott 1987; Tarrow 1989.

2. It is important to note, of course, that not all people who by this definition will be considered political subjects would choose this as an acceptable self-description. This applies equally to the early modern "burgher" and the modern "citizen." Still, the individual liberties or collective sovereignties typically claimed by burghers and citizens notwithstanding, the basic fact of political life is that the "many" are always governed by the "few." See Morgan 1988 for a particularly searching historical account of the "opinions" or "fictions" that can be said to sustain this fact in modern America.

economic, or cultural sense could hardly be described as ordinary are nevertheless usefully seen as "ordinary" political subjects. By extension, what makes "popular" politics popular is its position relative to the domain of rulers and the politics of the official "elite."

To see politics as an interactive bargaining process, however, is also to insist that variations and changes in the realm of popular politics cannot be treated in isolation from variations and changes in the structures of political power or, broadly speaking, the history of state formation. This means that a history of popular politics in early modern Europe, in particular, must take into account not only the long-term consolidation (or disintegration) of power within specific polities but also the gradual elaboration of an interactive system of states within Europe as a whole. But how are we to conceive of the relationship between the history of popular politics, often enacted at the local level, and the history of state formation on a much grander scale? A volume of essays on the relations between cities and states in Europe suggests a useful point of departure that allows us to build on the most recent literature: "In Europe before 1800 or so, most important changes in state structure stemmed from rulers' efforts to acquire the requisites of war, from resistance to those efforts, and from bargains that ended—or at least mitigated—that resistance" (Tilly and Blockmans 1994:10). In this way, the ongoing bargaining process between subjects and rulers, which includes, for example, the pattern of tax revolts and conscription riots that punctuated the political history of Europe from the sixteenth to the nineteenth century, necessarily becomes a central concern within any convincing account of European state formation. But even more important, such a focus on political interaction takes us beyond the motives and intentions of political actors and highlights instead the often unintended consequences of the political bargaining process. This is not to say, of course, that motives and intentions are irrelevant; rather, in the absence of reliable or unequivocal evidence in this regard, as is often the case, we can nevertheless treat popular political action as an integral part of the political process.

It is fundamentally mistaken, however, to assume that the history of popular politics is for the most part the tragic story of an essentially reactionary and futile *resistance* to the inexorable rise of a system of national states. First, we know that not all resistance to the claims of European governments was or is futile. Indeed, as we shall see in the account that follows, in the most obviously successful cases of resistance to Habsburg dynasticism, popular political action helped to precipitate and fashion entirely new polities like the Swiss Confederation and the Dutch

Republic (Brady 1985; Parker 1985; Duke 1990). In other less spectacular cases, like the widespread and predictable resistance to increasing taxation, popular action could bend and shape public policy in significant ways even though resistance was not always expressed in open revolt and most tax revolts did not result in revolutionary transformations of power (see Dekker 1982; Schulze 1984; Scott 1987; Briggs 1989; Robisheaux 1989). Second, it is obvious that the claims that European rulers made on their subjects varied significantly in time and place. In the realm of taxation alone, both the character and the extent of the state's fiscal exactions separated the more agrarian regions of Europe from their more commercialized neighbors, creating disparities not only between states but also within them (see 't Hart 1989; Tilly 1990; Collins 1995). Likewise, the patterns of military recruitment and judicial authority in Europe offered quite variable challenges and opportunities to rustics and city folk, to the inhabitants of Europe's urban, commercialized core and its more rural, agrarian periphery. But in this period it was frequently the forceful claims of a variety of rulers to an unprecedented degree of cultural sovereignty— that is, final decision-making authority in matters of religious ritual and belief for whole polities—that were met variously with resistance or approval among their subject populations. It is precisely the relationship between the resistance or cooperation of subjects and the variably enforceable demands of rulers that we need to explore through broadly conceived and systematic comparison. Finally, and perhaps most important, it is clear that not all popular political action was simply reactive; indeed, as I shall argue below, when it was directed toward the reformation of religious ritual and belief, the political action of ordinary people could serve to legitimate or extend the authority of their rulers in surprising ways. For all these reasons, then, it is important to replace the easily romanticized concept of popular "resistance" with the less colorful but more flexible and inclusive concept of "popular political practice."

The Spatial and Cultural Dimensions of Political Interaction

To reconstruct the social history of politics, then, we need not only to examine the variable forms of popular political practice but also to situate them within the different political contexts in which popular political action takes place. Traditional accounts of European state

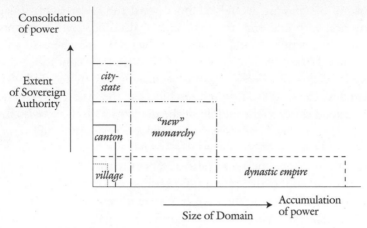

Figure 1. Variable dimensions of political space

formation, highlighting selected aspects of the experience of a few relatively centralized and autocratic monarchies, suggested a fairly direct, linear development from feudal monarchies to national states in the period between, say, 1200 and 1850 (cf. Strayer 1970). In fact, however, Europeans lived in a wide variety of political contexts at the end of the Middle Ages and, having started in different circumstances, experienced the process of state formation along widely divergent paths. To look simultaneously and comparatively at political interactions in these diverse and changing contexts, then, it is useful to think of the interactive bargaining process of politics in spatial terms. A "political space" can be defined as an arena, bounded in terms of both authority and territory, within which political bargaining can occur. The dimensions of such a political space vary, on the one hand, according to the extent to which those who rule within it exercise sovereign authority—that is, they can make independent, enforceable decisions with regard to issues of importance to their subjects—and, on the other, according to size of the domain—the physical territory and the population—over which that sovereign authority extends. Figure 1 suggests how we might visualize the dimensions of different kinds of political space.

Using this formulation of the concept of political space, it is possible to highlight graphically the differences among polities in a particular era. Around 1500, for example, city-states like Venice, with a broad range of authority concentrated in its ruling oligarchy, would stretch toward the upper left of the diagram. Dynastic empires like the expansive Habsburg imperium, by contrast, would extend toward the lower right. Village communes, with authority to make critical decisions over communal property, for example, would show up in the lower left whereas a small canton like Luzern within the Swiss Confederation concentrated an impressive degree of sovereignty, short of making war, in the hands of its magistrates. The so-called new monarchies, like the France of Francis I, would extend closer to the middle of the diagram with the proviso that the sovereign reaches of their royal governments typically exceeded their grasps.

This concept of political space also allows us to distinguish more fundamentally between two important dimensions of historical change that are frequently conflated in the notion of state formation, which in most iterations bespeaks the teleology of the modern "national" or "consolidated territorial" state (cf. Ertman 1997). In the early modern period especially—the period in which the European system of states first took shape—one must distinguish between the *accumulation* of power that typically resulted from a dynastic policy of adding new pieces of territory to an existing domain through skillful marriage alliances, inheritance, and conquest and the *consolidation* of power that was entailed in the extension of governmental authority over matters of consumption, welfare, and religion. Such distinctions obviously reflect, at bottom, the pretensions or claims of putative state makers because it is these claims that frame the extended conversations that constitute the political processes we are considering here. But the political bargaining process does not follow the directional schemes and tendencies of rulers alone. From the point of view of their political subjects, of course, movement toward the upper right along the diagonal of figure 1—that is, essentially the old, idealized linear development from feudal principalities to national states—undoubtedly seemed less desirable or inevitable than it did from the perspective of those who sought to augment and consolidate claims to sovereignty within territorial states. The point is, however, that neither the state maker's nor the state resister's perspective is sufficient. On the contrary, the actual trajectories of political development in Europe must be seen as the product of the interacting claims and counterclaims of rulers and subjects in changing times and variable spaces. To be sure, the pretensions of Europe's many rulers conditioned and channeled the political choices available to ordinary people, but choices there always were.

Since a political space can only be entered or filled by actors who are able to mobilize or deploy resources appropriate to it, the mobilization or deployment of resources within a political space can be usefully seen as both a political and a cultural process.[3] Among the existing opportunities for meaningful action afforded by specific social and political circumstances, all actors—both rulers and subjects—make choices that are bounded and mediated by cultural experience. As circumstances change, however, these actors learn to express new kinds of claims and to invent new forms of claim making.[4] Indeed, to describe and account for the choosing, the learning, and the inventing that ordinary people do in the course of filling the political spaces available to them may be considered one of the central analytical problems of the social history of politics. For it is precisely in the realm of choosing, learning, and inventing that ordinary people can be said to be making their own political history—to be shaping and enforcing essential, if often informal, bargains with their rulers.

Looking at the history of popular politics from a cultural perspective entails several different kinds of analysis. At the microhistorical level of particular communities and specific events, it is important to try to discern the political significance of often symbolically expressive collective action; for within the larger comparative history of popular politics, it is important to think of expressive actions like demonstrations and riots as an integral part of an interactive political process—as statements within an ongoing conversation. Since political bargaining requires communication, the various signs and symbols of popular collective action afford us invaluable glimpses of the range of social and cultural resources that ordinary people draw on in entering and filling the political spaces available to them. But given that repression or reprisal is a constant threat in most forms of political domination, much of the political action of subordinate populations "requires interpretation precisely because it is intended to be cryptic and opaque" (Scott 1990:137). Though it is fraught with epistemological uncertainties, the careful description and explication of various forms of popular collective action is a well-established problem in microhistorical research; indeed, it continues to be one of the most inventive and inspiring developments within the realm of "history from below."[5]

On a rather different plane, it is important to analyze and account for

3. For useful summaries of the considerable literature on resource mobilization, see especially Tilly 1978 and Tarrow 1989.
4. For a penetrating analysis of this kind of transformation at a fairly early date in England's history, see Justice 1994.
5. Excellent examples of this kind of microhistorical examination of particular events abound, but the work of historical anthropologists emphasizing the need for "thick

the cultural dynamics and consequences of multiple political interactions within particular polities, those that occur in concentrated clusters in revolutionary situations as well as more attenuated series of challenges and responses.[6] In his general accounts of the changing "repertoires" of contention in France and Great Britain, Charles Tilly (1986, 1995) explicitly uses the metaphor of jazz improvisation to suggest the cultural dimensions of the long-term history of popular political action. In his work on social movements, Sidney Tarrow (1989, 1994) also suggests more generally how we might link cycles of protest (as distinct from revolutionary situations) to cycles of reform, stressing in particular how these cycles produce and replicate innovations in the language and techniques of popular collective action. What is especially important about such relatively rare events as revolutions and widespread cycles of protest is that they usually reveal the hidden dimensions of a particular political culture.[7] But it is equally important to be attentive to subtler and less spectacular yet equally direct challenges that are often allowed within the rules of established regimes (cf. Beik 1997). Taken together, the generally accepted rules of political behavior—that is, the culturally specific "legitimacy" of political action undertaken by both subjects and rulers in specific historical settings—as well as the overall dimensions of what

description" is certainly the most sophisticated. For practical examples of historical-anthropological analysis as well as important discussions of theoretical orientation, see especially Isaac 1982 and Burke 1987. For the continuing inspiration of the work of E. P. Thompson and Natalie Davis, in particular, see the article by Suzanne Desan in Hunt 1989. James C. Scott's work (1990:esp. chap. 6) seems indispensable, however, in that it draws on the historical research on popular collective action in Europe but challenges us to go beyond the narrow definitions of political behavior that are often embedded in that literature. For examples of the distinctive genre of microhistory in Italian studies, see Levi 1988; Muir and Ruggiero 1991; Muir 1993.

6. Aya 1990 argues that in order to "bring the people back in" to the study of revolution, we must try above all to understand the *rationality* of the multiple, complex, and often difficult political choices that ordinary people have to make in such conflicted and anxious circumstances. To that end, he not only invokes the example and critical methods of cultural anthropologists but also insists on distinguishing in particular revolutionary situations between the intentions, the capabilities, and the opportunities of collective actors. Much of this comports well with what I am arguing for popular politics more generally, except that instead of "intentions" I have spoken of the "claims" of popular political actors. While I agree that ordinary people must be considered intentional actors, I am not so sure that we can with very great certainty infer their intentions from the claims they make on their rulers in the course of political negotiations.

7. This seems to be true not only because established authorities (and contemporary observers) document them with special care but also because political subordinates are often emboldened to express, in such exceptional circumstances, opinions and political claims they might normally keep hidden (see Scott 1990).

James C. Scott (1990) calls the "official transcript" may be said to constitute the dominant political culture of any given political space.

This last point brings us to the critical question of cultural innovation and, in particular, the role of ordinary people in the process of political-cultural change. This problem especially requires both a long-term and an internationally comparative perspective; for, as it happens, the most profound changes in political culture often emerge only gradually over long stretches of time, and they are often confirmed and maintained as a function of conflict and change within the larger system of states.[8] Meanwhile more or less routinized oppositions within a particular polity sometimes belie fundamental agreements in the realm of political discourse that are only evident when they are compared to other more or less routinized oppositions (cf. Schulze 1984; Prak 1991; Underdown 1996). The gradual rise and ongoing mutation of a militarily competitive system of variously sovereign states and within those states the gradual assertion and legitimation of a variety of forms of political sovereignty are but the most obvious and perennially intriguing political-cultural transformations in modern European history. The central argument of this book is that none of these innovations can be said to be the product of a specific era or of a particular polity; neither can they be said to be the work of rulers alone.

Ordinary People in European Politics (ca. 1500)

To understand more clearly the history and significance of popular political practice, we must come to a fuller appreciation of both the variety of political opportunities that political subjects enjoyed and the larger consequences of the choices that popular political actors made. The analysts of modern social movements often speak of political opportunity structures outside the "normal" channels of electoral politics; stripped of its present-minded assumptions about electoral politics, this

8. The assertion of monarchical absolutism and the consolidation of territorial states was characteristically a gradual, long-term process in both eastern and western Europe (e.g., Prussia, Austria, France, and Spain), whereas the confirmation of new revolutionary regimes typically involved both international conflict and multiparty treaty agreements recognizing their independence (e.g., the Swiss Confederation and the Dutch and American republics).

idea of geographically and temporally variable structures of political opportunity can be especially useful in the study of "informal politics" in other times and places, especially in those circumstances in which most people are excluded from formal political participation altogether.[9] In the first instance, of course, political opportunities are framed by the specific institutional structures through which rulers exercise their authority, and in this regard the relative openness of formal political structures to popular political bargaining is conditioned by the historically specific limits of governmental coercion or repression. But beyond that we can identify a number of significant variables: the relative stability of political alignments within the polity; the availability to popular political movements of influential allies; and the degree of political division among established political elites. But what is especially important (if also complicated and confusing) for understanding popular politics in the early modern period is to disentangle the multiple and overlapping structures of political opportunity that were obviously inherent within composite states.

At the beginning of the early modern period, around 1500, most Europeans lived within composite states that had been variously cobbled together from preexisting political units by a variety of aggressive "princes" employing a standard repertoire of techniques including marriage alliances, dynastic inheritance, and direct conquest. Some composites, like the Kingdom of England and Wales or the complex mosaic of *pays d'élections* and *pays d'états* in France, were composed of largely contiguous territories; others, like the Spanish Habsburg monarchy (created by the dynastic union of Castile and Aragon, each in itself a composite) or the Habsburg imperium more generally under Charles V, were separated by other states or by stretches of sea (Koenigsberger 1986; Greengrass 1991; Elliott 1992). Since the dynastic "prince" promised to respect the political customs and guaranteed the chartered privileges of these constituent political units, ordinary political subjects within composite states acted in the context of overlapping, intersecting, and changing political spaces defined by often competitive claimants to sovereign authority over them.[10] To the extent that they were oriented to a variety of political spaces defined by a variety of rulers, ordinary people could

9. I am especially indebted here to the excellent summation and theoretical extension of this literature in Tarrow 1989. See also Tilly 1978, 1986.

10. The generic "prince," in the sense of a political force accumulating territory, need not be a singular or a dynastic actor. In the case of the republic of Venice, for example, it was a closely knit oligarchy that added territory to its domain during the conquest of the terra

choose not only when and how to challenge the authority of their rulers but also where. As we shall see below, it was often in the interstices and on the margins of these composite early modern state formations that ordinary people enjoyed their greatest political opportunities.[11] By choosing to oppose the claims of some putative sovereigns, ordinary Europeans were often deliberately reinforcing the claims of constitutionally alternative or competitive rulers who were willing, at least temporarily, to meet their demands or to discuss their grievances and thereby to legitimate their political actions. In composite states especially, political opposition usually entails political alignment as well.

But what practical difference might the choices of popular political actors make? At the very least, a composite state involves three sets of actors: local rulers, national claimants to power, and ordinary political subjects. Figure 2 not only illustrates the obvious political alignments possible within such a state, it specifies the consequences that these different choices/alignments imply. In the first of these alternatives, ordinary political subjects align themselves with local rulers who are willing to champion their perceived interests vis-à-vis a more distant overlord and thereby help to consolidate local self-regulation and decision-making authority. In the second, local rulers align themselves with national claimants vis-à-vis their mutual subjects, thereby reinforcing their political interdependence in what I have called elite consolidation. In the third case, ordinary people align themselves with a more distant overlord who is willing to champion their interests vis-à-vis less responsive or more demanding rulers at home, thereby underwriting the consolidation of a broader territorial sovereignty at the expense of local self-determination.

By its very nature, this kind of complex political arrangement may be said to be particularly volatile because an alignment between any two of the actors promises to exclude the third; at the same time, the continued existence of the third represents the potential for two alternative alignments that implicitly threaten the status quo. Figure 2 nevertheless

---

firma; typically the newly conquered territories were guaranteed local "privileges" in return for their submission. See Finlay 1980; Guarini 1995.

11. James Scott's work (1987, 1990) is exemplary in the way that it explores the enormous ingenuity that ordinary people display in "working the system to their minimum disadvantage." In contrast to my approach here, however, Scott's descriptions of the relations of domination and (everyday) resistance tend to be neatly singular and linear, focusing on one set of relations at a time. It is critically important to apply a wide-angle lens to the analysis of the variable dimensions of domination and to the plurality of power in early modern Europe.

a. Local consolidation   b. Elite consolidation   c. Territorial consolidation

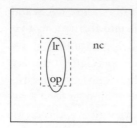
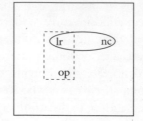
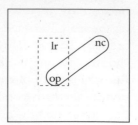

☐   Composite state
⌐ ̄ ̄⌐   Local sovereignty
lr   Local rulers
nc   National claimants to power
op   Ordinary people

Figure 2. Alignments of political actors within composite states

underestimates the complexity of politics within composite states in at least two important ways. As we shall see below, the constitutional layering of authority can entail more levels than "local" and "national," with district and regional or territorial rulers frequently claiming a piece of the existing "sovereignty."[12] At the same time, each of the principal actors is as often as not subdivided by internal rivalries and competing interests/objectives, producing situations in which all of these competing alignments appear at once; such situations might then be considered "revolutionary" if and when the alternative alignments make and attempt to enforce exclusive political claims that, if accepted, would eliminate their rivals.[13] For our purposes, what is especially instructive about even the stylized alternatives represented in figure 2 is the way in which ordinary people remain salient and potentially decisive actors even under political conditions that appear to guarantee the long-term survival of elite consolidation.[14]

Emphasizing the spatial and cultural perspectives on popular political

12. For the most part, this discussion treats the domain of the local ruler as its basic unit of analysis, but it is clearly evident that within even the local domain a variety of institutions, such as guilds, monasteries, brotherhoods, and families, might claim a significant degree of "private" self-determination.
13. On the nature and significance of exclusive or revolutionary claims, see Tilly 1978.
14. Obviously, these broad principles of alignment and opposition do not apply exclusively to early modern composite state formations. Unfortunately, the teleological myopia of most of the literature on European state formation obscures this element of "modern" state formations like the United States or the European Union.

practice within late medieval composite states, then, the chapters that follow explore the variety of ways in which ordinary people actively lived the "big changes" in European political history during the early modern period. Chapter 2 begins the story in the first half of the sixteenth century and focuses on the political process of religious reformation in the fragmented political context of the German-Roman Empire; it nevertheless locates the popular reformations of Germany and Switzerland within a larger comparative analysis of the role of popular political action in the Comunero Revolt in Castile and the "princely" reformations of Scandinavia and England. Chapter 3 examines the political dimensions of the "Second Reformation" in France and the Low Countries where the initial repression of religious dissent yielded to decades of civil war and revolution in the second half of the sixteenth century; again the emphasis is on the character and significance of popular engagement within these complex struggles over political and religious sovereignty that by the end of the sixteenth century produced three very different paths of political development. Chapter 4 analyzes the political dimensions of the Crisis of the Seventeenth Century, focusing in turn on distinct clusters of revolutionary struggles in Iberia and southern Italy, the British Isles, and France; against the backdrop of the sixteenth-century reformations, this chapter explores the significance of popular political action in accounting for the varied outcomes of large-scale revolutionary challenges to the rulers of composite states.

Each of these chapters—which together constitute a sort of dramatic development in three chronologically sequential acts—takes us from one region to another investigating the variant patterns of interaction among national powerholders, local rulers, and ordinary people; each chapter also develops a framework for understanding the particular interactions and historically specific range of variation evident in the cluster of conflicts in question.

Chapter 5 takes stock of the larger historical patterns brought out in the previous chapters; it assesses the cumulative outcome of some one hundred fifty years of political and religious conflict in specific polities, not in terms of an essentially static ancien régime, but as a set of variant trajectories of political development in which the interactions of subjects and rulers, in one time and place, limit and channel the next round of interaction but do not strictly determine the outcome. In conclusion, then, this book argues that the political engagement of ordinary political subjects needs to be taken systematically into account in any explanation of the political features of the "new regime" that gradually came into focus across the European continent in the second half of the seventeenth century.[15]

This, I hasten to add, is not an exclusive argument. It does not suggest, for example, that ordinary people were either the principal architects or the primary beneficiaries of the new structures of European politics or the new system of European states that rose from the ashes of "religious war." On the contrary, this work seeks to improve on previous accounts of the varieties of European state formation by tempering essentially ruler-centered or structurally determined models with the perspective of popular political practice and to augment the generally teleological research on the unitary sovereignties of territorial states with a specific concern for the consolidation of fragmented and layered sovereignties. Nor does this argument eclipse or undermine the value of more focused analyses of the modes of political action within specific polities or of detailed local research on particular events. Rather, it seeks to develop an analytic vocabulary and articulate a comparative framework through which it will be possible to ask sharper and more discriminating questions about the efficacy of popular politics in specific instances.

To accomplish all this in the course of a small book, my aim has been illustrative rather than comprehensive, and treatment of any given polity or region within the European political landscape is episodic at best. To some extent, this is simply reflective of the existing literature, which tends to be localized, discontinuous, and geographically uneven. To the extent that my choices of illustrative material were not merely dictated by the literature (or my limited access to it), however, I have generally placed more emphasis on exploring the broadest range of variation in each of these eras than on providing uniform or continuous coverage of any or all polities. Thus, while I have drawn a disproportional share of my examples from those parts of Europe north of the Pyrenees and Alps and west of the Oder, I am reasonably certain that I have encompassed the broad range of political variations evident within all of Europe's composite states. In any case, it was by no means my intention, in my choice

---

15. The prevalence of the term "ancien régime" to describe Europe between, say, 1660 and 1780 is doubly unfortunate in that (1) it embodies a retrospective anachronism in which the era of the French Revolution stands as the frame of reference through which we view the preceding period; and (2) it obscures the novelty of the political and religious arrangements that emerged after the religious wars, suggesting instead that these were, at bottom, holdovers from the distant past.

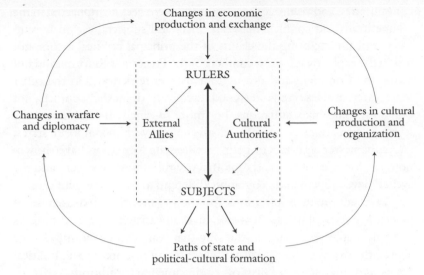

Figure 3. Historical dynamics of political interaction

of examples, to marginalize southern or eastern Europe or to privilege the politics of Latin Christendom.

Before setting out on this broadly comparative and essentially episodic exploration, however, it is important to ask how we might conceive of the more continuous dynamics of political development in any specific polity in the longue durée. Since our basic problem is to describe and account for the specific histories of state and political-cultural change that were embedded in the European system of states as it emerged in this period, figure 3 represents an axial model of the general argument that popular political actors were an integral part of these large-scale historical processes of political development in European history. As the diagram suggests, the heart of the story is the interaction or bargaining between governmental authorities (rulers) and popular political actors (subjects) which can be said to account for the path of state and political-cultural formation within specific political domains. Yet, as the figure also suggests, the interactions of rulers and subjects are channeled and limited in a variety of ways. In the early modern period especially, it is important to recognize two analytically distinct sorts of secondary actors who were implicated in politics at all levels. On the one hand, those who claimed cultural authority—often by virtue of their positions within more or less formal institutions like churches, schools, learned academies, religious communities, and voluntary associations—were deeply implicated in the competitions and conflicts between rulers and subjects, variously reinforcing or undercutting the claims of the principal political actors, not just in the explicitly religious conflicts of the Protestant Reformation but across the Continent and throughout the entire period. On the other hand, external allies often intervened directly in "domestic" conflicts, not only in revolutionary situations, but more routinely in constitutionally layered articulations of fragmented sovereignty within composite states.

As the newer accounts of path-specific state formation have shown, both the fortunes of war and diplomacy within the state system and the cyclical development and geographic differentiation of emergent capitalism have important implications for the organization and exercise of power. My account insists, however, on their variable impact on subjects and rulers alike, especially in the way that wars and economic change altered the distribution of politically important resources to all political actors. To this standard list of environmental conditions—that is, large-scale changes that transcended the boundaries of particular polities—I have added changes in the organization and production of culture. Especially during this period the spread of new printing techniques, the disintegration of the Roman Catholic church, and the rise of mass literacy helped to reconfigure the choices and channel the cultural resources available to all political actors within any given space. Altogether, then, the environmental conditions and the specific dimensions of the political domain can be said to structure the political opportunities but not to determine the choices of rulers as well as subjects. On the outcome side of the diagram, the closely linked trajectories of state and political-cultural formation can be seen as the institutional and cultural residue of historically specific interactions between rulers and subjects, which, in turn, influenced the environmental conditions and channeled the next round of political interaction.

A comprehensive or authoritative account of the big changes in European politics during this tumultuous period might well treat the environmental conditions and the political interactions in equal measure. This work focuses, however, on political interaction within historically specific political spaces and, by comparison, generally takes the changing environmental conditions for granted. While I want clearly to acknowledge the importance of these changing conditions, I want equally clearly to undermine the assumption that one can reason directly from structural conditions to political outcomes. On the contrary, what this work aims to demonstrate is that by starting in the middle—by focusing on political interaction as the heart of the story—we will finally be able to move beyond both elite-centered and structurally determined accounts of European state formation to describe and account for the various ways in which ordinary people were active and creative participants in the formation of the modern political landscape.

2

Revolt and Religious Reformation in the World of Charles V

First of all, the gospel does not cause rebellions and uproars, because it tells of Christ, the promised Messiah, whose words and life teach nothing but love, peace, patience, and unity. And all who believe in this Christ become loving, peaceful, patient, and one in spirit. This is the basis of all the articles of the peasants. . . : to hear the gospel and to live accordingly. . . .

    Second, it surely follows that the peasants, whose articles demand this gospel as their doctrine and rule of life, cannot be called "disobedient" or "rebellious." For if God deigns to hear the peasants' earnest plea that they may be permitted to live according to his word, who will dare deny his will?   The Twelve Articles, 1525

You are robbing the government of its power and even of its authority—yea everything it has, for what sustains the government once it has lost its power?   Martin Luther, 1525

    In the midst of what was surely one of the most dramatic popular political challenges of the sixteenth century, the representatives of three large peasant armies assembled at the town of Memmingen and drew up "The Twelve Articles of the Peasantry of Swabia" in late February or early March 1525. The articles not only listed specific grievances and demands that reflected a profound crisis of agrarian society and religious authority but also expressed a set of principles that were at once revolutionary and capable of encompassing the hopes and aspirations of a broad coalition of political subjects throughout southern Germany. Thus, the third article joined an attack on serfdom with an alternative vision of the political and social future: "It has until now been the custom for the lords to own us as their property. This is deplorable, for Christ redeemed and bought us all with his precious blood, the lowliest shepherd as well as the greatest lord, with no exceptions. Thus the Bible proves that we are free and want to be free" (Blickle 1981:197). In this sense, Martin Luther, whose theological challenge to the established Church had inspired and emboldened the peasant leaders, was surely right in arguing that the peasants' demands threatened the established political order. The peasants' protestations to the contrary notwithstanding— "Not that we want to be utterly free and subject to no authority at all," the third article continued—this most famous of the manifestos associated with the Revolution of 1525 promised to transform Swabian society according to the lofty principles of "godly law."

At the time the peasant leaders were assembled in Memmingen, they can be said to have enjoyed a brief military advantage over their opponents; for the armies of the imperial Swabian League were temporarily distracted by other, more traditional military challenges. Once they turned their attention to the massive insurrections, not only in Swabia but in Franconia and Thuringia as well, the established rulers and their more practiced and professional armies easily defeated the popular challengers, sometimes even without a fight. By the end of the year, virtually all of the peasant insurrections had been subdued and a massive repression had begun throughout the area. Indeed, never again would this region be rocked by popular insurrection on such a massive scale.

Because of the well-deserved fame of the Revolution of 1525, not to mention the explosion of revolutionary religious enthusiasm at the city of Münster ten years later, it is tempting to identify popular religion with popular rebellion in the early years of the sixteenth century. As it happened, however, popular movements for the reformation of religious belief and practice took a variety of forms short of open rebellion—from the submission of humble petitions to the formation of secret "conventicles." Moreover, "successful" reformations were as often magisterial as popular in origin. Thus the political dynamics of the English and

Scandinavian reformations, where rulers actively aligned themselves with religious reform movements, were strikingly different in the 1530s and beyond. In England, for example, in the absence of massive popular demands for religious change, the king took the initiative to separate the Church from Rome and to introduce modest changes in the ritual life and dogma of the Church of which he now claimed to be the head. The most obvious popular response in 1536 was an abortive rebellion in Lincolnshire and what has come to be known as the Pilgrimage of Grace.

The leaders of these English movements, like the leaders of the German revolution, put together broad but immensely fragile coalitions that could not withstand the counterchallenges of the king and his allies. Also like their German predecessors, they articulated an eclectic set of grievances and published specific demands regarding the regulation of public affairs and social relations in an agrarian society. But in the English case, instead of demanding reform or liturgical innovation, the leaders of a broadly based popular mobilization were emphatically demanding the restoration of the established Roman church and the religious practices associated with it. Meeting at Pontefract in December 1536, for example, they demanded vigorous actions against "the heresies of Luther," among others, and insisted that "the privlages and rights of the church . . . be confirmed by acte of parliament, and prestes not suffre by sourde onless he be disgrecid" (Fletcher 1983:111–112). In response, a publicist for the king asked rhetorically,

When every man wyll rule, who shall obeye? . . . No, no, take welthe by the hande, and say farewell welth, where lust is lyked, and lawe refused, where uppe is sette downe, and downe sette uppe: An order, and order muste be hadde, and a waye founde that they rule that beste can, they be ruled, that mooste it becommeth so to be. (Ibid., 112)

Despite their obviously different demands with regard to the reformation of religious practice and belief, then, the rebels in both Germany and England were seen by contemporaries to threaten the foundations of established authority and to promise a fundamental reorientation of the essential relationships between rulers and their subjects.

Such was the nature of the Reformation era in Europe: though dissenting theologians like Martin Luther, Huldrych Zwingli, and Jean Calvin may not have intended it, their direct challenges to the authority of the established Church intersected with and had profound implications for the interactions of subjects and rulers more generally. As Euan Cameron sums up the process in his recent survey,

Politically active laymen, not (at first) political rulers with axes to grind, but rather ordinary, moderately prosperous householders, took up the reformers' protests, identified them (perhaps mistakenly) as their own, and pressed them upon their governors. This blending and coalition—of reformers' protests and laymen's political ambitions—is the essence of the Reformation. It turned the reformers' movement into a new form of religious dissent. . . . [I]t promoted a new pattern of worship and belief, publicly preached and acknowledged, which *also* formed the basis of new religious *institutions* for all of society, within the whole community, region, or nation concerned. (1991:2; emphasis in original)

Consequently, the sixteenth-century Reformation was a unique transition in the history of Western Christendom in the sense that it laid the foundations for divergent paths of closely linked religious *and* political development that endured throughout the early modern period.

This chapter focuses on popular political action during the first act of the European Reformation, especially within the composite domain of Charles V of Habsburg. The consummate late medieval dynastic prince, Charles combined a collection of patrimonial lordships in the prosperous commercial centers of the Low Countries with a composite kingship in Iberia, created just half a century earlier by the marriage of Ferdinand of Aragon with Isabella of Castile, and the emperorship of the vast German-Roman Empire in central Europe. It was within or on the fringes of Charles's imperial domain, to which he was elected in 1519, that popular enthusiasm for religious reform was first concentrated in the 1520s; and as I will argue, popular engagement in the essentially political process of religious reformation took a variety of forms in Germany—including, of course, the Revolution of 1525—which precipitated, by midcentury, a political and religious settlement that extinguished Charles's unambiguous claim to cultural or religious sovereignty over the whole of his empire. To underscore the significance of these political and religious conflicts for the subsequent history of central Europe, this chapter also sets the German Reformation in the larger comparative context of the Scandinavian and English reformations where, by contrast, popular engagement in the reformation process helped to consolidate princely claims to cultural sovereignty. I begin, however, with a brief examination of the first major challenge to Charles's sovereignty—the Comunero Revolt of 1520–1521 in Castile, at the heart of his Iberian domain—for two principal reasons: on the one hand, the Comunero Revolt did not directly invoke the question of religious authority and thus reminds us that not all sixteenth-century conflict was associated with or inspired by the challenges of Protestant theology; on the other hand, the Comunero Revolt involved all the important political actors within a composite state—local rulers and ordinary political subjects as well as national claimants to power—and thus illustrates clearly the long-term significance of the alternative alignments among them.

Communes and Comuneros in Castile

On May 30, 1520, just ten days after Charles I of Castile had left Spain to assume his new role as Charles V in the German-Roman Empire, an unruly collection of artisans, mainly textile workers in the woolen industry, invaded the city hall of Segovia and seized Rodrigo de Tordesillas, one of the city's official delegates to the recent meeting of the Cortes that had been summoned by the king at Santiago. Incensed by the apparently boundless fiscal demands of their young monarch—demands that seemed to support little more than Charles's dynastic ambitions in Germany—the crowd brought their defenseless victim, who was condemned for having betrayed local interests, first to the city jail and eventually to the place of public executions where they hanged him. Stephen Haliczer describes the aftermath:

Tordesilla's murder was the signal for a wholesale attack on the representatives of royal government in the city of Segovia. The *corregidor* (royal official of the town), his lieutenants, and police officials were stripped of their offices and forced to flee. New officials were appointed by a revolutionary committee composed of members of the city council, delegates from the cathedral chapter, and parish representatives. The *Comunero* revolution had begun. (1981:3)

In the next four months, delegates of the city of Segovia joined delegates from no less than eighteen other revolutionary cities in Castile to constitute the Sacred League (Sancta Junta), which claimed power as the sole legitimate government of Castile in place of Charles's regency government, which had quickly collapsed in the face of this powerful wave of urban insurrection.

In many respects, the revolution of the Sacred League, also known as the Comunero Revolt, represented a classic form of local resistance to an aggressive dynast (see Blockmans 1988). The Sacred League was a coalition of many, though not all, of the leading cities of the Kingdom of

Castile, whose sovereignty Charles had seized from his own apparently insane mother in 1516. Collectively, the members of the league, whose efforts were welcomed by the deposed and psychologically unstable Queen Juana, sought to abolish the *alcabala* (a general tax on commerce), to reduce the power of the king, and to transform the Cortes, in which they were represented, into the primary institution of the state (cf. Bonney 1991; Lynch 1991). The political demands of the Comuneros may thus be considered fundamentally revolutionary in the sense that they were exclusive of the claims to political sovereignty that Charles was making as king; to accept the rebels' claims, indeed, would be to transform fundamentally the structure of political authority in Castile.

As the events in Segovia suggest, however, the Comuneros' opposition to the royal government involved as well a political realignment within the local community as officials appointed by and oriented to the royal administration were replaced by others who were more responsive to local demands and who were selected by, among others, the representatives of popular parish assemblies. And once they joined the Sacred League, the leaders of the rebellious communes of Castile deepened their political orientation toward ordinary political actors within the urban community by building the league's defenses on the basis of urban militias mobilized and recruited locally. There is certainly more than a little historical irony in the fact that the Comunero Revolution adopted the defensive form of a sacred league because less than fifty years earlier, in 1476, Queen Isabella had encouraged the chartered cities in her Castilian domain to act as a sacred league—the Sancta Hermandad—and to raise urban militias to maintain public order and support her in her efforts to tame the powerful Castilian nobility. Though the league of cities had been disbanded in 1498, when the Crown once again shifted its dynastic policy toward dependence on the rural nobility, the lessons of this earlier political process had clearly not been lost on the municipalities involved. To deploy the civic militia in opposition to the new king, however, was to create a new kind of internal political dynamic that also entailed the creation of independent municipal councils, or "communes" (hence the name "Comunero"). For the duration of the revolt, at least, the local rulers of the rebellious cities were to be fundamentally dependent on the approval and support of their subjects (see fig. 2a).

In the late summer of 1520, the political situation in Castile became even more volatile and threatening to the established political order when political disturbances in the countryside began to threaten noble landlords as well as the king. In the village of Dueñas, not far from the capital of Valladolid, for example, rebellious peasants, spurred on by a group of radical monks, rejected the lordship of the local count of Buendía and replaced the count's officials with others chosen by a popular assembly. The rebels then proceeded to encourage rebellion in other parts of the count's local domain, and they seized nearby fortresses belonging to the count (Haliczer 1981:185). In October, there were also a number of antiseigneurial revolts in Tierra de Campos, where eventually some twenty-seven localities sent representatives to a rebel league that met at Palencia. In principle, the peasant revolts might have offered the urban Comuneros potentially important allies in their fight against the king and the powerful nobility with which he was allied, but in the end the Comuneros' failure to take advantage or ally themselves with the rising tide of rural discontent exposed the limits of this sort of urban resistance to aggressive dynasts. The fact is that the political bargains by which dynastic princes typically constructed their composite states created local privileges that distinguished one piece of the composite from another. Indeed, the extent to which municipal charters privileged urban communes over their rural hinterlands militated against urban-rural alliances vis-à-vis a common enemy like an aggressive dynast or his noble allies; and in this case, the extent to which the Comuneros' militias indiscriminately exploited defenseless country folk in the course of their military campaigns made such alliances extremely unlikely.

Thus the rebellious cities' political isolation in an essentially rural environment underscored the fragility of their revolutionary coalition. At first, the urban militias were able to hold their own against the royal government's feeble counteroffensive, but inasmuch as the rural rebellions served as a serious warning to the nobility of the obvious dangers of a general disintegration of royal authority to preserve peace and guarantee their privileges in the countryside, the king's regent was soon to be bailed out by the combined forces of the nobility's private armies. The first serious blow to the Comuneros came in December 1520 when a royalist army sacked their lightly defended capital at the town of Tordesillas and captured thirteen league delegates. The league was quickly reconstituted at Valladolid, though it was pared down to eleven cities, and briefly rallied by capturing all of Tierra de Campos. But in the spring of 1521, the military struggle finally turned in favor of the king's forces, and in a decisive battle at Villalar, the viceroy's infantry defeated the Comuneros' exhausted soldiers. On April 24, 1521, the three principal Comunero military leaders were condemned to death, and although the city of Toledo held out until February 1522, the revolution of the Sacred League had come to an end.

Though the Comuneros were thus defeated militarily, their resistance to the aggressive dynasticism of Charles of Habsburg was not without result. Indeed, Haliczer describes the postrevolutionary political situation in Castile as follows: "Charles did not return to a cowed and subdued Castile ready for unquestioning obedience; instead, it was a subdued king who came back [from Germany] to a restive and hostile kingdom in 1522 to face the task of rebuilding support for the monarchy" (1981:207). From this perspective it is not surprising that the cities of Castile gained some important concessions from the king following their defeat: a system of tax collection more favorable to the cities; a reorganization of the central government along lines favored by the cities; and a Cortes decidedly more receptive to the special grievances of the cities. Even the government's repression may be considered light because many of those who had been excluded from a general pardon in 1522 were eventually pardoned; in the end, only twenty-three persons were executed for their resistance to the monarchy.

Still, in the long run, the most important political development from the point of view of the ordinary citizens of the Castilian towns is that the Crown began channeling its considerable patronage to municipal representatives in the Cortes. In short, a political alignment of ordinary people with their local rulers—which underwrote a local consolidation of power vis-à-vis the king for the duration of the revolt (see fig. 2a)—was replaced by an alignment, lubricated by royal patronage, between local magistrates and the king—which consolidated the power of the elites vis-à-vis their local subjects (see fig. 2b). For the king, the not inconsiderable result was that the municipal representatives to the Cortes would henceforth be more likely to grant him his fiscal demands, but this kind of favorable treatment also helped to create a privileged set of urban oligarchs who were clearly more alienated from their political subjects than their predecessors had been during their defense of the local community in the face of monarchical consolidation. Indeed, effective municipal resistance to monarchical consolidation inevitably depended on coalitions of a variety of sorts: between municipal rulers and their subject populations; among cities with often disparate economic and political interests; or between rebels on opposite sides of the legal, social, cultural, and sometimes even physical barriers that differentiated cities from their rural hinterlands. In the aftermath of the Comunero Revolt, then, it can be said that to the extent that royal policies privileged cities over their hinterlands and oligarchs over their urban subjects, they helped to ensure that an urban revolt of this magnitude would not be repeated in Castile.

Revolution and Religious Reform in Germany and Switzerland

In the early years of his political career, then, Charles V was challenged in quick succession by revolts in both Iberia and Germany. At the other pole of his far-flung accumulation of political territory—in the Austrian Habsburg patrimonial domain and more generally in the diverse territories of the empire—the patterns of political contestation that Charles V faced were, at first blush, far more complex and confusing, and not only because German politics were infused by religious controversy and enthusiasm. The extreme segmentation of political authority in the German-Roman Empire—both geographically in hundreds of more or less self-regulating political units and constitutionally in the welter of overlapping and often competing hierarchies that characterized the governing institutions of the empire—preserved an immense variety of political spaces in which ordinary people could, and in fact did, initiate their own challenges to those who claimed authority over them.[1] Not surprisingly, then, by comparison with the Comunero Revolt, the Revolution of 1525 in Germany was both more diffuse and, at bottom, less of a direct threat to Charles's political sovereignty because it was most often directed at his political subordinates.[2]

This "revolution of the common man," as Peter Blickle has described it, was predicated on the creation of relatively loose and informal coalitions among locally mobilized peasant groups as well as artisans and common laborers on the fringes of southern Germany's many cities and in the adjoining cantons of the Swiss Confederation. What brought

1. For a brief introduction to the political structures of the German-Roman Empire, see Hughes 1992.
2. It is impossible in the short compass of this work to reflect the richness of the social-historical research that has been applied to the Revolution of 1525 and to the urban reform movements in Reformation Germany; in fact, this work has recently been summarized deftly by others: see especially Blickle 1992; Cameron 1991; and Scribner 1986. For our purposes, it will be necessary to draw on this extensive literature more selectively to locate the political engagements of ordinary Germans more clearly in the political spaces that constituted the Holy Roman Empire.

them together in a common cause was the ideal of a community-based church demanding faithful preaching of the "pure gospel" and a "godly law" that applied to rulers and subjects alike (Blickle 1981, 1992). Though it is tempting, in retrospect, to emphasize the breadth of the coalitions, to highlight the enormous geographic spread of the insurrection, and even to speak of the whole complex of events in the singular form of the term "revolution," it is important for our purposes to disaggregate this historical composite and to locate the political actions of ordinary people within their respective political spaces.

The basic, constituent unit of popular insurrection in sixteenth-century Europe, as many scholars have suggested, was the local community—whether that of the rural village or that of the chartered town—and the Revolution of 1525 was no exception (cf. Sabean 1976). As it happened, the German peasant mobilization began at Stühlingen in the Hegau in June 1524 when several hundred tenants of Count Siegmund von Lupfen rebelled against the exactions imposed by their lord. They chose as their leader a former mercenary, Hans Müller, and quickly worked out an alliance with the nearby town of Waldshut, where a popular preacher named Balthasar Hubmaier had galvanized opposition to the town's more distant Austrian overlord. When these in turn allied with the city of Zürich, the authorities were forced to play for time while the peasants of Stühlingen, where it had all started, submitted their grievances formally to the Reichskammergericht (Imperial Chamber Court) for adjudication within the legal framework of the empire. Meanwhile, the rebel forces led by Müller forced the capitulation of Freiburg-im-Breisgau.[3] Finally in 1525, following inconclusive talks between the rebels and the Austrian officials, the revolt burned itself out.

Similar scenarios—albeit often with more violent endings—were played out in Swabia, Franconia, Thuringia, and the Tyrol, as local resistance to lordly, princely, or imperial exactions aggregated under the leadership of skilled soldiers, urban artisans and lawyers, or popular preachers. The soldiers and their military skills were important to such movements because as local resistance fused into regional insurrection, the most likely response from established rulers was a military campaign.[4] The artisans and lawyers were important because they helped to

3. See T. Scott 1986 who clearly demonstrates the structural difficulties that stood in the way of an enduring alliance between town and countryside.
4. For a brief account of the movement's spread and the military campaigns associated with it, see Thomas A. Brady and H. C. Erik Middelfort, "Translators' Introduction," in Blickle 1981.

bridge the political and social gap between city and countryside. The preachers were important because their radical religious populism served powerfully to unite otherwise very diverse people in a common cause: the cause of "godly justice."[5] Still, the most basic political interaction was between a variety of local rulers and their immediate subjects—rulers and subjects as various as the many fragments of sovereignty that dotted central and southern Germany, including many parts of modern-day Switzerland and Austria. The individual stories of the many popular actors in this complex drama converged on the theme of opposition to what were considered the illegitimate or excessive exactions of rulers. Undoubtedly the most common, but by the same token the least visible, form of this opposition was simple evasion, often by individuals but sometimes collectively in the form of rent strikes or refusals to pay the tithe. But in the previous hundred years, this basic dynamic had spilled over with increasing frequency into larger collective actions in the form of violent rebellions. In the first half of the fifteenth century there were seven such regional revolts; in the second half of the fifteenth century, fourteen. In the first twenty-five years of the sixteenth century, there were no less than eighteen (Blickle 1979).

In this sense, the scenario of 1524–1525 was well rehearsed; the claims, the claim makers, and the basic forms of claim making must at least have been familiar to those involved. What was truly unprecedented was the magnitude of the historical convergence: in all, hundreds of thousands of ordinary people served at one time or another in the "peasant" armies; as many as 130,000 may have died in the fighting or in the subsequent repression; virtually all areas of central and southern Germany, with the notable exception of Bavaria, were touched by the conflicts.[6] We must be careful, however, neither to overestimate nor to underestimate the achievement of the rebels. The convergence of so many discrete rebel movements was far from complete. Though they clustered in a very concentrated period and shared many essential characteristics, the regional uprisings were not directly connected with one another; nor were they well integrated on a regional scale (in both Swabia and Franconia, for example, there were multiple armies under discrete leadership). Never-

---

5. See Scott 1989 on the tumultuous career of Thomas Müntzer, one of the most famous of the rebel preachers who was executed after the defeat of the peasant armies he led.

6. There were, in fact, insurrectionary movements as far away as Samland in the northeast, but these appear to have been rather different from those in central and southern Germany; see Scribner and Beneke 1979.

theless, these popular mobilizations outstripped, for a time at least, the ability of established rulers to repress them—not only individual lords and princes, but even imperial aggregations like the Swabian League.

In this regard, we cannot but be impressed by the leaders of the movements, often of relatively humble origin themselves, who organized massive armies within the narrow limitations of an agrarian society. Because so many were active in agriculture, the soldiers in the rebel armies often were allowed to serve for only short periods, so that each would in turn be able to tend to his own crops at regular intervals.[7] Besides fielding massive armies, the movements' leaders frequently brought together deliberative "peasant" assemblies, negotiated informal alliances with other rebels across existing territorial boundaries, and produced manifestos like that of the peasants of Swabia. From some three hundred grievance lists, the authors of the Twelve Articles not only distilled a common list of grievances regarding the disposition of common resources, the collection of tithes, and the imposition of unpaid labor services, they also articulated a vision of the future that could inspire and unite very diverse people across a broad terrain. In a "godly" society, indeed, ordinary people would be both personally "free" (see article 3, quoted above) and collectively in charge of their religious welfare (see article 1 by which the local community asserts the right to choose its own pastor); rulers, meanwhile, would be clearly limited by the precepts of divine justice.[8] The "Revolution" of 1525 may in this regard be considered the most dramatic example of the way in which the sixteenth-century Reformation provided ordinary Europeans with, to borrow Euan Cameron's expression, "their first lessons in political commitment to a universal ideology" (1991:422).

Still, on the face of it, this broad challenge to the political and religious establishment was, like the Comunero Revolt, a failure: in the immediate sense that the many armies of the various movements either gave up without a fight or were soundly defeated in lopsided battles; and in the larger sense that the leaders of the movement were, on the whole, unable to institutionalize their radical religious reforms and to realize their populist visions of a more egalitarian "godly" society. In the absence

---

7. See Brady and Middelfort, "Translators' Introduction," in Blickle 1981:xxi.
8. Peter Blickle, in making a forceful argument for the revolutionary qualities of the movement, identifies two broadly conceived alternative visions of the political future: the corporative-associative constitution and the constitution of territorial assemblies (Blickle 1981; cf. Blickle 1986).

of major defections from the ranks of the political elites or significant outside support, this massive popular mobilization gave way to the firm consolidation of elite control in the German countryside (see fig. 2b). This is not to say, however, that the peasant uprisings in southern and central Germany were completely unsuccessful. As recent research has shown, in some areas the movements achieved both specific concessions with regard to some of their immediate demands and long-term reforms of the political and judicial systems. In the long run, the judicial changes in particular had far-reaching implications for the interactions of rulers and subjects within the fragmented jurisdictions of the German Empire because they legitimated the formal appeal of popular grievances to imperial authorities (Schulze 1984; Trossbach 1987).

The failure of the Revolution of 1525 to dislodge the established political order within the empire was also, of course, relative to the boundaries of the empire itself. Just beyond the effective reach of imperial authorities—in the complex jurisdictions of the Swiss Confederation—the process of religious reformation intersected with the process of revolutionary conflict in a rather different sense that opened greater opportunities for the success of religious reformations in the countryside (Peyer 1978; Blickle 1992; Gordon 1992; Greyerz 1994). There the Oath Confederation (Eidgenossenschaft) of just three forested mountain districts or cantons had first been formed as a common defense against feudal domination already in the late thirteenth century, and it went through several phases of crisis and expansion before its armed citizens, in one of their most heroic moments, defeated the formidable armies of Emperor Maximilian I in 1499 and thereby seemed to secure their de facto independence and the principle of communal self-governance for the foreseeable future. Within the diverse territories of the confederation, then, the more or less accomplished fact of revolution ensured that rural communities stood in a rather different relationship to the political process of religious reformation (Bonjour, Offler, and Potter 1952; Luck 1985).

In the large city-state cantons of Zürich and Bern, for example, municipal authorities formally adopted Protestant worship in the 1520s and began actively promoting the reformation of religion in their rural hinterlands as well. In the smaller core cantons of Luzern, Uri, Schwytz, and Unterwalden, by contrast, Protestantism made few inroads, and local authorities stalwartly defended the established religious order (cf. Blickle 1992:167). In several remarkable situations, however, the question of religious orientation—the choice for or against the new evangelical preaching and experimentation in worship—was left to individual rural communities within a canton. In 1528, the city-state of Bern, as part of the process of introducing Protestant worship, conducted a systematic consultation (*Ämterbefragung*) of the rural population which, as expected by its organizers, produced a handsome majority—though by no means unanimous consent—for the Reformation. Meanwhile, in the rural cantons of Appenzell and Glarus, *Landesgemeinden* (general meetings of all full citizens) decided that each individual community should have the right to choose for or against the religious reforms; in both cases, the subsequent decision-making process left the cantons religiously divided (Fischer, Schläpfer, and Stark 1964; Wick 1982). A similar pattern of religious division as a consequence of local decision making emerged to the southeast of the confederation in Graubünden (Blickle 1992; Head 1997). But what is particularly instructive about these Swiss examples is that when an essentially completed process of political revolution gave them the truly extraordinary opportunity to choose either for or against the Reformation, they did both: The various rural communities of Switzerland chose both for and against the project of religious reform and not necessarily one or the other.

Patterns of Urban Reformation

As it unfolded in southern Germany and Switzerland, the process of religious reformation intersected only partially and imperfectly with the process of revolutionary political conflict. Only rarely did successful challenges to the cultural dominance of the Roman Catholic church entail simultaneous and direct challenges to the sovereignty of established political regimes, but when they did, they were most likely to take place within the relatively concentrated political spaces of self-governing cities. These self-governing cities were scattered throughout Europe's urban core from northern Italy[9] to the Low Countries and the Baltic coast, but within the empire alone there were some 80 imperial "free" cities, subordinate only to the emperor, and more than 2,000 ter-

9. Even though there were no popular insurrections associated with the Protestant Reformation in northern Italian cities, one must surely recall that the city of Florence had been the political arena for a religiously inspired popular insurrection led by the priest Savonarola just a few decades earlier. See Weinstein 1970.

ritorial cities, chartered by territorial lords and princes. Only a few of these were large population centers, and many had fewer than a thousand inhabitants. Regardless of size, however, the chartered municipalities were free to conduct their own affairs unless and until their "sovereigns" chose to intervene. It is thus within cities that we can see with special clarity the political processes of the sixteenth-century religious reformation.

The political process of religious reformation, including the active participation of ordinary people, was well under way within many German communities before the events of 1525. This process, in the broadest sense, began with the rapid diffusion of Martin Luther's new, evangelical theology by means of cheaply published pamphlets and broadsides, written for the most part by and for a well-educated reforming clergy. Vigorous popular engagement was usually predicated not so much on the spread of printed material as on the success of evangelical preaching. The preachers might be established religious leaders within their communities or newly trained converts, insiders or outsiders, but where they became effective leaders, they went beyond mere criticism of the established Church to suggest a variety of concrete means by which their audiences might identify themselves with the movement and become actively involved in the process of spiritual renewal (cf. Wuthnow 1989). The popular response, in turn, took a variety of forms that ranged from presumably private decisions to withdraw from active participation in the established ritual life of the Church—especially to stay away from the confessional and the Mass—to much more public and demonstrative acts like the mocking of priests and the desecration of sacred images (see, e.g., Wandel 1992, 1995). In many places, popular movements for reform were led by guildsmen—artisans as well as petty merchants—who organized formal petitions urging municipal authorities to intervene: to mandate "biblical" preaching, to reform or abolish the Mass, to call evangelical preachers, to establish a "common chest" for poor relief, or to expel priests.

At almost any point, this interaction between preachers and people might become a problem for civil authorities. Urban magistrates were officially charged with the maintenance of public order within their circumscribed domains, yet having limited coercive resources at their disposal, they depended to a considerable degree on popular assent, without which daily governance would not be possible. Given Charles V's zealous defense of papal orthodoxy and the imperial condemnation of Luther's teachings at the Diet of Worms in 1521, then, even the passive toleration of radical preaching might be considered an act of insubordination, but any attempt to discipline, expel, or otherwise limit popular preachers risked opposition from within the community. Caught between their nominal, often distant sovereigns and their immediate subjects, most civic leaders simply tried to buy time—to stay neutral—but the informal coalition between reforming preachers and an active laity often proved irresistible. In many cases the city councils started out as the reluctant arbiters of growing conflicts over religious practice and belief, but in the end it was they who enacted the essential reforms, not only by mandating changes in religious practice and changing ecclesiastical personnel but also by appropriating Church property for the use of the community.

In Augsburg in the early 1520s, for example, civic authorities obstructed the local bishop's efforts to discipline Lutheran preachers and published, but did not enforce, imperial mandates concerning religion; by the same token, however, they took no steps to appoint evangelical preachers, to establish religious reforms, or to attack the Catholic church. This middle course proved untenable in the summer of 1524, when a radical Franciscan monk gained a popular following in the city; in the words of one unsympathetic chronicler,

He preached critically of the spiritual and temporal authorities and against the customs of the Church. He also preached frivolously about the Sacraments and went around flippantly with the Holy Sacrament. . . . [H]e spoke in his sermons as if all things should be held in common. With these and similar sermons the monk attracted many people, indeed the majority of the populace. (Quoted in Broadhead 1979:82)

When the preacher Hans Schilling was surreptitiously removed from the city, a large crowd of perhaps two thousand of his supporters besieged the town hall, and the municipal council was forced to promise to recall Schilling. After the crowd had gone home, however, the council sent for six hundred mercenaries, imposed martial law, and punished the leaders of the crowd. The council was nevertheless forced to call a preacher to the post at the Franciscan church who was acceptable to the parishioners— as it happened, a Zwinglian (rather than a Lutheran) who was a zealous advocate of religious reform. In the end, then, the civic authorities were forced, for the sake of domestic peace, to appoint an evangelical preacher against their original wishes and in defiance of both the bishop and the emperor (Broadhead 1979, 1980).

Such interactions involving preachers, priests, magistrates, bishops, "princes," and ordinary people were common in the cities of the empire both before and after the Revolution of 1525. Typically, they involved only short-term confrontations and only incremental changes; in fact, in Augsburg there would be two more rounds of confrontation and compromise, in 1530 and 1533, before the council would commit itself and the city openly to the Protestant faith. Yet the aggregate effect of thousands of such incidents is what historians often call the urban reformation—the most dramatic example of popular pressure leading directly to institutional change in the Latin Church. There was no standard scenario for this urban reformation, however; much depended on specific interactions within variable contexts. Some groups proved to be more receptive of the reforming preachers, better organized, more resourceful, or more determined to act than others, while some urban authorities were more open to the new evangelical message, more critical of the established Church, or enjoyed greater latitude for independent action than others.[10] In short, the structures of urban political opportunity varied considerably, not only within the empire but also across the European terrain.[11] What was, in any case, essential to the process of urban reformation was a political space within which civil magistrates, religious authorities, and ordinary people might interact without the immediate intervention of outsiders.

Without pretending to catalog or narrate exhaustively the many complex stories that constitute the urban reformation, it is important at least to describe and account for the patterns of variation and to indicate the duration of the larger process.[12] Given the generally agreed upon importance of the urban reforms, there have already been several attempts to construct paradigms of urban reformation—usually divided into the "imperial city," the "Hansa city," and the "late city"—or to distinguish between its "popular" and "magisterial" phases (see Scribner 1990). What I should like to highlight here, however, is not the significance of one or

10. Accounting for these variations in the strength and determination of the central actors is obviously critical to a convincing account of the urban reformation as a whole; my more modest goal here is to show that it is at least necessary to take these popular actors into account if were are to understand the political process of religious reformation in Germany.
11. On the very different structures of political opportunity in the cities of France and the Low Countries, see chapter 3 below.
12. The following analysis of the dynamics and chronology of the urban reformations differs from but is fundamentally indebted to Euan Cameron's (1991:210–263) excellent synthesis of the monographic literature. Please note that the specific examples have been chosen with an eye to illustrating the range of variation that needs to be explained; other examples might have served these illustrative purposes just as well.

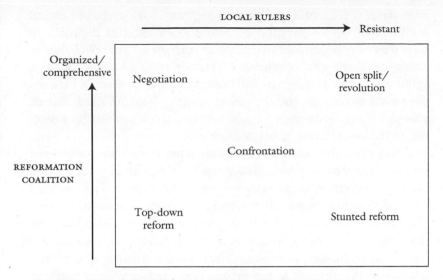

Figure 4. Political dynamics of the reformation process in Germany

the other type but the more generally observable patterns of *interaction* between different sorts of reformation coalitions (subjects) and variously receptive municipal authorities (rulers). Figure 4 suggests how we might imagine the array of possibilities.

In one dimension, figure 4 notes variations in the size and coherence or organization of the reformation coalition—that is, in the collabora-tion between evangelical preachers and laity. In some cases the urban reform movements were remarkably well organized, drawing on preex-isting institutions such as guilds or creating new worshiping communi-ties. At the other extreme, popular support for religious reform remained scattered and the cooperation between reforming preachers and respon-sive laity was too fleeting to be expressed in enduring networks or insti-tutions. In the other dimension, the figure highlights clear differences in the posture of the urban authorities—most often the municipal coun-cils—who, whether they might wish it or not, typically ended up medi-ating between popular demands for religious innovation and official edicts to the contrary.[13] Their relative resistance or receptivity to popu-lar demands for reform might be predicated on a variety of personal

13. The analysts of "new social movements" often distinguish analogously between inclu-sive and exclusive regimes.

interests as well as structural constraints, but in the end the political conflicts that the Reformation unleashed rarely afforded the rulers of cities the luxury of unmixed motives—whether motives of political expediency or of religious conviction.[14] Putting these variables together, figure 4 suggests how we might understand the differences between communal revolutions and top-down reforms, between the failure of reform and the achievement of negotiation and compromise, as a function of the interaction of rulers and subjects.

Where a broadly based or well-organized popular coalition interacted with a relatively open or nonresistant regime, the political process, as we have already seen in the case of Augsburg, often resulted in a negotiated settlement and a more gradual or piecemeal transition toward a reformed Church order. This occurred especially in many of the imperial free cities of southern Germany (indeed, it is often identified as *the* imperial-city reformation), but the same dynamic appeared in a variety of episcopal and territorial cities and in the urban-dominated cantons of northern Switzerland as well.[15] In several Swabian cities, such as Ulm, where those most likely to mobilize in favor of religious reform were more closely associated with the structures of municipal power, the guilds alone, or a faction of the oligarchy allied with them, might successfully push for official action in favor of reform. After attempting to forestall a decision for nearly a decade, the municipal council at Ulm finally submitted the question of religious reform to a vote of the guilds, fraternities, and master craftsmen in 1530, and by an overwhelming majority those who were polled rejected the largely anti-Lutheran imperial edict issued at the close of the Augsburg Reichstag that year. In this way, councils like those at Ulm or at Augsburg, which were torn between imperial decrees and popular sentiments, often chose to compromise with popular demands to survive. In other cases, such as at Strasbourg, where the established regime was more thoroughly divided, popular agitation might easily link with a reforming faction within the oligarchy to produce action in favor of the Reformed church order (Abray 1985; Brady 1985). A similar process of gradual displacement of old patricians occurred at Zürich between 1524 and 1528, which helps to explain the rel-

14. In focusing on popular politics, this analysis clearly begs some important questions regarding especially the constraints on official action. A fuller analysis of this side of the political interaction would require a more complete specification not only of local coalitions and patron-client relations but also the relative availability and proximity of external allies and/or political competitors (including religious and imperial authorities).

15. The standard work on the so-called imperial-city reformation is Moeller 1972.

ative delay in the abolition of the Mass in the very seat of the Zwinglian reformation (cf. Cameron 1991:245–246). In the terms of figure 4, this experience may be represented as a fairly straightforward movement from confrontation toward negotiated reform (and sometimes back again).

Where a coalition of ardent agitators faced off against more resistant authorities, however, the movement for religious reform might succeed only by overwhelming or partially displacing the existing regime. This occurred especially in the northern port cities of the Hanseatic League and some smaller inland territorial cities, where guildsmen were typically excluded from the town councils and local patricians identified themselves with the old Church hierarchy. In these situations, popular mobilization often led to the creation of a burgher committee (*Bürgerausschuss*) that demanded both a more open constitution and religious reform (Mörke 1983; Schilling 1983). In Lübeck, for example, after five years of unsuccessful negotiation, the burgher coalition seized control of the town council in 1533 and elected their leader as *Bürgermeister*. Following an unsuccessful involvement in the Counts' War in Denmark, however, the old oligarchs regained power in Lübeck in 1535. Even so, retaining the religious reforms proved to be a useful way for the returning oligarchs to quiet popular discontent. Thus, although successful antipatrician political agitation was often short-lived and the burgher committees eventually disappeared, the mostly Lutheran religious reforms remained as the most obvious token of the political interaction. Tracing this experience in terms of the framework provided by figure 4, the political process of religious reformation, having begun with confrontation at the center of the diagram, moved first toward revolution in the upper right but eventually veered toward a negotiated compromise following the political restoration of 1535.

Undoubtedly the most spectacular example of an open split or revolution came at the episcopal city of Münster in 1534–1535 (Hsia 1988b). There popular pressure led by the local guilds yielded initially to negotiated Lutheran reforms in the early 1530s while an increasingly radical millenarian movement encountered considerable resistance from the local elite. In early 1534, however, this radical movement, strengthened by an influx of Anabaptists from the Netherlands, seized power, expelled those opposed to it, and instituted a radical religious regime that awakened the fears of Lutherans and Catholics alike. Eventually outside military intervention defeated the millenarian rebels and resulted in the restoration of Catholicism. In the terms of figure 4, then, the complex political process of religious reformation in Münster moved successively from confrontation to negotiation to revolution and finally to a Catholic restoration.

Rather different political dynamics were evident in cities where there was relatively little popular support or largely ineffective popular agitation for religious reform (Mörke 1991). This might be the case where popular evangelical preaching was effectively suppressed; where the preachers gained a following too weak to cause problems serious enough to force official action; or where unprovoked official action might make religious reform seem genuinely "unpopular." The fact is, of course, that the urban reformation was not a universal experience, even in southern Germany. In the small imperial city of Schwäbish Gmünd, for example, evangelical preachers were driven out in the aftermath of the revolts of 1525, and in the 1530s the magistrates responded to guild-based pressure for religious reform by supervising the clergy more closely and by curtailing some of their privileges, but they did so in terms of the old faith, leaving no scope for the institution of a reformed Church order. In the archepiscopal city of Cologne, too, the fear of losing significant privileges and exemptions granted by the prince-bishop appears to have prompted very quick and remarkably effective action to nip Lutheranism in the bud, with the municipal authorities burning Luther's books, supporting the very conservative theology faculty at the university, censoring the press, and closely controlling the city's pulpits.[16] At Leipzig, by contrast, it was Duke Georg of Saxony's ardent Catholicism that not only disallowed Protestant preaching but also led to the expulsion of a number of "closet Lutherans" who had taken to avoiding the confessional and to crossing the border into electoral Saxony to hear Protestant sermons. In the latter two cases especially, the obvious limit to urban reformation was (the fear of) intervention from an external authority, but several cantons of Switzerland—Luzern, Zug, Fribourg, and Solothurn—rejected the reform without such immediate external constraints. In short, confrontation between a weak reformation coalition and a resistant magistracy might lead simply to stunted reform.

Finally, there were a number of cases in which religious reform was clearly initiated and controlled by the political elite. Most often this occurred within principalities or monarchies, but this authoritarian sort of reformation occurred within the more compact political spaces of

16. Cologne may perhaps be considered typical of a number of episcopal cities that successfully suppressed the tendencies toward reform, including Paderborn, Würzburg, and Bamberg; Cameron 1991:262.

cities as well. In Zwickau, for example, the local elite very early on established a sort of gospel of civic obedience, preached by Nikolaus Hausmann but favored by few of the local population (Karant-Nunn 1987). When some of their subjects more enthusiastically followed disciples of the radical theologian Thomas Müntzer and the so-called prophets of Zwickau, the council clamped down with its stricter Lutheranism to preserve order and to prevent both radical reform and Catholic reaction. And as late as 1575 the changing opinions of the political elite led to an official reformation in the Alsatian town of Colmar (Greyerz 1980).

It is safe to say, however, that in the vast majority of cases urban reformations were precipitated by popular agitation in the wake of evangelical preaching in the early years of the Protestant revolt and that in each case there were ebbs and flows in the political process in which confrontation might yield to a variety of transient outcomes. Figure 5 illustrates these complex and variant experiences and accounts for them in terms of the interactions between variously resistant local rulers and variously constituted reformation coalitions. Although many German and Swiss cities followed a fairly simple trajectory from confrontation to compromise, this was by no means a simple or universal experience. But in the final analysis, what is striking about all of these urban reformations is that they involved a *political process*—that is, an interaction between subjects and rulers—in which the local officials of the established Church often played relatively minor roles.

Of course, the Roman Catholic church itself was weakened and divided by the defection of prelates and priests, especially in the early years of the Reformation, but more generally it is true that the terrain of cultural/religious authority was quite effectively contested by evangelical preachers.[17] Not surprisingly, the Catholic church was most successful in fending off the reformation process in those urban political spaces where it claimed both temporal and ecclesiastical authority. But even in ecclesiastical states, the Church was vulnerable because the prince-bishops were so frequently absentees who ruled only indirectly. Thus in the episcopal city of Geneva, on the southwestern frontier of the empire, for example, the prelude to religious reform was political revolution against the bishop's temporal authority in the 1520s (Monter 1967; Kingdon 1974).

---

17. Many communities arranged debates or disputations between Catholics and evangelicals as part of the political process leading toward the adoption of reform; that the result was in many cases a foregone conclusion did nothing to enhance the Church's ability to speak authoritatively on matters of faith.

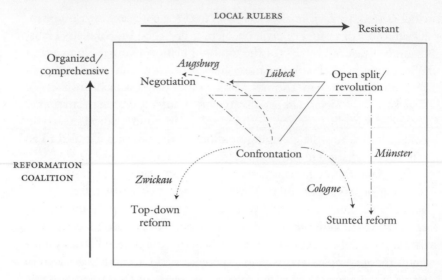

Figure 5. Variant experiences in the local reformation process

Supported by the city-state of Bern, a local coalition of "patriots" declared the city's independence from both its absentee bishop and the Duchy of Savoy on which the bishopric was dependent. After fending off a dramatic military siege in 1530, the city's new rulers only gradually began to adopt religious reforms and then by fits and starts that included, in 1538, the expulsion of the most prominent evangelical preachers in the city, Guillaume Farel and Jean Calvin. Eventually, however, a growing reformation coalition did prevail over the hesitancy of Geneva's magistrates, with the external support of Protestant Bern on whose protection the city depended. Calvin returned in the fall of 1541 to lead the Genevan Reformation but continued to face profound political difficulties until 1555. Only then did Geneva emerge as the international center of the second phase of the European Reformation (Naphy 1994).

Dynasties, Princes, and Cycles of Protest

The political dynamics of the reformation process that were especially visible in the compact urban spaces of the German-Roman Empire were not fundamentally different from the interactions of subjects and rulers more generally in the Reformation era. Variations in both the character of the reformation coalition and the receptivity of established rulers can also be said to account for a variety of political interactions in the German countryside prior to, during, and after the Peasants' War (see esp. Blickle 1992). In literally hundreds of rural juris-dictions, locally formidable coalitions were mobilized to press for redress of a range of social, economic, and religious grievances. In the short term at least, many locally vulnerable rulers were either temporarily displaced or forced into negotiations to buy time. But in the long run, the radical visions of social and political revolution that were articulated by leaders like Thomas Müntzer in the course of 1525 were not likely to find a recep-tive audience among the established lords and princes who claimed polit-ical sovereignty in the south German countryside. Moreover, as the ini-tially local conflicts aggregated into a general war, the likelihood of a well-organized and durable popular political challenge on that scale may be said to have diminished considerably while the collective strength and determination of the "princes" increased inversely. In any case, the deci-sive defeat of the peasant armies and the rural repression that followed can be said henceforth to have shaped the choices and interactions of all rulers and subjects in the German countryside.

If, prior to and during the crisis of 1525, the political engagement of ordinary German rustics implicated them in a variety of revolutionary sit-uations and tense negotiations regarding the political and religious future (see top half of figure 4), in the years after the Peasants' War, the reformation process in the German countryside yielded to a variety of more authoritarian outcomes (lower half of fig. 4): either religious reform was decisively stunted by elite resistance or it was imposed from above by authoritarian reformers. In the end, then, a large swath of ter-ritories in northern and central Germany would gradually be "Protes-tantized" as a consequence of the conversions of their immediate over-lords while (among others) Bavaria, the lands under direct Habsburg control, and the territories controlled by the major prince-bishops and most other ecclesiastical states would remain officially Catholic and even-tually subjected to a "counterreform" designed to promote a new sense of popular piety.[18] Some territories, such as the small principality of Braunschweig-Wolfenbüttel, might even be reformed, counterreformed,

18. For a useful chronology of the gradual religious changes in the German countryside, see the table in Cameron 1991:269; for a map of the religious coloring of the German prin-cipalities at the time of the Schmalkaldic War (ca. 1547), see Cameron 1991:264–265.

and re-reformed as a consequence of military interventions or dynastic successions. Surely ordinary people were not the principal architects of these essentially authoritarian reformations in the German countryside, but it is important nevertheless to recognize their instrumental roles in initiating the reformation process and moving it forward.

To reconstruct the many pieces of the German reformation process into a larger story, it may be useful to conceive of the scattered events of the urban reformation as well as the widespread explosion of peasant revolts in 1524 and 1525 as constituting a massive cycle of protest within and on the fringes of the German-Roman Empire—a cycle that began in the early 1520s and faded away in the early 1540s.[19] At the beginning of the cycle, news of the experimental reforms of religious practice that began in Wittenberg under Luther's guidance in the aftermath of the Diet of Worms in 1521 quickly spilled over a variety of political boundaries, and the "Luther question" perforce implicated a variety of rulers and subjects in an accumulating and intensifying struggle over the definition of religious and political authority. In such a cycle of protest, the generally operative limits of knowledge, communication, and solidarity are often broken; patterns of success or failure in one place and time lead to imitation or rejection in the next; and in general, a variety of political actors are emboldened to seize political opportunities that they hardly could have imagined to exist before the cycle began (cf. Giugni 1992). In this case, the military defeat of the peasant armies contrasts sharply, to be sure, with the relative success of the urban reform movements. Still, it is important to take seriously their coincidence in time and place, if for no other reason than that the defeat of the peasant armies and the rural repression that followed undoubtedly had a chastening effect on rulers and subjects alike—not only within the empire but throughout Europe as well.

The powerful confluence of so many extraordinary events across such a broad terrain cries out, then, for more than a calculation of the relative strengths and weaknesses of political actors within particular cities, territories, and regions of the empire. Indeed, it is clear that the German cycle of protest coincided with a general crisis of imperial power. Despite the emperor's intrepid support of Catholic orthodoxy and a succession of imperial edicts, it became brutally obvious in the wake of the Diet of

---

19. For a definition and an explication of the essential characteristics of (modern) cycles of protest, see Tarrow 1989:41–56.

Worms that neither Charles V nor his brother and regent, Ferdinand, was in a position to stem the tide of popular protest and unsanctioned religious innovation.[20] Not only were the imperial authorities powerless to punish, quickly and efficiently, those officials who violated imperial policy—for example, neither the municipal council of Augsburg nor the Elector of Saxony who protected Luther—but they were equally unable to protect or reward those nominal subordinates who might valiantly try to defend the established Church order—for example, the council at Lübeck—against popular demands for reform. Even the repression of the peasant revolts, which was predicated on an unusual consensus among the diverse rulers of southern Germany, was more clearly the work of the Swabian League of local and regional authorities than of the emperor.

It was, thus, in the context of a general crisis of imperial authority that there emerged an unprecedented array of coalitions in favor of religious reform—coalitions formed locally by the alliance of evangelical preachers and a newly emboldened laity in both the cities and the countryside. Especially in the heady months leading up to the conflagration of 1525, the general cycle of protest was fueled by the quite reasonable perception of extraordinary opportunities to act decisively and in some cases by apocalyptic visions of a better future. The defeat of the peasant armies severely limited or even closed down entirely the opportunities for many thousands of actors in the countryside of southern and central Germany, but the cities and more generally the cantons of the Swiss Confederation remained basically unviolated spaces within which ordinary people could continue, under the varying conditions we have already observed, to engage in the political process of religious reformation.

How long could these conditions last and the cycle of protest continue? Not long, for at least two reasons. First, the progressive division of the constituent parts of the empire and the Swiss Confederation into armed and openly hostile "Protestant"[21] and Catholic alliances clearly limited the room to maneuver for all political actors, including popular reform coalitions. Still, within the empire the defenders of the new reforms managed to forestall an armed confrontation and to bargain for

20. Charles's political options in Germany were severely limited by both constitutional and strategic constraints; see Brandi [1937] 1980; Bonney 1991.
21. The term "Protestant" was, indeed, first used in 1529 to describe a faction of the Reichstag that formally protested the authoritarian drift of imperial policy; it therefore had more clearly political than theological content.

time by demanding a general council of the Church to resolve the out-standing religious issues. Second, the reformation coalitions that were the driving force of protest and reform were transient entities. As the early destructive phase of the Reformation gave way to the immensely more difficult task of constructing a new religious order, the initially powerful coalitions between clerical reformers and ordinary people gave way to a more general estrangement of the newly professionalized Protestant clergy from what they often perceived as a "superstitious" and sometimes hostile laity (Cameron 1991:389–416). At the same time that magistrates and princes claimed increasingly to speak for and to control the new Protestantism, the initial popular enthusiasm of the reforming coalition diminished. With the gradual demise of the reformation coali-tions, then, the cycle of protest began to fade away.

Thus the summoning of the Council of Trent in 1545 and the defeat of the Protestants in the Schmalkaldic War (1545–1547) may be said to have ushered in a new phase of reformation politics. After another round of warfare in the early 1550s, the Reichstag at Augsburg in 1555 finally adopted a thoroughly authoritarian settlement encapsulated in the prin-ciple *cuius regio eius religio* (roughly, "whose rule, his religion"). By the terms of the Peace of Augsburg, the rulers of what were the culturally "sovereign" principalities of the empire would be empowered to choose either the Lutheran Augsburg Confession or Catholicism and in doing so determine the religion of their subjects, who were "free" to emigrate if they disagreed; imperial cities could adopt Lutheranism only with the proviso that they accept some form of Catholic worship as well; and ter-ritorial cities were expected to follow the decisions of their immediate overlords.

In the end, it is critical to recognize that the political variables that may be said to have governed the interactions of subjects and rulers in the beginning of the cycle of religious protest and reform in Germany are not the same as those that determined the long-term outcome of the reformation process. The point is, of course, that the local and relatively compact or dense political spaces within which the interactions origi-nated were not inviolable, and eventually the networks of alliance or lines of competition that evolved among the various rulers of Charles V's vast domain could be as important to the outcome of the process as the rela-tive strength or resolve of the locally mobilized popular political actors. In some cases, popular reformation coalitions might be allied with local authorities, as a result of local negotiations or compromises, but opposed by an array of territorial and imperial authorities (see fig. 2a); in others, where revolutionary splits divided rulers from subjects, reform coalitions might find themselves facing a formidable threat of outside intervention from transient alliances of local, territorial, and imperial rulers (see fig. 2b). But even if those interlocal networks of political power can be said to account generally for the religious geography of Germany at the end of Charles V's tempestuous reign as emperor, this does not obliterate the critical roles that ordinary people played in initiating the reformation process in the towns and villages in which they lived and worshiped. Nor does it diminish the long-term importance of these interactions—as embedded in new structures of power and in inevitably partial and locally partisan historical memories—for domestic political interactions once the immediate cycle of protest and reform had passed.

In the final analysis, a simple tabulation of winners and losers in this complex historical process is impossible for at least two reasons. First, it would involve an infinitely complex comparison of the intentions and transient achievements of an enormous range of political actors. But even if we could, despite the obvious documentary and epistemological uncertainties involved, execute such a comparison, we would certainly find that no one could have willed or intended the bundle of political and religious compromises that were legitimated by the Peace of Augsburg. Though the peace was formally promulgated in Charles V's name, it was an outcome of the political process that he personally could not accept; indeed, prior to the meeting of the imperial diet he had abdicated the imperial throne and turned over his authority in the complex negotiations to his brother, Ferdinand, who would later be crowned the new emperor. Apparently the ever-pious Charles could not bring himself to recognize the legitimacy of Protestant churches within the empire; in any case, it is clear that the ever-political Charles could not have lived with the permanent limitations on his sovereign authority as emperor. Though, as we shall see in chapter 4, another round of conflict culminating in the Thirty Years' War redrew the religious map of Germany and the imperial constitution continued to preserve an important degree of imperial "sovereignty," the Peace of Augsburg laid down the parameters of Germany's subsequent political and cultural development. The official cultural monopoly of the Roman Catholic church had been broken, and both the cultural and political "sovereignty" of the empire had been fundamentally segmented.

Patterns of Princely Reformation

To understand the political significance of the reformation process in Germany in a broader comparative context, it will be useful to examine briefly the "princely" reformations that took place simultaneously in Scandinavia and England. In terms of sheer numbers of ordinary people whose religious experience was transformed by the reformation process, the princely reformations in northern Germany and beyond were obviously more important than the popular urban reformations since in most of Europe only a small minority of the population lived in cities.[22] It would be as misleading, however, to imagine a singular "princely" type of reformation as it is to posit a uniform and unchanging experience of urban reformation. Here we will take as our point of departure the assumption that a princely reformation is one in which the reform of religious ritual and belief occurred with at least the tacit support of the territorial lord or prince. Given this obviously broad and inclusive baseline, it will be possible not only to describe a range of variation in princely reformations but also to underscore once again the importance of popular engagement in the political process of reformation. In Scandinavia alone, Ole Peter Grell (1992, 1995) distinguishes three different patterns of princely reformation: in the duchies of Schleswig and Holstein and in the composite monarchies of Denmark/Norway and Sweden/Finland. But before we look at each in turn, we need to recognize their common historical background in the Union of Scandinavian Kingdoms.

Originally the dynastic achievement in 1397 of the Danish queen, Margrethe I, the Union of Scandinavian Kingdoms (including Norway, Denmark, and Sweden, along with Finland and the duchies of Schleswig and Holstein) was at the beginning of the sixteenth century on the verge of collapse (Kirby 1990; Metcalf 1995). Christian II's aggressive attempts to consolidate his control over this vast dynastic composite served only to antagonize both the lay and the ecclesiastical elites whose authority at the local and regional levels he threatened (Grell 1995). Following the massacre of some eighty lay and ecclesiastical lords in Stockholm in 1520,

---

22. Clearly there were great variations within Europe, with the highest concentrations of urban population in northern Italy, the Rhineland, and the Low Countries; by contrast, the least urbanized parts of Europe were on the peripheries of the southwest and the northeast, including Scandinavia. See especially De Vries 1984.

a noble revolt led by Gustav Vasa reestablished the independence of the Swedish kingdom in 1521, with Vasa as regent.[23] Meanwhile, the growing opposition of the Danish aristocracy led in 1523 to the overthrow and exile of Christian II, followed by the election of Duke Frederik of Schleswig and Holstein, Christian's uncle, as king. Gustav Vasa and Frederik I, as usurpers, had a common interest in preventing the return of Christian II, and despite Gustav's suspicion that Frederik sought to reunite the composite under the Danish Crown, they cooperated to fend off Christian's intermittent attacks until his final defeat in 1532. It was against this backdrop of political instability and uncertainty—what we might regard as a classic political crisis within a composite state—that the Protestant Reformation first took root in Scandinavia.

The duchies of Schleswig and Holstein illustrate the enormous political complexities of late medieval dynasticism. The duke of Holstein was a vassal of the German-Roman Empire while the duke of Schleswig was a vassal of Denmark, but in 1460 the two units had been declared to be administratively "inseparable and indivisible" (Lausten 1995). Under Christian II, the duchies had been ruled separately by Duke Frederik, but with his election as king they were once again brought closer to the Danish kingdom. In 1525, Frederik's son, Christian, who eventually succeeded to the Danish throne as Christian III, took over administration of Haderslev and Tönning, which were part of the duchy of Schleswig, and it was under his sponsorship that Lutheranism was first institutionalized in the region (Grell 1992; Lausten 1995). Although there had been evangelical preachers in the area since 1521, where possible Christian intervened directly to dismiss prelates opposed to reform, to appoint evangelical preachers, to provide training for evangelical pastors, and to design new ecclesiastical regulations—first in Haderslev alone, but after 1526 (when he became regent of the two duchies) more generally in Schleswig and Holstein. By 1528, according to Grell (1992:97), the "Reformation was a *fait accompli*" when the Synod at Haderslev, called by Christian, enacted the Haderslev Church Ordinance. One of the first of what would be many Lutheran church ordinances in Europe, the Haderslev Church Ordinance was intended to guide the parish clergy in their pastoral activities; besides advising the ministers to preach the Gospel as spelled out by Luther, it obliged them to swear an oath of allegiance to the duke.

Within the small domain of Haderslev (and more generally in

23. Gustav Vasa was not crowned king of Sweden until 1528.

Schleswig and Holstein), a modest popular base aligned with the active support of the local lord was sufficient to prevail over the modest opposition of the episcopal establishment. The result was an essentially peaceful and official reform with a strong dose of civil regulation of formerly ecclesiastical affairs such as education and poor relief. Within the larger kingdom of Denmark, by contrast, the political dynamics of the reformation process were significantly different. In the first place, King Frederik owed his position to the combined lay and ecclesiastical elite who had deposed his nephew; indeed, according to the coronation charter that he was required to sign in 1523, Frederik promised, "[We will] not allow any heretics, disciples of Luther or others to preach and teach, either openly or secretly, against God, the faith of the Holy Church, the holiest father, the Pope, or the Catholic Church, but where they are found in this Kingdom, We promise to punish them on life and property" (quoted in Grell 1992:104). Though Frederik clearly violated this oath in several instances, he was nevertheless forced in some measure to honor it at least publicly as long as the return of Christian II, who had converted to Lutheranism in exile, was a real threat. Consequently, the process of reformation in Denmark proceeded more clearly from the bottom up, building on the base of popular reformation coalitions in the cities (see Grell 1992; Lausten 1995). The earliest successes of popular evangelical preaching were in the small city of Viborg in Jutland where Hans Tausen, a former member of the Order of Saint John of Jerusalem, was able to build up a popular following and a colleague, Jorgen Jensen Sadolin, established a school for evangelical preachers in 1526; both men were supported by royal letters of protection, granted at the request of local magistrates.[24]

In the same year, a Danish Herredag (Parliament) meeting in Odense transformed the Catholic church in Denmark into a national church as a means of dealing with clerical abuse without transforming religious practice; in practice this meant that locally appointed bishops were not to seek confirmation from Rome and that revenues that had earlier been sent to Rome should now flow to the Crown. In the following year, however, Frederik publicly proclaimed a neutral stance with regard to matters of ritual and belief, declaring that "'the Holy Christian Faith is free' and that he governed 'life and property, not the soul'" (Grell

---

24. Frederik justified these letters of protection, in apparent breach of his coronation oath, by claiming that he only protected preachers of the pure Gospel, not heretics (Lausten 1995:20).

1992:106). With this kind of tacit support, the evangelicals gathered strength in Viborg, appropriating the Franciscan and Dominican monasteries for their own use, closing down many parish churches, and restricting Catholic worship to the Cathedral; by the end of 1529, public disturbances had ended public Catholic worship altogether. Meanwhile, the reform-minded magistracy of Malmö in Scania (today part of Sweden) began actively recruiting evangelical preachers. At first evangelical preaching was only allowed outside the walls of the town, but as the services became more popular they were moved into a chapel and finally a larger church. The reform movement suffered a temporary setback in Malmö in 1528 when the archbishop of Lund threatened the magistrates with a heresy trial, but by 1529, again with the tacit approval of the king, the evangelical preachers and magistrates of Malmö were emboldened sufficiently to seize church properties, including the mendicant houses, and to rid the city of a restive Catholic minority (Grell 1988, 1990). By 1530 the evangelical reform movement had gained a significant following in all the towns and cities of Denmark (Lausten 1995), but in Copenhagen it had been denied comparable political success, in part because of the strong defense of the Catholic establishment by the local bishop. At the same time, however, the effectiveness of popular support for religious reform was deflected by factionalism that paralyzed the municipal council. Although there were at least four evangelical preachers in the city and the city council had managed to take over most of the monasteries, Copenhagen remained divided between Protestants and Catholics prior to Christian II's last attempt to regain his throne in 1531—this time with the support of his brother-in-law, Charles V of Habsburg, at whose insistence Christian had reconverted to Catholicism.

The final defeat and arrest of Christian II in 1532 might have signaled the beginning of a more comprehensive princely reformation had it not been for the untimely death of Frederik I. When a conservative minority of aristocrats on the royal council prevented the immediate election of Frederick's Lutheran son, Duke Christian of Schleswig and Holstein, the stage was set for civil war: the Grevens Fejde, which was precipitated by the revolt of Malmö against the royal council, ostensibly in defense of its municipal reformation (cf. Grell 1988). Although the aristocrats quickly backed down and elected Christian a month later, the alliance of Malmö and (more reluctantly) Copenhagen with the Hanseatic cities of northern Germany defined the essentially political struggle between the king and key elements of his composite domain (with both sides supporting Lutheranism) until Copenhagen finally surrendered in 1536. Once

Christian III had won the war, he immediately imprisoned the Catholic bishops and summoned a parliament, composed of an unusually large number of gentry, burghers, and peasants, to create a Lutheran territorial Church (Metcalf 1995). In light of its broad base of popular support after a full decade of evangelical preaching, especially in the cities, the Church Ordinance of 1537 proved to be an excellent tool for Christian III, in the wake of nearly two decades of political instability, to consolidate his "sovereignty" in a remarkably uniform and direct fashion throughout his domain.

In the kingdom of Sweden, the reformation process followed yet another course (Grell 1992; Kouri 1995; see also Roberts 1968). Though Gustav Vasa is often said to have been less keenly interested in evangelical religion than his Danish counterparts, that he charted a far more hesitant course toward the creation of a Lutheran national church reflects real political constraints as well. For our purposes, what is most telling is the general consensus that evangelical preaching failed to build a broad base of popular support for the cause of religious reformation in either Sweden or Finland. Thus popular support for the Protestant cause was strongest in Stockholm, particularly among the large German population, which was always in some sense suspect because of its extensive ties with the (Lutheran) Hanseatic cities of the Baltic coast. By the same token, prior to 1540 Vasa was faced repeatedly with rural uprisings that not only protested the heavy taxation that Vasa demanded to repay the significant debts he incurred in fighting for Swedish independence but also defended traditional Catholic religious practice. The latter reflected, in all likelihood, not so much a generalized peasant conservatism as the considerable success of Catholic priests in gaining popular support by identifying with peasant grievances against the fiscal exactions of the new monarch (Kouri 1995).[25]

To be sure, none of this prevented Vasa from "nationalizing" the Swedish Church as a means of solving his financial difficulties. Indeed, very early on Vasa began secularizing monastic lands, claiming that "the church consisted of all believers and that its resources had been given for public ends: in other words the church's wealth belonged to the nation" (Grell 1992:113). In 1527, despite rural unrest, a Riksdag (Parliament) meeting at Västeras forced the return of ecclesiastical fiefs to the Crown.

---

25. The episcopal hierarchy was, it should be noted, fundamentally weakened during the war of independence by continued vacancies in key Church positions.

Significantly, as part of this bargain, the king took over the administration of all lay properties belonging to monasteries and the Church, but the lay nobility was allowed to reclaim all properties donated to the Church since 1454.[26] Still, in response to the ongoing danger of popular opposition, Vasa promised to retain the religious status quo, claiming that modest changes in religious ceremonies and ecclesiastical discipline (a "compromise" enacted by the national synod in 1529) had neither been forbidden nor enforced by him. When the national synod went even further in the 1530s to mandate that all services be conducted in Swedish and that Swedish manuals be used for baptisms and marriage, royal directives pointed out that the clergy were not empowered to introduce religious changes; the king also attacked the most prominent spokesmen for an independent evangelical church (indeed, they were his former advisers) for "failing to teach obedience towards secular authority" (Grell 1992: 116). Finally, the Riksdag meeting at Örebro in 1539 authorized the king to take full control of the Swedish Church, and the king, as "protector of the Holy Christian faith in the whole kingdom," promptly issued instructions for a new Church government. Still, throughout Gustav Vasa's reign (1528–1560), the Swedish Church managed to accommodate a variety of theological tendencies and ritual styles. It did not adopt a full Protestant church order until 1571, and it was not until 1593 that it adopted a strictly Lutheran theology (Kouri 1995).

As these three cases suggest, "princely" reformations, too, were complex political processes that yielded a variety of often transient outcomes that served primarily to structure the next round of interaction rather than to freeze any particular state of affairs. For our purposes, it is particularly important to note that the different dynamics evident in the reformation processes in Schleswig/Holstein, Denmark, and Sweden reflect variations both in the relative strength of reformation coalitions and in the size and character of the political spaces within which they interacted with a variety of "sovereigns." In all three cases, it is important to recognize the political significance of popular support for the evangelical cause, but to judge by the contrasting experiences of Denmark and Sweden, in large composite states a substantial base of popular mobilization was the sine qua non of a thoroughgoing transformation of religious ritual and belief. Conversely, it was only in the relatively com-

---

26. Metcalf 1995 argues that this bargain helped to reduce the need for new exactions on peasants and thus to buy domestic peace for the new regime.

pact space of a semiautonomous feudal principality like Haderslev that a thoroughgoing reformation of religious practice *and* ecclesiastical politics could be enacted experimentally, largely from above.

Turning finally to England, it would seem that the better-known events of the English Reformation in general and the Pilgrimage of Grace in particular would easily fit within this range of variation. To be sure, it is no more possible to summarize the rich results of the last thirty years of research on England's experience of religious reformation than it is to do justice to the richness of reformation research on Germany and Scandinavia.[27] Much has changed in the way historians approach and disagree about the reformation in England, but for our purposes there are two new perspectives that are particularly important. First, much like students of Germany and Scandinavia, historians of the English Reformation have moved away from grand explanations of a singular "event" or even a discrete set of events; instead they are more likely to imagine an especially long and drawn-out *political process*, full of contingency and spiced with dramatic reversals of fortune, in which the transformation of ecclesiastical politics—that is, the formal separation of the Church of England from Rome—was distinct from the reformation of religious practice, not unlike the Swedish experience in this regard. At the very least, according to Christopher Haigh, one can say that England experienced a whole complex of discontinuous and parallel reformations: "There were three political Reformations: a Henrican political Reformation between 1530 and 1538, much of it reversed between 1538 and 1546; an Edwardian political Reformation between 1547 and 1553, almost completely reversed [by Queen Mary] between 1553 and 1558; and an Elizabethan political reformation between 1559 and 1563—which was not reversed" (1993:14). Haigh goes on to distinguish a parallel "evangelical" reformation: "The Protestant Reformation of individual conversions by preachers and personal contacts, the Reformation which began in London, Cambridge, and Oxford from about 1520, and was never completed" (ibid.).

The political process of these transient and discontinuous political reformations includes a whole series of well-known skirmishes and showdowns among different kinds of rulers: between high churchmen

27. I am especially dependent in what follows on Christopher Haigh's work, both in exploring the recent research (1987) and in surveying the critical events (1993); for a broader range of opinion, especially with regard to ordinary people, see Scarisbrick 1984 and Whiting 1989. The standard account, emphasizing religion as opposed to politics, has long been Dickens 1964.

and royal officials; between different claimants to national political and religious sovereignty; between national claimants and local rulers. But as the recent literature has shown, the political processes of the English reformations also emphatically included ordinary people. Again, Haigh summarizes the results:

"People" mattered in these Reformations because they were there and they took part. Sometimes, some rebelled: in 1536, 1549, 1554, and 1569 there were major risings caused partly by religious discontents; there were lesser but potentially dangerous disorders in 1537, 1541, 1548, and 1570. Sometimes, and especially in London, some actively advanced the cause of Reformation, pulling down images in 1547, mocking the mass in 1548, pulling down altars in 1550. Some were converted by Protestant proselytizing; some were outraged by such heresy, resorting to personal violence or informing to authority. And everywhere, always, people obeyed or did not obey rules of Reformation or de-Reformation, and their obedience or disobedience is Reformation history. (Ibid., 19)

Here again there is much that is familiar about the English reformations: the critical importance of popular engagement; the broad range of possible responses, from individual acts of disobedience to mass collective action; the episodic quality of large-scale action. The point, however, is not to make the English reformations look just like all others but to use the peculiarities of the English experience to highlight critical aspects of the Reformation era more generally.

In this regard, I should like to return to the story with which I introduced the English Reformation at the beginning of this chapter, the Pilgrimage of Grace. In 1536, amid the first of the political reformations—the Henrican reformation in which the Church of England was separated from Rome and monastic property was expropriated by the Crown—large numbers of ordinary English subjects chose to protest the fiscal demands of their government and took up arms in defense of their parish churches. Imagine the scene. In the summer and fall of 1536, royal commissioners were fanning out throughout the kingdom, closing monasteries, suppressing superfluous saints' days and popular festivals, and allegedly confiscating the movable wealth of local churches. The very embodiment of "negative confiscatory policies which seemed to be the hallmark of the changes of the 1530s" (Davies 1985:83), these agents of a distant but very aggressive sovereign met with a variety of forms of resistance ranging from passive noncooperation to humble petitions and direct threats, but at the beginning of October a relatively minor confrontation at Louth in Lincolnshire set off a chain of events by which rumors, alarms, and musters called tens of thousands of ordinary people into action in defense variously of God, faith, Church, king, and the common good. A great assembly of these common folk at Lincoln boldly supported a series of demands, drafted by the gentry, regarding taxation, heresy, suppression of monasteries, punishment of those responsible for oppression, and pardon for the rebels, but when the king refused to negotiate, the aristocratic leaders of the movement persuaded the commoner to disperse within ten days of the original incident.

A parallel movement farther north in Yorkshire shared many of the symbols, goals, and oaths of the Lincolnshire mobilization but proved to be considerably more organized and durable. Led by an obscure and slightly mysterious lawyer, Robert Aske, this "Pilgrimage of Grace" eventually mobilized more than twenty thousand men who represented a significant challenge to the fiscal and ecclesiastical reform policies of King Henry. On October 16 rebels from throughout Yorkshire and beyond converged on York and entered the city. From there the forces marched under the banner of the Five Wounds of Christ (a crusading symbol) to Pontefract, where Lord Darcy surrendered the royal castle and joined the rebellion, and on toward Doncaster where they confronted a small royal army. Though some of the rebels wanted to march all the way to London, on October 27 the royal and rebel armies agreed to a truce, in the expectation of negotiations with the king, and most of the rebel army disbanded, though Aske and his fellow leaders remained in effective governmental control of the north.

Once again Henry was inclined to refuse negotiations, but it was clear to his advisers that he had little choice but to offer to negotiate. Consequently hundreds of representatives of the rebel movement met in late November and early December to formulate a statement of their grievances. As in the German peasant assemblies of 1525, a variety of economic and political issues mingled somewhat awkwardly with administrative and religious issues, but it is clear that it was the religious issues and symbolism and the common defense of a locally integrated church that bound the uneasy coalition of ordinary people and elite leaders together (Davies 1985). Finally formal negotiations at Doncaster on December 6 appeared to yield significant royal concessions, and on December 8 Aske convinced the pilgrims to go home. Later, when it became obvious that the rebels had been duped and that the king had no intention of satisfying their demands, an unsuccessful attempt to re-create the initial mobilization called forth a violent repression in which many of the gentry elite who had initially joined this broadly based regional coalition against the king's reform polices now participated in rounding up and executing nearly two hundred rebel leaders.

In the most general sense, the Pilgrimage of Grace highlights the reality of popular *opposition* to the reformation process. Largely invisible, especially during the first phase of the European Reformation, because it so often took the form of individual acts of disobedience, opposition was nevertheless predictable, if for no other reason than that the religious questions of the day divided people at all levels of society. Even more, then, the political process by which the Reformation was enacted was sure to divide rather than unite people for whom the Reformation entailed much more than shifting religious sensibilities. This is, of course, the essence of what it means to say that religion and politics were inextricably entwined. Moreover, the political struggles of the reformation process not only required ordinary political subjects to make choices they might rather have avoided, but it taught them willy-nilly how (and how not) to be political. In short, despite all the research that focuses on popular support for the reformation of religion, we must remember that this was always a matter of choice and that in choosing either for or against the Reformation ordinary people entered a much larger political process in which even apparently modest and essentially private choices in one round of interaction laid down the parameters of choice for the next round.[28]

In a more specific sense, the Pilgrimage of Grace—precisely because it affected the form of a pilgrimage toward the center of power—highlights the critical relationship between the scale of popular collective action and the qualities of the political space in which the power to reform "religion and regime" was being contested. In 1536 the people of Yorkshire were fighting a whole complex of battles simultaneously, the points at issue ranging from enclosures of commons land to the preservation of monastic communities (Elton 1980; Fletcher 1983; Davies 1984, 1985). But what is striking, from a broader comparative perspective, is that these battles were being fought within the political space defined by an almost uniquely uncomplicated monarchy. To be sure, England had previously been the core of a much more complex composite state that spanned the English Channel, and it would soon serve again as the core of a composite that included Ireland and Scotland. By 1536, however, the political

28. This important lesson is especially relevant, I think, in the second phase of the European Reformation, which will be addressed in the next chapter.

incorporation of England and Wales was more or less secure, and for the time being the political dimensions of England were remarkably simple. In this political context, the constituent unit of popular mobilization was still the local community—as it was elsewhere in Europe—but the effective arena for political contestation regarding the critical questions of "religion and regime" had effectively been "nationalized" inasmuch as the pilgrims of Yorkshire sought the redress of their grievances from their royal—as opposed to provincial or local—"sovereign." To have an impact within this comparatively vast arena, it was clearly necessary for local mobilizations to be aggregated into a larger "pilgrimage" oriented toward negotiations with London. Ordinary political actors inevitably turned for support to allies or brokers who could exploit networks of communication with the king through which their grievances might be satisfied. In retrospect, we may think them naive for trusting that the aristocratic leaders of their broad coalition would represent them effectively, or for imagining that the king might be willing to engage and treat with them so directly. Nevertheless, in choosing to enter the national arena in this dramatic way, they helped immeasurably, though unwittingly, to confirm for succeeding generations the notion that questions of religion and regime were appropriately national questions requiring solutions that applied to the whole kingdom in equal measure.

Official Reformations and State Power

From the perspective of England, then, the multitude of reformations on the Continent take on rather clearer political hues. In the first half of the sixteenth century, all Protestant reformations, regardless of who inspired or instigated them, were "official" reformations in the sense that wherever they succeeded, they were formally enacted or instituted in law for whole populations by political officials. For the most part, Europe's new Protestant rulers gladly expropriated Church property and diverted Church revenue for their own use, but they also willy-nilly took on vast new responsibilities, formerly within the domain of the established Church, for the regulation of public welfare and the education (and employment) of pastors.[29] In this sense, the political process of

29. Though Protestant reformations varied considerably with regard to the pace and direc-

religious reformation clearly entailed a broader transformation of the essential relationships among various kinds of rulers and their political subjects—what we might usefully call state formation, not in the dynastic sense of accumulating new territory, but in the qualitative sense that specific rulers consolidated unprecedented claims to cultural sovereignty within their domains (see fig. 1). But if the German principle of cuius regio eius religio captures the culturally authoritarian drift of these outcomes, then the most telling question to ask in assessing the larger political consequences of the reformation process is, Which rulers in what domains?

To answer that question as precisely as possible for those places where the Protestant Reformation was institutionalized is to begin to describe the various trajectories of state formation that emerged from the first phase of the political and religious conflicts of this tumultuous era. Suffice it here to summarize the general tendencies. In the German Empire as well as neighboring Switzerland, Protestant reformations were enacted by local rulers—usually urban magistrates or territorial princes, but occasionally by peasant referenda—at the expense of Charles V and his imperial claim to cultural sovereignty (see fig. 2a). In England, Denmark, and Sweden, by contrast, Protestant reformations were enacted nationally by kings and parliaments at the expense of local self-determination (see fig. 2c). In both of these trajectories, ordinary people were essential to the political alignments—what I have termed the reformation coalitions—that both precipitated and sustained them over time. But what, then, of those parts of Germany where, amid the tumult of a general cycle of protest and reform, reformation coalitions tried and failed to break the religious monopoly of the Catholic church? Though the repression of religious dissent certainly enjoyed the encouragement and support of the emperor, it was not necessarily a victory for his exclusive claim to cultural sovereignty. On the contrary, in the absence of popular support for the ecclesiastical establishment, it is clear that the alignment of local rulers with the emperor in defense of the Catholic church resulted in the consolidation of elite power at the expense of popular political actors who might advocate religious reform or at least liberty of conscience (see fig. 2b). This outcome was not unlike the settlement that followed the Comunero Revolt in Castile where there was little popular

---

tion of change in dogmatic belief and ritual practice, they invariably involved the destruction of a religious establishment previously oriented toward Rome.

support for the king but a substantial accommodation of elite interests. As we shall see in chapters 3 and 4, only in the second half of the sixteenth century, following the Council of Trent, did the Catholic rulers of Europe learn to tap the resurgent popular piety of the Counter-Reformation church to enable new forms of territorial consolidation at the expense of local elites.

3

Religious Dissent and Civil War in France and the Low Countries

1. Firstly, no church should aspire to any precedence or domination over another.

2. Each colloquy or synod should elect a president to preside over it. This office to come to an end at the conclusion of each synod or council.

3. The ministers should take with them to each synod an elder or deacon, or several. . . .

6. The ministers shall be elected by the elders and deacons of the consistory, and presented to the congregation to which they are ordained; if there is opposition, it shall be for the consistory to adjudicate. . . .

15. Those [ministers] who teach bad doctrine, and after having been admonished do not desist, those also of scandalous life meriting punishment by the magistrate or excommunication, or disobedient to the consistory, or insufficient in other ways, shall be deposed. . . .

20. The elders and deacons are the senate of the church, and the minister shall preside. . . .

27. Heretics, despisers of God, rebels against the consistory, traitors against the church, those accused and condemned for crimes worthy of corporal punishment, and those who bring scandals upon the church, are to be excommunicated and cast out, not only from the sacraments, but also from the whole assembly. As for other vices, it will be left to the discretion of the church to decide whether those excluded from the sacraments will be admitted to hear the word of God preached. Articles of Discipline,
Synod of Paris, 1559

There is no province which is not infected, and in some of them the contagion has spread even to the countryside, as in Normandy, almost all of Brittany, Touraine, Poitou, Guyenne, Gascony, a large part of Languedoc, Dauphiné, Provence, Champagne—together making almost three quarters of the kingdom. In many places, the heretics hold their meetings, which they call assemblies, wherein they read, preach, and live in the way of Geneva, without any regard for the king's ministers or his commands. The contagion extends to every class, and (a strange thing!) even to ecclesiastics. . . . All the harm done has not yet appeared openly. . . .

Giovanni Michieli,
Venetian ambassador to Paris, 1562

In May 1559 representatives of a handful of the many fledgling Protestant churches in the kingdom of France met secretly in Paris to draft a common Confession of Faith and to adopt Articles of Discipline for a national church. Though the famous leader of the Genevan Reformation might not have approved of every detail, the work of the Synod of Paris bore unequivocal witness to the immense influence of Jean Calvin in his estranged homeland. And although the delegates to the synod might very well have bridled at the charge of separatism, their work betrayed an acceptance of their inability to capture the Gallican Church from within. Instead of reforming the old Church root and branch, they created an entirely alternative and distinctively "Reformed" ecclesiastical structure modeled on Geneva's Ecclesiastical Ordinances (Duke, Lewis, and Pettegree 1992:72–76). Thus, according to the Articles of Discipline, the new French Church would be ruled by a pyramidal structure of elected bodies extending from local consistories to national synods, all of which would include both clergy and laity. Ministers would be elected by and responsible to local consistories, and local consistories, including elected elders and deacons as well as clergy, would be responsible for the discipline of the faithful. To be sure, there were ambiguities and unresolved issues in the documents of 1559, which later synods would attempt to correct, but there is no doubt about the course that the Synod of Paris charted for French Protestantism: the "true" church would be a separate church including only the faithful who were willing to submit to the authority and discipline of the consistory.[1]

On the face of it, the spring of 1559 may be considered an inauspicious time for a clandestine meeting to organize a revolutionary church. Just one month earlier the kings of Spain and France, Philip II and Henry II, had signed the Peace of Cateau-Cambrésis, thereby ending a long series

---

1. This is not to say that the French Protestants had given up all hope of eventually controlling the French Church through the conversion of the king; Greengrass 1994.

of Habsburg-Valois wars. This pivotal agreement not only reversed the diplomatic alignment of Europe but also "bound the Catholic monarchies in a joint endeavor to crush Protestantism" (Salmon 1975:117). While the synod was meeting in Paris, then, the French royal government was redoubling its efforts to persecute "heretics." Indeed, given the history of official intolerance of Protestants in France, extreme Catholic partisans like the duke of Guise felt entirely justified in resolving to "exterminate all those of the Huguenot religion as guilty of divine and human *lèse majesté*."[2] Still, the situation changed dramatically when in July Henry II died from the wound he received in a tournament celebrating the treaty with Spain; the genuine political uncertainty that ensued resulted in unprecedented opportunities for the new Reformed Protestants.[3] Increasingly public in their worship and organization, Reformed preachers seemed by 1562 to be gaining new adherents everywhere.[4] With a touch of the paranoid exaggeration that characterized the defenders of the Catholic faith, the Venetian ambassador reported that the "contagion" seemed to be spreading throughout France and that "the heretics . . . read, preach, and live in the way of Geneva, without any regard for the king's ministers or his commands" (Coudy 1969:96). It was soon evident, however, that the Protestants' greatest expectations and the Catholics' worst fears would not be quickly realized, for in the course of 1562 France was torn by the first of a series of nine civil wars that would last until 1598 and would end in a temporary stalemate.

Meanwhile, the intended repression of Protestant dissent fared no better in the Low Countries domain of Philip II.[5] After concluding the peace with France, Philip departed the Netherlands for Spain, leaving his half-sister, Margaret of Parma, as governor-general and opening up a period of genuine political uncertainty. Following an aborted attempt by local noblemen to reverse the most aggressive religious policies of the new government, however, there was an explosion of popular religious dissent in the Low Countries as well. Like their counterparts in France,

2. Quoted in Greengrass 1983a:376; on the origins of the term "Huguenot" to designate French Protestants, see Gray 1983.
3. See Benedict 1981:9–94. The term "Reformed" may be preferable to the term "Calvinist," for despite the obvious influence of Jean Calvin, not only in France but more generally in Europe during the second half of the sixteenth century, we should not exaggerate the unity of the movement or the influence of a single leader; what is more, "Reformed" along with the originally derogatory "Huguenot" is what the actors themselves used.
4. See the map of French Protestantism in Mandrou 1977:127.
5. On the character and fate of Protestant dissent in Spain, see Kamen 1994.

Reformed preachers in the Low Countries attracted thousands of people to their illegal assemblies on the outskirts of the region's many cities, and in 1566–1567 a spectacular wave of popular iconoclasm spread from Flanders in the southwest to Groningen in the northeast.[6] The seventeenth-century historian Gerard Brandt describes the beginning of the process in Flanders:

At first, [the Mob] attacked the Crosses and Images that had been erected in the great Roads of the Country; next, those in Villages; and lastly, those in Cities and Towns: All the Chappels, Churches, and Convents which they found shut they forced open, breaking, tearing, and destroying all the Images, Pictures, Shrines, and other consecrated things they met with. . . . Swift as lightning the evil diffused itself, insomuch that in the space of three days above four hundred Churches were plundered. (Rowen 1972:34)

Philip responded to the iconoclasm by sending the duke of Alva at the head of a sizable Spanish army in 1567, but a military countermobilization by a broad coalition of religious and political dissidents set the stage for eight decades of intermittent warfare that by 1600 resulted in the de facto independence of the United Provinces of the Northern Netherlands in which the new Reformed Church enjoyed a public and privileged position.

These developments in France and the Low Countries are central to the second phase of the European Reformation, which unfolded in the second half of the sixteenth century. The first phase had been especially associated with two prominent German theologians—Luther and Zwingli—and had enjoyed only limited success outside the relatively autonomous cities and territories of the German Empire and the Swiss Confederation. In the absence of royal or princely conversions as in Scandinavia and England, there were, as it turned out, only limited opportunities for popular reformation coalitions to accomplish the formal religious reformation of whole communities and the institutional transformation of territorial churches.[7] Conversely, initially promising reform movements were effectively repressed or at least driven underground in Iberia, Italy, France, and the Low Countries. Following a series of Protestant reversals in the 1540s, however, there was a new explosion of popular religious dissent beginning in the late 1550s that immediately

6. See the map of Netherlandic iconoclasm in Parker 1985:77.
7. On the limited success of the early Reformation, see the articles collected in Pettegree 1992a, especially the introductory survey by Andrew Pettegree.

and directly challenged the authority of the established Church and boldly announced the beginning of the "Second Reformation."[8]

The religious conflicts and civil wars in France and the Low Countries bear many striking similarities.[9] In both cases, the new Reformed churches grew out of the experience of official repression and the formation of secret conventicles; they were nurtured by truly international networks of support, rooted in exile communities like those in London, Emden, Wesel, Strasbourg, and Geneva; they drew much of their popular support from urban artisans; and they depended for their survival on the political and military support of powerful noble factions. They were also quickly caught up in the maelstrom of very long and destructive civil wars. By 1600, however, these parallel, even interdependent, developments had yielded remarkably different ecclesiastical and political outcomes.[10] In France the Edict of Nantes (1598) established a limited toleration for Reformed Protestant worship and even allowed the continued fortification of Protestant strongholds—at royal expense!—but nevertheless set the stage for the forceful reconstruction and extension of royal power in the coming decades. By contrast, the northern Netherlands territories that joined the Union of Utrecht in 1579 and formally abjured their sovereign in 1581 emerged by 1600 as a permanent confederation of sovereign provinces in which the Reformed church enjoyed a privileged status and Catholics a variable but severely limited toleration. In between, in the southern Netherlands the Catholic church was restored to its monopoly position, but at the cost of a massive emigration of Protestants and permanent constitutional limitations on its "foreign" sovereign, the Habsburg king of Spain. These very different outcomes established, in turn, clearly divergent trajectories of constitutional and political-cultural development that lasted for nearly two centuries.

Against the backdrop of broadly similar experiences during the First Reformation, these clearly divergent historical trajectories in France and the Low Countries represent the comparative problem that is at the heart of this chapter. Not merely a matter of the success or failure of "The

8. On both the utility and difficulty in adopting this term, see Schilling 1992 and Scribner 1994.
9. For an early and very suggestive comparison, see Van Gelder 1930; unfortunately, suggestive beginnings like this have rarely spawned systematic international comparisons in the largely "national" historiographies of the Reformation era. See also Van Nierop 1995 for a comparison that is very similar to my own except that it focuses more clearly on elite politics on a grander scale. Woltjer 1994 presents a very useful comparison on the question of popular violence in particular.
10. On the interdependence of these histories, see Parker 1985 and Sutherland 1980.

Reformation"—and thus not easily reducible to universalizing arguments regarding regional culture or social structure in either a Weberian or a Marxian mode—the religious settlements that emerged from the Second Reformation were the unintended and thoroughly ambiguous consequences of many decades of political and military struggle that pitted religious dissenters against the defenders of the Catholic church. Rather than narrate the military/political struggles at the (inter)national level, however, I highlight the varieties of popular mobilization during the civil and religious wars of the second half of the sixteenth century and explore variations in the patterns of political interaction across time and space. Throughout my goal is to show how the divergent trajectories that were the consequence of the religious struggles of the Second Reformation need to be understood in terms of differences in the character and fate of popular mobilization for political action in relation to both local rulers and national claimants to religious and political authority (see figs. 6 and 7 below). In this phase especially, the political process of religious reformation entailed deep and enduring divisions within as well as among communities and polities.

Building "Churches under the Cross"

In the 1560s and beyond the history of political revolt intersected powerfully with the history of religious dissent to precipitate several decades of intense civil strife in both France and the Low Countries. In retrospect, the conjunction of dissent and revolt often seemed logical, even inevitable, to Protestant and Catholic apologists alike, though for obviously different reasons. Catholics equated evangelical Protestantism with sedition whereas Protestants justified their insurrections as morally necessary resistance to religious and political tyranny (Nicholls 1984b; Duke 1990; Van Gelderen 1992). General historical accounts of the era further reinforce the connection between religious and civil conflict by including the French civil wars and the Dutch Revolt in a larger conception of an "age of religious wars," which reached its deadly climax in the Thirty Years' War. One Dutch scholar has even characterized the earliest phase of the Dutch Revolt as a "revolutionary reformation" (Van Gelder 1943). For our purposes, however, it is important to break down these monolithic constructs and to locate the engagement of ordinary people more precisely within the fragmented spaces of sixteenth-century civil and ecclesiastical politics and within the larger chronologies of religious dissent and political insurrection. Indeed, a more prospective view of the Dutch and French conflicts suggests that the confluence of the histories of dissent and insurrection was neither automatic nor complete; and in the experience of most political subjects, the direct connection between Reformed Protestantism and political revolt was short-lived indeed.

The early decades of the Reformation era would certainly not have predicted the kind of Reformed Protestant mobilization that emerged in the 1560s. In cosmopolitan centers like Antwerp and Paris, the theological debates surrounding the "Luther question" immediately attracted considerable attention, and the Lutheran critique of established religious ritual and belief was easily translated into calls for local reform of the Church. The initial attraction appears to have been among the educated elite,[11] but as always the key to building popular enthusiasm for religious renewal was effective popular preaching, which in France was for a brief time even nurtured officially by the bishop of Meaux.[12] As in Germany, charismatic preachers in the many cities of northern France and the Low Countries might meet with a variety of responses, ranging from a private withdrawal from the ritual life of the Church to very demonstrative attacks on the symbols of Catholic piety and clerical abuse.[13] Despite evidence of locally significant popular response, however, the cause of religious reform was effectively stunted in both France and the Low Countries by the 1540s.

Whereas Charles V was largely powerless to stem the tide of evangelical protest in imperial Germany, he was in a much better position to combat heresy within his patrimonial territories in the Low Countries where his personal rule was much less compromised by locally powerful elites. It is critical to note here that Charles was neither king nor emperor in the Low Countries. Rather, he served variously as duke, count, and lord of his accumulated territories, and as a territorial lord, his day-to-day authority was more direct and less mediated than in his role as emperor

11. On the connection between humanism, municipal schools, and early interest in reform, see Pettegree 1992b and Nicholls 1992.
12. For a brief survey in English of the history of the French Reformation, see Greengrass 1987; there is no equivalent for the Low Countries, though the collection of pathbreaking essays in Duke 1990 comes close.
13. See Greengrass 1987:11–12 on eating meat on Friday and stealing the Host ("a surprisingly frequent occurrence"). The first iconoclastic attacks in the Netherlands occurred in Antwerp and Delft in 1525 (Pettegree 1992b:9); in Paris an image of the Virgin was smashed in 1528 (Nicholls 1992:125).

or even king (in most of Iberia). The provinces of Flanders, Brabant, Zeeland, and Holland formed the core of his patrimonial lands, and from the beginning of his rule in 1516, Charles aggressively sought to expand his domain, especially in the north. In 1521 he added the small southern province of Tournai, but his most extensive acquisitions were in the northeast: Friesland in 1524, Overijssel and Utrecht in 1528, Groningen (with Drenthe) in 1536, and Gelderland finally in 1543 (cf. Pettegree 1992b:2). At the same time, he attempted to consolidate his control of the core provinces through the creation of new fiscal and political institutions (De Schepper 1987; Tracy 1990).

Since the Netherlands quickly became the most important center of evangelical publishing outside Germany, the first of a series of steps that Charles took to combat heresy was a placard aimed at controlling the book trade in 1520. Then in 1521 Charles promulgated a special Dutch/French version of the Edict of Worms that condemned Luther's teachings; attendance at gatherings where the Scriptures were read was prohibited in 1525; and as soon as the first editions were published in 1526, those who possessed vernacular versions of the Bible were ordered to surrender them to authorities. By 1529 all those who were found in possession of forbidden books faced the death penalty. When, in July 1523, two Augustinian monks were burned at the stake in Brussels for being "obstinate heretics," they were the first martyrs for Lutheran belief anywhere in Europe. As Alastair Duke describes the situation,

The degree of political pressure which [the Habsburg administration in] Brussels exerted in the provinces of Brabant, Flanders and Holland, which together with Zeeland and the Walloon towns comprised the heartland of the Habsburg Netherlands, ensured that the Reformation could not survive for long in the open. The relatively large number of persons executed for heresy and related offenses under Charles V from these provinces tells its own tale. (1992:146)

Duke estimates that during Charles's reign, there were 63 executions in the Walloon towns of Mons, Tournai, Lille, and Valenciennes; 100 in Flanders; and 384 in Holland.[14]

At first the investigations of heresy focused on prominent supporters of the new learning, but by 1527–1528, there were investigations of small

14. Altogether at least 1,300, and perhaps as many as four or five times that number, were executed between 1523 and 1566 under the combined reigns of Charles V and Philip II (see Duke 1990:71, 99). This was clearly the most sustained and destructive persecution of Protestants anywhere in Europe.

groups of artisans as well, especially in the industrial cities of Flanders and Brabant where the climate was most forbidding (Duke 1990; Pettegree 1992b). As a result, it became clear that a German-style reformation, predicated on the more or less public formation of a broad reformation coalition, did not have much of a chance in the Low Countries. The authorities' worst fear that the "contagion" might spread more generally to the mass of the population was nevertheless realized by the growth of an Anabaptist movement in the early 1530s, especially in the northern provinces of Holland, Friesland, and Groningen. The Anabaptists shared the Lutherans' contempt for the elaborate rituals of the Catholic church, but they further marked themselves by symbolically separating their "brotherhoods" from the existing Church, usually by means of the ceremony of (adult) believer baptism; and rather than appeal primarily to the learned elite, they drew their greatest support from the urban poor, who were most receptive to the apocalyptic message of preachers like Melchior Hoffman. The Dutch Anabaptist movement reached its first peak in 1534–1535 with the rise and fall of the anabaptist "kingdom" in Münster. After several thousand Dutch militants were intercepted on their way to defend Münster from attack, there were abortive conspiracies to seize control of the cities of Leiden and Amsterdam. In the aftermath of the fall of Münster, there were more than two hundred executions in those areas of the north where authorities had previously been most complacent in rooting out heresy among "simple" folk.

Such resolute persecution could not eradicate "heresy" altogether, of course, but it effectively deprived the early reform movement of its leadership and drove it underground. The evangelicals who survived gathered together in small conventicles where they met regularly to read the Bible and discuss theological issues (Duke 1990; Pettegree 1992b). Some of these were Anabaptists who, in the aftermath of Münster, followed the more pacific leadership of Menno Simons, but others remained more cautious and essentially nonconfessional.[15] Those reform-minded intellectual leaders who remained in the Netherlands tended to hold themselves aloof from the common folk of the conventicles, but there was a

15. Reformation historians use the term "confessional" to denote the various strands of theological and ecclesiastical difference (often articulated in formal, propositional "confessions" of faith) in European Christianity during the Reformation and Counter-Reformation era and beyond; the most general confessional tendencies (each with regional variations) are, thus, Catholic, Lutheran, [Swiss] Reformed (i.e., Zwinglian or Calvinist), and Anabaptist, each with its own increasingly distinctive confessions.

growing political opposition among the urban elite to ongoing religious persecution—opposition that at times bordered on open confrontation with the central authorities in Brussels (Decavele 1975). At the same time, each wave of persecution brought with it a wave of emigration that eventually resulted in the establishment of exile churches in Wesel, London, and Emden. Of these, the most important was the Dutch exile community in Emden, just across the Groningen border in East Friesland.[16] Indeed, by the later 1550s the Dutch exile church in Emden had become the "Mother Church" of a new, more clearly organized Reformed Protestant movement in the Low Countries (Pettegree 1992b).

By comparison with the Low Countries, the initial opportunities for elite discussion of evangelical ideas may have been slightly greater in France. As David Nicholls (1983) describes the situation under Francis I, a combination of elite protection and competition among civil and ecclesiastical authorities may have afforded a "cultural space for heretical thought" both among the intellectual circles of Paris and in the bishopric of Meaux. At the first sign of popular enthusiasm, however, there was enormous pressure to clamp down on "Lutheranism." Thus the first "martyr" for the evangelical cause in France was a modest weaver from Meaux who was burned at the stake in 1524. In 1525 all translations of the Scriptures were suppressed, and early the following year the first list of forbidden Lutheran doctrines was issued by the Parlement of Paris. In 1528 the smashing of an image of the Virgin in Paris, which seemed to indicate something a good deal more menacing than private, intellectual speculation—perhaps even a clandestine sect—drew an official response involving all civil and ecclesiastical authorities: expiatory processions were organized, and rewards for information about the guilty were offered to the public (Nicholls 1992).

As it happened, the persecution of evangelicals in France tended to be cyclical, reflecting in part the course of events internationally. The first cycle (1524–1526) coincided with and was surely reinforced by the Peasants' War in Germany; the second (1534–1535) was sparked by the so-called Affair of the Placards, a famous incident involving the simultaneous distribution in several cities of broadsides attacking the sacraments, and coincided with the Anabaptist revolution at Münster. Another cycle, beginning in the late 1540s, followed the end of Francis I's involvement

16. Though the Dutch exile church in London was very promising when it was established in 1550, it was quickly closed down following the death of its patron, Edward VI, in 1553 (see Pettegree 1986).

in the Schmalkaldic War in the empire, during which he had toned down his attacks on heretics at home in deference to his Lutheran allies abroad. Though the cumulative death toll from judicial prosecutions was certainly not as high in France as in the Low Countries, the number of formal heresy investigations was formidable: at least five thousand and perhaps as many as eight thousand by the 1550s (Greengrass 1987:32–38). In addition, the first of a devastating series of religious massacres in France was inflicted on the Vaudois (Waldensians) of Provence in 1543 and 1545. The Parlement at Aix-en-Provence apparently feared that the Vaudois might rebel and "turn Swiss"; thus they ordered what appears to have been a preemptive strike that destroyed the Vaudois villages, the viciousness of which, in turn, provoked an international outcry and the prosecution of those responsible.[17]

As a result, the growth of a popular reform movement was also effectively stunted in the domain of Francis I. Indeed, as in the Low Countries, each successive wave of persecution brought with it a wave of emigration: first primarily to Strasbourg but in the late 1540s and 1550s, especially to Geneva, where a magisterial reformation had established Calvin as the leader of a radically new ecclesiastical organization based on the combined authority of clergy and laity (cf. Denis 1984). There, the stream of French exiles may have been as high as ten thousand by mid-century. Meanwhile, the Protestants who remained in France appear to have organized themselves into informal conventicles similar to those in the Low Countries. These clandestine meetings appear to have attracted their membership from a cross section of urban society, though the bedrock of their support was to be found among skilled artisans, and as at Meaux, they might even organize a Protestant church with an elected leadership and a sizable membership (Heller 1986; cf. Meyer 1977). Still, the cycles of repression continually forced the nascent evangelical movement to remain largely invisible until the late 1550s, except in the south where it enjoyed a variable degree of noble protection and encouragement in the countryside.[18] The growing contact between the exile community in Geneva and the pockets of Protestant sympathizers in France nevertheless created the framework for a more organized Reformed Protestant movement capable of challenging the hegemony of the

17. See Audisio 1984 and Cameron 1984. Unfortunately, most historians have considered these events as largely peripheral to the French Reformation considered on a "national" scale.
18. On the limited growth of Reformed Protestantism in the countryside of Languedoc, see Le Roy Ladurie 1979 and Molinier 1984.

Catholic church on a scale that seemed to the Venetian ambassador, at least, to amount to three quarters of the kingdom when it became suddenly visible in 1562.

In both the Low Countries and France, then, embattled evangelicals began building "churches under the cross" that were separate from the established Church and dependent, at least in part, on the theological and pastoral leadership of "mother" churches outside the immediate scope of official repression. In retrospect, it is tempting to emphasize both the organizational and the theological coherence of these embattled minorities, but prior to the 1560s there was little evidence of unity or uniformity in either movement. According to David Nicholls, early French Protestantism, in the cities at least, "retained something in the nature of a religious debating society" in which a number of distinct tendencies might be visible:

There were militant prophetic Protestants, some influenced by millenarian ideas, who wished to overthrow the papal Antichrist and impose the new religion on the unregenerate; peaceful Protestants, who merely wanted to be left alone to practice their religion; Protestant sympathizers, who kept their feelings secret, partly through fear and social convention, but also partly for genuine religious reasons; and the Protestant nobility, who never stopped being nobles, with a concomitant mentality and lifestyle. (1992:129)

The same might be said of the evangelicals of the Low Countries, where, Alastair Duke emphasizes, the movement was both regionally and socially diverse. Still, in the 1560s and beyond, the outbreak of open hostilities and civil war not only revealed the extent and diversity of the underground movement but also ensured that the most coherent, organized, and militarily resourceful among them would set the tone and direction of the Protestant movement.

Popular Mobilization and the Coming of Civil War

In the first half of the sixteenth century the cumulative effect of the many and various attempts to suppress evangelical dissent in France and the Low Countries was the criminalization of not only a wide range of religious beliefs but also a variety of fairly commonplace behaviors. Indeed, in France by the 1550s heretical *belief* could legally be inferred from the *behavior* of the subject being investigated. This might include interpreting Scripture without official sanction, attending secret meetings of all kinds, attacking sacred images, selling and distributing forbidden books, even speaking "words contrary to the Catholic faith and the Christian religion." Individuals were also, not surprisingly, forbidden to associate with the French exile community in Geneva, and those who were found to possess books or letters from Geneva were subject to arrest as "heretics and disturbers of the public peace and tranquility" (Greengrass 1987:34; see also Sutherland 1980). In short, virtually any outward sign of affinity or association with evangelical ideas in general and with Geneva in particular was equated with public unrest and even sedition, which was, of course, punishable by death (cf. Duke 1990:73–74).

In this climate of heightened fear and suspicion, becoming a member of an underground church or even attending an evangelical worship service must be considered a deliberate act of defiance of, if not quite outright rebellion against, both civil and ecclesiastical authority. But this is precisely what thousands of ordinary French and Netherlandic subjects did during the "wonderyears" of the 1560s. Though there were only a handful of churches represented at the clandestine Synod of Paris in 1559, evangelical preachers were attracting increasingly large numbers of enthusiastic followers, some of whom defied authorities by openly chanting psalms in the evangelical fashion or holding public worship services (*prêches*) outside the towns. By March 1562 one of the most prominent patrons of the French evangelical movement, Admiral de Coligny, tried to assemble a list of more than two thousand churches then extant. Even a much more conservative estimate of the number of organized congregations (see Garrisson 1980) yields an estimate of the adult Protestant population in the neighborhood of two million or perhaps 10 percent of the total population of France (Greengrass 1987: chap. 6; see also Benedict 1981: appendix 1).

Likewise, in the Low Countries there was an explosion of openly defiant evangelical activity. The first Calvinist church was formally organized at Antwerp in 1555, and before the decade was out there were churches in all the major towns of Flanders; in 1561 in the Walloon towns of Valenciennes and Tournai psalm-singing crowds of evangelicals even demonstrated publicly in the streets (Duke 1990; Steen 1985; cf. Le Barre 1989). Even more impressively, however, beginning in May 1566 evangelicals began to hold open-air services (so-called *hagepreken*, or hedgepreaching) just outside the walls of the cities; at first these bold demonstrations of popular support drew modest crowds, but by July they had swelled in some places to more than twenty thousand.[19] Then, in August, there began the wave of iconoclastic attacks, described above, that spread from Flanders all the way to Groningen, permanently damaging hundreds of churches as well as the relative calm that had prevailed under the cloak of official repression.

How are we to understand these sudden demonstrations of evangelical strength in both France and the Low Countries? Though the religious appeal of evangelical theology in general and of Calvinism in particular may be considered to have remained relatively constant, the perceived opportunities for individual religious choice and for open dissent had changed so dramatically as to set off what may usefully be considered a cycle of religious protest analogous to that which had begun in Germany in the early 1520s (see chap. 2). In the first instance, the sweeping claims that both the Valois and Habsburg regimes made for an unprecedented degree of control over religious ritual and belief belied the obvious limits of royal/princely repression, even if that was significantly more potent than imperial control in Germany. Despite evidence of the pervasive recourse to exemplary justice, indeed, the rulers of these relatively novel composite states were necessarily dependent on a variety of more or less independent institutions, with variously pliant personnel, to implement their repressive policies. In the Netherlands, for example, municipal governments insisted on the primacy of their own jurisdictions in the face of a threatened Spanish-style Inquisition, but they remained reluctant to persecute even small cultural minorities within the very populations on whose immediate goodwill the viability of their rule depended. Likewise, the growing attraction of the high French nobility to Calvinist ideas clearly compromised the repressive capacity of the Valois regime in those places where religiously suspect nobles, by virtue of their positions of local and regional authority, were the filter through which royal policy necessarily passed. This was especially true in those regions with functioning provincial estates, the pays d'etat, which were clustered especially in the south and west of France.[20] Thus it was clear that at the peripheries of these extensive and variegated domains—especially in the north of the Low Countries and the south of France—the reach of princely pre-

19. The largest gathering appears to have been approximately 25,000 at Laer on July 14; meetings of 20,000 were reported at Ghent and more than 10,000 at Valenciennes and Tournai. See Crew 1979; Pettegree 1992b:chap. 5.
20. See the map of France prior to the civil wars in Salmon 1975:28.

tensions to control religious practice and belief far exceeded their effective grasp.

Closely related to these structural constraints on royal action, another factor that appeared more immediately to open significant new opportunities for religious experimentation and choice, if not general reform, was the availability to the clandestine religious movements of politically influential allies. In some places in the north and south significant numbers of both urban notables and rural nobles were attracted to the new evangelical spirituality as well as to Calvin's emphasis on lay religious leadership, but even where that was not so obviously the case, any attempt by the central administration to perform judicial and ecclesiastical end runs around locally and regionally powerful elites might easily invoke a familiar sort of resistance in the name of established privilege and traditional rights. For Brabant and Flanders, in the heart of the Habsburg domain, Wim Blockmans (1988) has described a "Great Tradition" of revolt that helped to establish both the political and the ideological foundations of the Dutch Revolt. In this view the many important urban centers of the Low Countries not only anchored an ongoing resistance to Burgundian/Habsburg fiscal and political ambitions but also actively developed institutionalized, practical alternatives to monarchical centralization in the Low Countries. More recently, Marc Boone and Maarten Prak (1995) have argued that this Great Tradition of urban revolt was complemented by an equally long-standing and impressive "Little Tradition" of internal opposition to the domination of powerful and wealthy oligarchs in both town and countryside. Indeed, from the Flemish Peasants' Revolt of the early fourteenth century (1323–1328)[21] to the tragic revolt of Ghent against Charles V in 1540,[22] the complementary traditions of elite and popular revolt had revealed myriad possible alliances against an unwanted consolidation of central authority or administration. As embedded in both historical memory and constitutional reality, then, the multiple histories of political insurrection or

21. For the better part of five years, the peasants of coastal Flanders staged the most sustained rural insurrection of the otherwise rebellious fourteenth century, which not only demonstrated the revolutionary potential of rural communities but also modeled a remarkably successful political alternative to seigneurial domination of the countryside. See Te Brake 1993.

22. This heroic, if unsuccessful, defiance of Charles V's various attempts to consolidate his control in the Low Countries resulted in the complete revocation of Ghent's traditional liberties as a chartered city, but not before Charles had traveled from Spain to preside personally over the symbolic humiliation of the whole community. See the vivid contemporary account of both the revolt and the city's humiliation in Rowen 1972:16–25.

revolt afforded the new evangelical communities with a repertoire of fairly familiar collective actions that might complement the organization of independent churches and some very powerful allies, if not always spiritual brothers, when the long-standing traditions of local autonomy and self-government were at stake.

Though these urban-centered models of the "Great" and "Little" traditions of revolt are clearly rooted in the most urbanized provinces of the Low Countries, they may still be useful in thinking about the more rural provinces of the Low Countries and the kingdom of France more generally.[23] Rural insurrections are, not surprisingly, more clearly the dominant theme of French history from the fourteenth-century Jacquerie onward, but it is clear from Henry Heller's (1991) survey that French history, too, betrayed elements of multiple traditions of revolt—of internal division and conflict within communities as well as collective resistance to outside control. Heller presents an impressively diverse collection of tax protests, food riots, and peasant insurrections with peaks of activity in the 1520s and 1540s (ibid., 42–44 table), but he notes, in addition, the appearance in the mid-1540s of religious issues amid the political agitation, especially in the cities. The more general point may be that, in both France and the Low Countries, corporate communities—whether rural communes or chartered towns—could (and frequently did) serve as an arena for local political contention as well as the bedrock for a more generalized opposition to the intrusion of unwanted outside authority (cf. Blickle 1986).

In the short term, however, the precipitant for this new cycle of religious protest was neither the structural limits of dynastic state making nor the long tradition of opposition to it; rather, it appears to have been a genuine uncertainty about the government's commitment to the policy of repression. Despite the announced intentions of Philip II and Henry II to redouble their efforts to suppress heresy after the Peace of Cateau-Cambrésis in 1559, a constellation of forces pushed central authorities in precisely the opposite direction in both France and the Low Countries. Following the untimely death of Henry II, the enfeebled government of Francis II (1559–1560) briefly renewed the government's long-standing commitment to enforcing religious uniformity, but under the regency of

23. And more generally in Europe as well. The Comunero Revolt in Spain, for example, may be seen as a classic example of Blockmans's Great Tradition, but there, too, urban resistance to the monarch was predicated on a pattern of urban riots that would seem to be evidence of the Little Tradition of popular challenges to urban oligarchs; see chapter 2 above.

Catherine of Medici during the minority of Charles IX (1560–1563), government policy moved decisively in the direction of moderation and compromise. By the Edict of Amboise (March 1560), the government effectively admitted that the persecution of Protestants had become unenforceable. Then after the regent failed, amid increasing tumult and political pressure, to achieve a theological compromise between Catholics and Protestants in the famous Colloquy at Poissy (September 1561), the Edict of St. Germain (January 1562) granted a limited toleration of evangelical worship (see Christin 1995, 1997). It was precisely in this context that an increasingly organized religious protest movement was emboldened not only to petition formally for official sanction but also to demonstrate its popular strength more openly and defiantly on the local level.

Likewise, following Philip II's departure from the Netherlands to Spain in 1559, although the government of Margaret of Parma was formally committed to his policies of repression, a series of unforeseen challenges brought that policy into serious question. In particular, broad elite opposition after 1561 to a plan to reform the primitive ecclesiastical structure of the region—reforms that undermined or threatened a broad range of local and regional officials in favor of a starkly centralized ecclesiastical regime—resulted in the dismissal in 1564 of Cardinal Granvelle, one of Philip's most trusted advisers in Brussels. Inasmuch as many local officials were refusing to enforce the government's heresy laws against otherwise law-abiding subjects, several high-ranking noblemen strongly urged revision of the heresy legislation in favor of a more tolerant policy. When Philip steadfastly refused all compromise, however, some four hundred lesser noblemen, who were derisively called "Beggars," pledged to unite in opposition to the Inquisition, and in the spring of 1566 Margaret secretly agreed to moderate temporarily the enforcement of the heresy laws (Parker 1985; Van Nierop 1991).[24] It was thus amid exaggerated reports of Margaret's "concessions" that the enormous potential for a popular evangelical movement burst into full view.

What began in the 1560s in both France and the Low Countries, then, was a new, generalized cycle of religious protest that revealed both the weaknesses of government repression and the availability to popular religious dissenters of influential political allies. In this heady atmosphere, news of (successful) popular demonstrations traveled quickly and

24. By August 23 Margaret had conceded freedom of worship for Protestants where preaching had already taken place (Pettegree 1992b:132).

invited imitation elsewhere. For example, news of prêches in northern France emboldened evangelicals to do the same (the so-called hedge-preaching) in the southern Low Countries; notorious incidents of iconoclasm also begat imitation across a broad terrain. For a time, indeed, it seemed to Catholics and Protestants alike as if the established religious regime might be destroyed along with the harshest elements of dynastic political consolidation. To the extent that this seemed to be the fulfillment of apocalyptic hopes and visions nurtured in the darkest days of repression—the answer to fervent prayer—it helped to underwrite ever bolder evangelical action in a variety of contexts. Yet to the extent that it awakened the worst fears of those dedicated to, if not personally invested in, the ecclesiastical establishment, it sparked a vigorous countermobilization in defense of the old regime. And very quickly in both north and south, what began as a spectacular series of relatively independent local mobilizations was overshadowed by the formation of political and religious alliances and the subsequent explosion of armed conflict on a much broader scale.

In France the first round of civil war followed quickly on the first public recognition of the Protestant movement. A massacre in March 1562 of evangelical worshipers at Vassy by the duc de Guise precipitated a massive military mobilization by the Huguenot leadership, and by summer civil war had begun in earnest. Indeed, the conspiracies and strategies of "national" leaders—that is, of high-ranking nobles or influential notables who could deploy military resources on a grand scale and who claimed to speak for far-flung alliances on one side or the other—are almost necessarily the principal mileposts for any coherent account of the long decades of conflict that ensued.[25] Likewise, in the Low Countries the massive hedgepreaching and iconoclasm of 1566 quickly gave way to an equally massive military repression under the duke of Alva in 1567 and the first military countermobilization by the rebels—the so-called Beggars—in 1568. These military conflicts were at first closely linked, and in retrospect, 1572 can be seen as a significant turning point in both cases: in France, the disastrous Saint Bartholomew's Day massacre of Huguenots in Paris signaled the stagnation and eventual decline of the Huguenot party;[26] in the Low Countries, by contrast, the Beggars achieved their

25. See, for example, the very impressive and useful chronologies in Salmon 1975:333–342 and Crouzet 1990:1:23–41; for a recent narrative account, see Holt 1995.
26. Not only was the most prominent Huguenot leadership summarily executed, but some 3,000 Huguenots in Paris and 8,000 more elsewhere were killed in the space of just a few days. See Benedict 1978; Diefendorf 1991.

first military success in the seizure of the small city of Den Briel in southern Holland.[27] In both cases the rebels began after 1572 to take concrete
steps toward the creation of independent, revolutionary governments,
but in the long run these complex religious/political/military conflicts
gradually separated into relatively discrete "national" histories, though
outside intervention remained an important element in both the French
civil wars and the Dutch Revolt.[28]

The Character and Fate
of Popular Protestantism

As popular protest gave way to civil war, the character and
fate of popular political action varied considerably, and it is this pattern
of variation that is our chief concern here. In retrospect, it is perhaps
tempting to conclude, as Henry Heller (1991) does with regard to the
French Huguenots, that the heavy hand of elite leadership in the context
of open warfare sidetracked or even stifled the growth of an otherwise
promising popular evangelical movement. At the local level and in the
short term, however, it often seemed as if the popular movement was in
the driver's seat, forcing otherwise tentative or cautious elites to make
choices or take risks that they would much rather have avoided (Benedict
1981:chap. 10). But rather than generalize in this strictly dichotomous
fashion, let us look briefly at a series of examples that illustrate the range
of variation and highlight the complex relationship between religious
dissent and political revolt.

To the extent that religious conflicts in France and the Low Countries
grew out of the political pressure of local reformation coalitions on variably receptive municipal authorities, they may be said to reflect the same
political dynamics as were evident in the urban reformations in Germany
(see fig. 4 above). As we shall see, however, the politicization and nation-
alization of the complex problems of religion and regime in France and
the Low Countries produced a distinctive pattern of direct political and

27. After earlier military failures, this modest success gave the Beggars a base from which
to "liberate" large parts of Holland and Zeeland. See Parker 1985.
28. For brief introductions, in English, to these very complex histories (and historiographies), see Knecht 1989 and Holt 1995 on the French civil wars and Limm 1989 on the
Dutch Revolt.

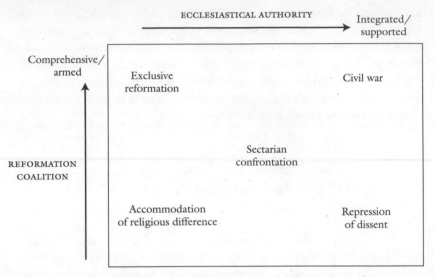

Figure 6. Political dynamics of religious contestation in the Second
Reformation

military contestation between two "religious" parties—Reformation and
Counter-Reformation coalitions. Indeed, the long years of often violent
struggle require us to imagine a rather different set of political interactions that tended toward rather different (though, in many cases, equally
transient) outcomes, including both civil war and the formal accommodation of religious difference, which was conspicuously absent in the
First Reformation.

Thus, Figure 6 describes and accounts for the distinctive features of
this second round of reformation conflict in terms not only of variations
in the character and capacity of the Reformation coalitions—highlighting its social comprehensiveness as well as its military capacity—but also
of variations in the character and capacity of established religious authority—highlighting especially the extent to which the Church was integrated with political elites and enjoyed the support of popular political
actors within a larger Counter-Reformation coalition. We shall return to
these broader comparisons later, but first we must disaggregate the larger
historical constructs—the French Wars of Religion and the Dutch
Revolt—and locate the variety of conflicts within concrete political
spaces. Let us begin with the example of Toulouse.

In the southern French city of Toulouse the leaders of the newly organized Reformed church—the consistory as well as some of the city's nota-

bles—met urgently on the evening of May 11, 1562, and decided, in light of the rapidly accumulating evidence of civil war more generally between Catholics and Protestants in France, to take immediate action.[29] Armed Protestants were surreptitiously let into the city, occupied the Hôtel de Ville, and took several *capitouls*, the city's chief magistrates, prisoner. They subsequently moved quickly to occupy several colleges of the university and to erect barricades across key streets so as to fortify those sections of the city in which they were able to establish themselves before dawn. Though this well-planned coup was initially successful, rumors of an armed Protestant uprising had compromised the element of surprise, and the Catholics were prepared to meet the Protestant challenge; indeed, the Catholics enjoyed a clear advantage in the numbers of armed men immediately available in the city, although the Protestants benefited from the armaments, including cannons, they captured in the arsenal of the Hôtel de Ville. Four days of very destructive urban warfare, beginning on May 13, finally yielded to a truce on May 16, which amounted to a capitulation by the Protestant forces.[30] A guarantee of limited safe passage afforded the Protestants only marginal protection from the vengeance of their Catholic enemies when their mass exodus from the city was completed by the evening of May 17. By the time the dust had settled, as many as four thousand people may have died.

These dramatic, albeit exceptionally fast-moving and destructive, events in Toulouse encapsulate clearly some of the most important general characteristics of political and religious conflict in the second phase of the European Reformation: the integral involvement of ordinary people at the community level; the deep religious/sectarian divisions within communities; and the final arbitration of armed might, more often than not in alliance with actors outside the community. But the conflagration at Toulouse also announced the more specific theme of short-term success followed by ultimate failure for the Reformed Protestants, a theme that was replayed with often devastating variations in many communities not only in France but in the Low Countries as well. In the Walloon town of Tournai, for example, we can see in rather slower motion and more vivid detail the political dynamics of what was essentially a revolutionary process that exploited the complex relationships among a popu-

29. This account of events in Toulouse is based on Greengrass 1983a, which includes a map of the Protestant and Catholic strongholds within the city; cf. Davies 1979.
30. Greengrass 1983a notes that the failure of anticipated outside support and a severe shortage of food as well as military reversals quickly demoralized the Protestant forces.

lar religious movement, locally vulnerable magistrates, and an implacable but distant sovereign (see esp. Steen 1985; Le Barre 1989).

As early as 1563 a crowd of perhaps two thousand evangelicals openly chanted psalms and listened to sermons in the streets of Tournai after authorities had broken up clandestine meetings in the countryside; some in the crowd even boasted, "They [the authorities] do not wish us to sing in the woods where we bother no one, so we will sing in the city; and if they put in a garrison of one thousand, we will raise two thousand" (quoted in Steen 1985:49–50). Such bravado notwithstanding, the local Reformed Protestant movement remained generally invisible until the surprising summer of 1566. Then, in Tournai as elsewhere in the Low Countries, the popular dimensions of the evangelical movement became fully visible in the massive crowds that thronged to worship services just beyond the immediate jurisdiction of the urban magistrates who were continually pressured to enforce the central government's uncompromising placards against heresy. On one such occasion, Pasquier de Le Barre, a local notable who chronicled these events, reports, "In open defiance of the magistrates, the flower of Tournai was in attendance, leaving so few people of quality behind in the city that no one could remember the like, even during times of war and adversity that the place has suffered" (1989:102).

Indeed, the steady growth of popular support for the evangelical movement produced a locally formidable coalition, led by the Reformed consistory and supported by the guilds, that local authorities were unable to resist.

Recognizing their own inadequacy in the face of the problem, some magistrates began to worry about [the governor general's] repeated warnings that the King would someday demand an account of their regime and find them wanting. However, the King who was far away inspired much less concern than did the people of Tournai itself, for the fervor of the masses of people who went to sermons began to make the magistrates anxious. (Steen 1985: 70–71)

And well they might be anxious, for after iconoclastic crowds "cleansed" the city's churches in August, the Reformed Protestants not only moved their services inside the walls and indoors, but the preachers and members of the consistory who claimed to speak for the movement forced their way into the exclusive domain of the local town council's deliberations, pressing a program of popular armament and religious reform. Still, a hastily assembled citizen's militia of about four thousand appeared to be no match for the small royal garrison and the army that Margaret of Parma raised to support it. Thus, following the defeat of a rebel "army" near Lille on December 27, Tournai was quietly occupied by royal troops in January 1567. Though there was little bloodshed inside Tournai, the city paid a very high price for its brief Reformed Protestant rebellion: a period of harsh persecution (with more than 1,000 condemnations) was followed by the complete dissolution of Tournai (and the Tournésis) as a separate province.

A similar scenario was played out in nearby Valenciennes where, in the absence of a local garrison, it took a siege that lasted until March 24, 1567, to end the city's defiance of Philip's authority (Clark 1972; Parker 1985:93–98). Likewise, at Rouen during the first French civil war, a royal siege forced the surrender of a rebel Huguenot regime (Benedict 1981). At Lyon, by contrast, the rebel Huguenot regime that seized power in the spring of 1562 lasted until 1567, but it, too, ultimately failed under pressure from a potent countermobilization in defense of the established Church (Davis 1975). What all of these cases have in common is that a locally formidable reformation coalition—which brought together notables, bourgeois, and artisans under the leadership of the local Reformed consistory—opted, in the heady atmosphere of escalating political crisis during the 1560s, for a course of action that amounted to local revolution;[31] yet lacking outside help in the face of a spirited defense of the established regime, these revolutionary regimes ultimately failed not only to bring on the Calvinist millennium but also to preserve even a limited space for public evangelical worship. In the terms suggested by figure 6, all of these cases moved quickly from a common starting point in the lower right—the repression of dissent—toward sectarian confrontation in the center; in addition, each was engulfed in the larger pattern of civil war that thrust them back toward the forceful repression of dissent.

In other cases, of course, the defeat of the Reformed Protestant movement was not predicated on a sudden coup or even the apparent pretense to found a revolutionary regime. In Amiens, for example, though Protestantism appealed to a broad spectrum of the local population, the Reformed community never joined the political alliances or took on the

---

31. Though these municipal conflicts will certainly not pass muster as "great" revolutions, they do pass the test of "revolutionary situations," which is predicated on the condition of multiple sovereignty and highlights exclusive claims by challengers and a significant level of popular support for those claims as proximate causes. Cf. Tilly 1978, 1993.

political aspirations of their coreligionists in Toulouse or Rouen—which had roughly similar levels of popular support in the total urban population—at the beginning of the French civil wars (Rosenberg 1978); having remained politically discreet at the height of Huguenot strength, then, the local reform movement quickly found itself on the defensive in Amiens as the conflict and warfare escalated elsewhere. Similarly, across the border in the Habsburg Netherlands, despite a sizable evangelical movement in the region, Reformed Protestantism was held in check in Lille (a close neighbor of Tournai and Valenciennes) as the local elite remained firmly united in its resistance to religious change; thus even in the summer of 1566 the Reformed Protestants of Lille were unable to exploit the fleeting opportunities for bold dissent that others seized where elite loyalties were more clearly divided or their policies uncertain (DuPlessis 1991). At the heart of the Valois domain, the city of Paris presents yet another variation on this theme. Home to a sizable Reformed community and torn by sectarian violence throughout the 1560s, Paris nevertheless remained the political *and* cultural capital of the "most Catholic" French kingdom; indeed, short of conversion of the monarchy to Protestantism and conquest by Huguenot armies, it is hard to imagine a scenario in which the people of Paris might have been free to establish an entirely new religious regime or even a publicly dissenting church.[32] In these cases, then, evangelical dissent did not in fact connect with political revolt in the experience of ordinary people for a variety of reasons, each of which reflects the locally specific structures of political opportunity as much as the absolute strength of the movement itself.

It would surely be mistaken, however, to dwell on examples of the failure of religious dissent during the Second Reformation, for eventually dissenting communities established themselves as public churches and drew on both elite alliances and popular support in large stretches of both France and the Low Countries. Here again, the character and the fate of local interaction were quite variable. La Rochelle, an important port on the west coast of France, is illustrative of a number of French cities, primarily in the south and southwest, where in the early 1560s Reformed Protestantism quickly attracted majority support among the

---

32. In the successive peace settlements of the civil wars in which the monarchy allowed limited freedom of worship to Huguenots, Paris was invariably excluded from the list of places where Calvinist worship was formally authorized; see Salmon 1975. On the divisions between Huguenots and Catholics and the bitter fate of evangelical Protestantism in Paris, see Diefendorf 1991 who emphasizes the critical importance of popular mobilization on numerous occasions between 1562 and 1572.

urban population without serious resistance from the religious and political establishment.[33] Indeed, despite considerable division between the
oligarchical *corps de ville* and the city's bourgeois citizens over alleged
abuses of power by municipal officials earlier in the century, the
Reformed church, which claimed at least forty-two of the one hundred
members of the corps de ville among its congregation, boldly but peace-
ably inserted itself into the public arena without an open break with the
local political regime. What is more, during the first civil war in 1562–1563
and against the backdrop of very serious municipal conflicts with the
Crown in the 1540s and 1550s, this openly Protestant city managed to
resist considerable pressure to ally itself with the Huguenot rebellion
more generally and even continued to proclaim its loyalty to the king.
Thus it was that the successful establishment of Reformed Protestantism
in La Rochelle invoked neither the "Great" nor the "Little" tradition of
revolt, both of which had been prominent features of recent Rochellais
history. The "moderates" who had managed to steer this remarkable
course were, however, temporarily swept aside in the second war
(1567–1568) by "zealots," who insisted on alliance with the Huguenot
party and the suppression of the Catholic church, and although the moderates quickly returned to power, they also formally negotiated an alliance
with the Huguenot party when the city was threatened with a royal garrison in the third war (1568–1570). Henceforth, La Rochelle remained an
important Huguenot stronghold until the Edict of Nantes guaranteed its
position as a place of Reformed worship and surety in 1598.

    Although the experience of La Rochelle was in some sense excep-
tional, it nevertheless illustrates the experience of those communities in
which the popular evangelical movement enjoyed explosive growth,
with or without the active support of local elites, and an increasingly
Protestant community as a whole managed to avoid outside intervention
to restore the Catholic church, with or without the support of the
broader Huguenot alliance. Thus Reformed Protestantism quickly
gained the upper hand and remained in a dominant cultural position in
cities like Nîmes, Montpellier, and Montauban as well as a broad range
of small towns in the south and west of France. In the course of the civil
wars, and especially in the aftermath of the Saint Bartholomew's massacres in 1572, the religious and political leaders of these places where
Protestantism had gained the upper hand moved to establish not only a

33. The following account of events in La Rochelle is based on Meyer 1977; see also Meyer
1984 and Trocmé 1976.

new national church but also a politically independent confederation—what Janine Garrisson (1980) has called les Provinces Unis du Midi—outside the immediate domain of a severely crippled monarchy. Although these self-governing communities would certainly be considered rebellious from the point of view of the monarchy, in the experience of ordinary people within these Huguenot strongholds, a fully institutionalized Reformed Protestantism, with its corporate discipline and generally austere morality, undoubtedly seemed the very opposite of rebellious (see, e.g., Segui 1933). In all these cases, then, amid the genuine uncertainty of the early 1560s, we can see an exit from the starting point of repressed dissent in the direction of initially local and informal accommodations of religious differences followed by locally variable movements in the direction of exclusive reformations.

Yet another scenario for Reformed Protestant success may be seen in the experience of the rebel cities of the northern Low Countries after 1572. Following the hedgepreaching and iconoclasm of 1566, the notoriously repressive regime of the duke of Alva had driven both religious dissenters and political opponents either underground or into exile. Yet the capture of the small town of Den Briel on April 1, 1572, set off what Geoffrey Parker (1985) calls the Second Revolt in which the Beggars established a more or less permanent territorial base within the Low Countries from which to challenge the Habsburg regime militarily. This outcome was far from certain as, at first, only widely scattered cities took the side of the Beggars (see Parker 1985:139 map). By September, following a strategic retreat toward the south by the duke of Alva, the map of rebel-held territory had begun quite dramatically to fill in especially in the north, only to be pushed back by a Spanish counteroffensive almost exclusively into the provinces of Holland and Zeeland by the end of the year—with the notable exception of cities like Middelburg and Amsterdam that remained loyal to the king (see Parker 1985:143 map). In this new cycle of revolt some cities like Valenciennes replicated the wonderyear experience of only short-lived success for religious and political revolt. In Holland and Zeeland, however, a number of cities established new political and religious regimes that survived the test of time and the depredations of intermittent civil war.[34]

In cities like Leiden and Delft, which had experienced both the iconoclasm of 1566 and the repression that followed, there was a residue of

---

34. On the ebb and flow of the rebels' military campaigns through the end of the century, see the maps in Parker 1985:210–212, 229.

resistance to Spanish tyranny that quickly reemerged in the form of popular demonstrations in 1572 in response to the news of rebel success elsewhere, but an official shift to the rebel cause awaited the arrival of rebel troops and a change in the local magistracy (Boogman 1942; Kooi 1993). Then, of course, religious dissenters suddenly enjoyed opportunities for both demonstrative and organizational activity, the latter aided by both the return of exiled leaders and the organization of district-level classes and regional synods on the Calvinist model. Even in places like Gouda, Dordrecht, and Rotterdam, which had not been touched by the iconoclasm of 1566, churches were "cleansed" of idolatrous images, Reformed pastors were installed, and consistories were organized, sometimes in opposition to local magistrates who advocated a less stringently confessional reformation (Hibben 1983; Ten Boom 1987; see also Spaans 1989). Though the newly public Reformed Protestant congregations usually attracted only very small minorities of the local populations as full members, the experience of local church building and intercommunity networking "under the cross" gave them enormous advantages in the contest for local position, virtually assuring them the biggest churches and eventually a formal monopoly on public worship.[35] Yet the same organizational discipline and confessional rigor that strengthened them internally made it difficult for these essentially *voluntary* congregations to assume the role of a *community* church: zealous and aggressive consistories often kept local magistrates at arm's length while the requirement of submitting to the spiritual discipline of the consistory appears to have made the transition to full membership in the worshiping community a comparatively difficult one for most people (Parker 1985; Duke 1990; Pettegree 1994). In each of these cases the local trajectory of the process of religious contestation went from repression (via sectarian confrontation) toward civil war and quickly veered toward exclusive reformations before reaching various forms of accommodation of sectarian difference.

By the mid-1570s, then, the basic geography of Reformed Protestant

---

35. Following the immediate failure of Spanish repression due to mutiny and bankruptcy, the Pacification of Ghent (1576) recognized the Reformed church as the official church in Holland and Zeeland; following the failure, in turn, of the Pacification (which included all the Low Countries provinces), the Union of Utrecht, negotiated exclusively by the northern rebel provinces and the city of Ghent in 1579, gave the Reformed church the status of a "public" church but prohibited the persecution of religious dissenters. Consequently, not only other Protestant confessional groups—especially Lutherans and Mennonites—but also Catholics continued to exist as worshiping communities albeit under occasionally severe limitations. See especially Spaans 1989 for an analysis of this confessional interaction within a single urban community (Haarlem).

success had begun to take shape in the south and west of France and in the north of the Low Countries—that is, on the peripheries of the Valois and Habsburg regimes where rebels enjoyed their greatest military success. In these areas, the Huguenot and Beggar coalitions began to fashion revolutionary governments that consolidated their political power on a regional scale and served to underwrite still costlier and more destructive civil wars.[36] In the southern Netherlands, which had always been the heartland of popular support for Reformed Protestantism, there would be one more round of popular religious/political revolution. There, in the context of the Pacification of Ghent (1576),[37] locally variable Reformation coalitions once again seized the initiative in Brussels, Antwerp, and Ghent, forcing reluctant elite leaders to open up new opportunities for popular political action as well as religious choice (Decavele 1984; Marnef 1986, 1987, 1994, 1996). In Ghent, which had lost its chartered self-governance in 1540, a radical Reformed Protestant regime came to power in 1577, reasserted the city's political independence, and in alliance with Holland and Zeeland anchored a significant pocket of rebellion in Flanders and Brabant until 1584. By the mid-1580s, however, the political/military tide had once again turned; in particular, the Walloon nobility had made a separate peace with the Spanish regime by the Treaty of Arras (1579), and with the urban rebels cut loose from their former allies, the Spanish were able to consolidate their reconquest of the southern provinces by attacking the towns one by one (Parker 1985). And by the same token the waves of popular evangelical mobilization, which had begun so dramatically and with great promise in the 1560s, had finally ended—either crushed by military failure or co-opted by the consolidation of elite leadership in rebel enclaves.

36. Although they did not formally abjure their "sovereign" until 1581 (and they did not give up their search for a replacement until the end of the decade), the provinces of Holland and Zeeland had effectively become independent of the Brussels government in 1572, and under their tutelage the other signatories of the Union of Utrecht—formally known as the United Provinces of the Northern Netherlands—had begun to create the conditions for fully independent self-government after 1579 (Te Brake 1992). Likewise, the "United Provinces" of southern France established a self-governing confederation after the debacle of the Saint Bartholomew's Day massacre. See Garrisson 1980; Parker 1985; Heller 1991:chap. 3.

37. Under this ill-fated agreement, the elite leadership of the amalgamated provinces, meeting extralegally as the Estates General, had extracted important political concessions from the incoming governor-general, Don Juan, in return for the restoration of Catholicism everywhere except in the provinces of Holland and Zeeland.

Popular Mobilization
and the End of the "Religious" Wars

Ordinary people did not simply disappear as political actors midway through the Second Reformation. Rather, the focus of popular mobilization shifted dramatically in the last quarter of the sixteenth century, especially in France: first, there emerged an increasingly bold and organized popular movement in opposition to the Huguenots and in defense of the Catholic church; and second, there were dramatic waves of nonsectarian opposition to the depredations of elite politics and seemingly unending civil war. Together, these new patterns of popular mobilization in France help us to understand the very different trajectories of political development that emerged in France and the Low Countries in the last quarter of the sixteenth century.

The potential for significant popular opposition to the apparent success of the Huguenot movement in the early 1560s was evident almost immediately. The dramatic failure of the Protestant coup in Toulouse in the spring of 1562, for example, was clearly due to a broad countermobilization, including large numbers of ordinary people, in defense of the municipal government and the Catholic church (Greengrass 1983a, 1983b). At the same time, ordinary people in many other parts of France undertook generally less organized—and less immediately effective—action to counter the growing audacity of evangelical attacks on "papists" and their ritual "idolatry." The cumulative result was a widespread pattern of very demonstrative, ritualized, and often violent competition in the streets (see esp. Davis 1975: chap. 6; Crouzet 1990). As the civil wars dragged on, however, local contestation between Huguenots and Catholics began generally to tip in favor of the most zealous Catholics in places like Rouen and Paris and culminated in the 1580s in a spate of local revolutions under the banner of the Catholic League (Sainte Union) which were intended to prevent the triumph of (or even a royal compromise with) the Huguenot party on a national scale. Though the Catholic League failed, in the end, to prevent a formal compromise with "heretics" in the Edict of Nantes, it prevented something much worse by prolonging the civil wars long enough to ensure that the monarchy would remain Catholic (Salmon 1975; Holt 1995).

The formation of Counter-Reformation coalitions in many parts of

France mirrored, in some respects, the process by which Reformation coalitions were formed more generally. Though the monarchy's vigorous defense of Catholic orthodoxy certainly validated and encouraged popular mobilization in defense of the established Church order, the latter, where it became visible and effective, was more directly a reflection of locally variable conditions: the history of relations between local clergy and laity, the density of religious institutions and the structures of ecclesiastical authority, the integration of ecclesiastical and political elites, and so forth (cf. Woltjer 1994). Yet, as with the Protestant reform movements, what appears to have been essential to the vigorous engagement of ordinary people on behalf of the established Church was popular preaching that went beyond mere criticism of "heretics" to suggest concrete means by which ordinary people might identify themselves with a larger movement and become actively involved in the process of spiritual renewal.[38] The popular response, in turn, might take a variety of forms, ranging from presumably private or individual acts of traditional piety to much more public or demonstrative acts such as participating in public processions and physical attacks on Protestants or the symbols of their worship and belief.[39]

Thus the local mobilization of a Counter-Reformation coalition necessarily involved an informal alliance between a segment of the clergy and the local population; it also appears almost everywhere to have drawn on one of the peculiar institutional legacies of the late medieval upsurge of popular piety in France: the religious confraternity (Benedict 1979; Harding 1980; Diefendorf 1991). Confraternities might take a variety of forms and be segregated by both class and occupation, but they were everywhere dedicated to the principles of mutual prayers and pious works. As Barbara Diefendorf describes them, "the whole popularity of confraternal associations in the later middle ages derived from the notion that salvation was at least in part a collective enterprise. Their members participated through their prayers and services in the salvation of their fellows, as well as the saving of their souls" (1991:34). Not surprisingly,

---

38. Robert Wuthnow (1989) uses the term "figural action" to denote the ways in which culturally critical discourses go beyond simple criticism of the status quo to suggest concrete and often symbolic actions by which ordinary people might mark themselves as part of a larger movement. Though Wuthnow uses this discursive element to explain the nonrevolutionary "success" of the Reformation (as well as the Enlightenment and European socialism), it may be just as useful in describing the discursive qualities of "successful" cultural innovations more generally, including the Counter-Reformation (cf. Delumeau 1977).

39. For a detailed analysis of this process in the city of Paris up to its deadly culmination in the Saint Bartholomew's Day massacre in 1572, see Diefendorf 1991.

confraternities were also at the cutting edge of the popular piety that the Counter-Reformation church sought to build following the Council of Trent (1545–1549, 1562–1563). As specific and voluntary subsets of the mystical *corpus christianum*, confraternities could serve as especially valuable mechanisms for mobilizing the most committed members of the orthodox Catholic community for action in defense of the faith, just as the conventicles and underground churches formed the organizational basis of powerful Reformation coalitions.

In principle, one might assume that a robust Counter-Reformation coalition—one that involved both charismatic preaching and an institutional base in confraternal associations—would be a comfort to officials, whether local magistrates or agents of the central government, dedicated to the eradication of Protestant heresies. Yet to the extent that the contestation between Catholics and Huguenots erupted in public confrontations and violence, popular Catholicism presented a serious problem for magistrates whose primary responsibility was the preservation of domestic tranquillity; at the very least, disturbances and riots of whatever sort simply made the local community more vulnerable to outside intervention. But even more serious, when in the course of the civil wars local Counter-Reformation coalitions allied themselves with the aristocratic faction of orthodox Catholics in the form of the Catholic League, zealous popular Catholicism became a real threat to those political elites— the so-called *politiques*—who sought to steer a delicate course toward accommodation and peace in the midst of an increasingly politicized and polarized population. In a number of cities, indeed, popular movements brought ultra-Catholic elite factions to power in the late 1580s, and in some exceptional cases, like St. Malo and Marseilles, popular Counter-Reformation coalitions helped to establish independent revolutionary governments that frightened even their noble allies in the Catholic League (Heller 1991:chap. 5). In its most extreme form, then, the Catholic League declared war on the state itself—in both its local and its royal manifestations—but in the end the league, which was in essence only a loosely amalgamated composite of local movements, fell victim to the exigencies of the civil wars that it had deliberately prolonged. With its political and military defeat, we see also the end of the cycle of popular Catholic mobilization that had sustained it locally.[40]

40. The league may be considered successful to the extent that it forced the Huguenot claimant to the French throne, Henry IV, to abjure his Protestantism in 1593 in order to establish his authority in the whole of the kingdom. This partial victory helped enormously

The general contrast with the Low Countries in this regard could not be more striking. Though Alastair Duke (1990:95) reports that in 1566 in Hainaut and Artois, "rural smallholders [were] prepared to stand up for their Catholic convictions" by reporting illegal assemblies and repulsing bands of iconoclasts, there is little evidence of sustained popular collective action on behalf of the Catholic church within the Habsburg domain despite the central government's best efforts to marginalize and eliminate religious dissenters. To be sure, there were signs of local political resistance to the establishment of a Protestant regime in the northern Netherlands in 1572 (Boogman 1942), and in the long run there is ample evidence that many inhabitants of the "liberated" provinces of the north were unwilling to abandon their affection for the Catholic church (Duke 1990; Elliott 1990); yet it is striking that, as was generally the case in Germany earlier in the century, there were no locally significant Counter-Reformation coalitions capable of competing with the Reformed Protestants in the local political arena. Although the reasons for this are undoubtedly many and various, two in particular appear to underscore what seems to have been peculiar about those places in France where a strong Counter-Reformation coalition did appear. On the one hand, Philip II's controversial attempt in the early 1560s to reform the ecclesiastical system within his Low Countries domain highlights the institutional marginality of the Catholic church, especially in the northern provinces.[41] On the other hand, cultural studies of the Low Countries prior to and during the early Reformation suggest a distinct pattern of lay spirituality that was expressed in the morality plays of very independent and frequently anticlerical *rederijkerkamers* (chambers of rhetoric) rather than devout confraternities (cf. Woltjer 1994).

In France there was also an important counterpoint to the mobilization of popular Counter-Reformation coalitions, which were largely urban phenomena, in a series of massive popular mobilizations in the largely rural south and southwest of France between the mid-1570s and

---

to depoliticize and demobilize the Counter-Reformation coalitions that were implacably opposed to a "heretic" king; by the same token it undercut the local political support of those elites who had used the league to establish their independence from the central government.

41. There was, for example, but one bishopric (Utrecht) in all of the northern provinces, and by contrast with France (with some 80 bishoprics) and even perhaps the southern Netherlands, where in many places ecclesiastical and political elites were often linked by family networks, the ecclesiastical establishment in the north was very much marginal to and in extreme cases estranged from those who occupied positions of local and provincial power. See Israel 1995.

the 1590s that ultimately served, in contrary fashion, to bring the civil wars to an end. One of the earliest of these, in the Vivarais between 1575 and 1580, illustrates the essential dynamics of this process. The Vivarais, a largely mountainous territory intersected by narrow river valleys to the west of the Rhône, was by the mid-1570s thoroughly divided politically and militarily between Huguenot and Catholic factions of the aristocratic elite. With each successive war, the towns and villages of the Vivarais were routinely subjected both to the violence of warrior bands and to the emergency taxation demanded by both sides to finance their war efforts; yet with each successive edict of pacification, the general demobilization that might have been expected to ease these burdens never materialized. In 1575 in the midst of the fifth civil war, a local chronicler noted,

The peasants removed tiles and beams from their houses and brought them to sell in Aubenas in order to keep alive through war and famine. The countryside was despoiled by the treachery of the soldiers of both religions. They [the warlords] cooperated with each other in betraying wealthy civilians, and in committing atrocities, thefts, and all kinds of evils. (Quoted in Salmon 1979:8)

When the Catholic faction of the provincial estates determined to deal with the growing anarchy by, yet again, increasing direct taxation to strengthen royal garrisons, they provoked a peasant mobilization that culminated in the formation of peasant leagues, which one official described as "combinations, conspiracies and rebellions perpetrated in the said region by *plusieurs Catholiques*, who have formed a syndicate to refuse royal taxes and all others, ordinary and extraordinary, imposed on the district, and resisting with united force and display of arms the sergeants and commissioners sent to execute our instructions" (quoted in Salmon 1979:9). As this tax revolt gained strength in early 1576, the elite factions of the province were induced to negotiate a local peace treaty that anticipated a national treaty by several months. This apparently sincere attempt at local conciliation in the interest of easing the burdens of war was, however, undermined by yet another war in 1577, and once again peasants mobilized to attack the garrisons as well as the tax collectors.

What was distinctive about this growing opposition to those deemed to be primarily responsible for the ongoing carnage was the nascent cooperation between Catholics and Huguenots. As one royal official reported in 1577, "I have received warning that the twenty-two parishes which have rebelled are on the point of joining the Huguenot party and have massed in force. If something is not done, there will be a rash of these evil beggars" (quoted in Salmon 1979:10). Though this fear that peasant rebels would actually join the "Huguenot party" appears to have been unfounded, the rebels in the Vivarais developed an ongoing cooperation between largely Catholic peasant communes and the small Protestant cities of the region. And the prediction that the "evil beggars" would proliferate certainly was prescient: not only did tax revolts continue in the Vivarais through 1780, but across the Rhône in Dauphiné a similar coalition between rural Catholics and urban Protestants mobilized in opposition to aristocrats deemed responsible for a thoroughly desperate situation in 1579–1580 (Le Roy Ladurie 1979; Hickey 1986). The most dramatic mobilizations of this sort occurred, however, in the mid-1590s. From the Bonnets-Rouges of Burgundy to the Tard-Avisés or Croquants in the southwest, there were locally significant mobilizations in opposition to perceived injustice and excessive taxation that through the mechanism of informal alliances and leagues were capable of shaking the very foundations of aristocratic rule.[42] These mobilizations varied significantly with regard not only to the issues they addressed and the claims they made but also in the effectiveness with which they could deploy armed force that was capable of frightening, if not defeating, those who were deemed to be responsible for prosecuting the civil wars and exploiting the ordinary political subjects of France for more than three decades. Yet what they all had in common was that they were independent of both the Catholic and the Huguenot alliances; these powerful revolts clearly transcended the deep polarization of French society along sectarian lines and thus signaled an end to the extreme politicization of the issue of religious reform.

    In this sense the popular revolts of the 1590s in France bring us full circle. On the one hand, they remind us of the larger histories of popular mobilization and political revolt that both preceded and survived the intensely sectarian religious conflicts of the Second Reformation. They are at once rooted in the multiple traditions of medieval insurrection and a prelude to the great peasant revolts of the seventeenth century; and for that reason, they are necessarily part of any convincing treatment of the

---

42. Cf. Bercé 1990, Salmon 1975, and Heller 1991 who differ relatively little in their sense of the essential chronology of what happened in the course of these revolts but disagree profoundly in their understanding of their political significance. Bercé sees them as vertically integrated coalitions against the central state whereas Heller insists on their anti-aristocratic thrust.

long-term continuities of popular political action in the larger political history of Europe (see Bercé 1987). On the other hand, these revolts remind us of the specific wave of peasant protest that so loudly heralded the beginning of the Reformation era in southern and central Germany in the 1520s (see chap. 2). Like the Revolution of 1525 in Germany, the composite French revolts were loose and highly transitory aggregations of countless small-scale mobilizations; their informal coalitions transcended local and regional boundaries and even occasionally the walls that typically divided cities from their hinterlands; their magnitude and intensity forced otherwise quarrelsome and religiously polarized elites to close ranks in the face of this obvious threat to their political authority; and for that reason they were ultimately military failures. Yet their essential difference is obvious: the deeply religious, almost millenarian ideology that underwrote the German revolts was conspicuously absent in the French revolts. And this underscores, in turn, the important fact that many elements within the repertoire of popular political action were essentially modular, capable of being deployed in a variety of settings in the service of a variety of short-term goals and long-term visions for the future.[43] Thus, while it is important to treat seriously the religious issues of the day, it is surely mistaken to associate all of the popular politics of the sixteenth century with the challenges of Reformation (or Counter-Reformation) theology.

Patterns of Religious Contestation

There remains the more specific task of sorting out the broader patterns of popular engagement in the religious contestation of the Second Reformation and assessing their significance for the outcomes of these conflicts. Let us begin with some general comparisons with the urban reformations in Germany (see fig. 4). Because of the direct threat of princely repression, municipal authorities in France and

43. I borrow the concept of modularity from Sidney Tarrow (1994) who (unfortunately from my perspective as an early modern historian) insists that it is an exclusive property of the repertoires of "modern" social movements. On the contrary, the evidence from sixteenth-century Europe suggests that both the modularity of popular political practice and the social movements of which modularity is said to be characteristic appear to have a longer and more complicated history than the current literature admits.

the Low Countries were generally much more resistant to demands for
the kind of magisterial reformations that took place in most of the imperial cities and even some of the territorial cities of Germany; this was true
even where the same magistrates were less than zealous in their pursuit
of heretics. Thus for most of the century and across much of the territory
from the North Sea to the Mediterranean Sea the political dynamics of
the reformation process tended toward either revolutionary splits or
stunted reform. Still, as we have seen, there were some places where,
especially in the heady atmosphere of the 1560s, municipal administrations no longer resisted popular pressure and negotiated an essentially
peaceful, though not always lasting, transition to Protestantism (e.g.,
Tournai and La Rochelle); or in the context of civil war, municipal
authorities might even, in some places, promote a kind of top-down religious reform as a result of a political/military shift to the rebel cause (e.g.,
in the rebel territories of southern France and the northern Netherlands
after 1572). Despite these similarities, however, it is important to recognize the extent to which the political dynamics of the Second Reformation were not merely minor variations on the themes established by
the First.

I have already argued that both the Valois monarchy in France and the
amalgamated Habsburg lordships in the Low Countries proved to be far
more effective in their attempts to crush religious dissent during the first
three or four decades following Luther's bold theological challenge to
Catholic orthodoxy.[44] Despite their obvious limitations as rulers of composite states and their historical vulnerability to multiple forms of
domestic revolt, Francis I and Charles V forcefully claimed an unprecedented authority to determine what was acceptable religious practice and
belief within their sizable domains. Under their successors, spectacular
and equally unprecedented waves of popular religious dissent exposed
the very real limits of those authoritarian claims; yet it is clear that most
of the chartered, self-governing cities of France and the Low Countries
would not be afforded the luxury of a gradual reformation process largely
exempt from outside intervention such as had occurred in the free cities

---

44. The political-structural comparison between an empire and a collection of (more or
less contiguous) territories under a single overlord (albeit with various sovereignties) is
especially telling in this case, because it was the same Charles of Habsburg who was
emperor in Germany and territorial lord in the Low Countries until his abdication in 1555;
presumably his personal determination to stem the tide of heresy did not vary and thus cannot be considered a salient factor in the very different histories of religious dissent in the
empire and the Low Countries.

of Germany. Although an exceptional place like La Rochelle might successfully avoid both tumult within and punishment from afar,[45] the experiences of Toulouse, Tournai, Valenciennes, and Rouen more clearly established the rule. The central governments in Paris and Brussels, despite their constitutional and strategic limitations, effectively made the promotion of unsanctioned religious change the legal equivalent of sedition and revolt.

Having thus politicized (and nationalized) the question of religious choice—for ordinary people as well as their local rulers—the "princes" of France and the Low Countries effectively stunted the growth of the Lutheran Reformation in ways that the emperor of Germany could not (cf. Koenigsberger 1989). Yet in their spirited defense of the established Church, they set the stage for distinctly different patterns of religious contestation in the Second Reformation. On the one hand, certainly the most important, albeit unintended, consequence of their harsh repression of locally vulnerable reform movements was the eventual creation of organized networks of underground churches; these clandestine networks, which were inspired and actively nurtured by exile communities in Emden, Geneva, and elsewhere, combined the discipline and dedication of a voluntary association with the formal solidarity and resources of an (inter)national alliance. Thus, as soon as new opportunities for religious dissent opened up in the 1560s, there were in many places well-organized groups of zealots ready to seize the initiative and lay claim to a new vision of the Church. On the other hand, princely penetration of the local political arena in the starkly propagandistic name of religious orthodoxy both spawned and valorized popular mobilization in defense of traditional forms of religious ritual and belief, with or without the active support of local authorities. For the most part these popular Catholic mobilizations were reactive and episodic, but by the 1580s the mobilization of robust Counter-Reformation coalitions in defense of established religion in France was instrumental in forming an array of revolutionary municipal governments under the general organization of the Catholic League, and thus steered France as a whole away from Protestantism and in the direction of a unitary "Catholic" monarchy.

In combination, these two specific legacies of the stunting of the first reform movements in France and the Low Countries underwrote what was surely one of the most striking features of the Second Reformation:

---

45. In fact, Judith Meyer (1977, 1984) argues that La Rochelle was more like an imperial free city than a typical French city in this respect.

a widespread pattern of sectarian confrontation and violence from the 1560s onward.[46] As we have seen, however, sectarian violence was not a uniform feature of the Second Reformation, nor was it synonymous with popular religious dissent. Rather it can usefully be considered the occasional, though not unpredictable, by-product of a much larger history of religious contestation. In terms of the frame of reference provided by figure 6, one might argue quite simply that the likelihood of violence increases as one moves from the lower left to the upper right—that is, toward the armament of both of the coalitions and thus the militarization of the conflict. Inasmuch as sectarian confrontations (in the middle of the diagram) were often played out using symbols rather than guns, civil wars (in the upper right) were necessarily more destructive even though they are less intriguing to most analysts; by the same token, consolidating and defending the victory of one side or the other (upper left or lower right) is as likely to produce bodily harm and physical destruction as an ongoing interaction in the middle of the diagram.

As we have seen, within the many and various corporate communities of France and the Low Countries the character and fate of Reformation coalitions varied considerably. At one extreme, they were often decimated by decades of determined repression, but even where the hand of official repression was not as heavy, Reformation coalitions might remain fragmented: segmented by social as well as confessional differences. In the face of official intolerance, however, these differences might be temporarily overcome, especially in the heady atmosphere of the explosive cycles of popular dissent that characterized the 1560s. At the other extreme, a truly comprehensive local coalition may be said to have entailed, in the political context of aggressively consolidating "princes" and civil wars, not only the submerging of local differences for the sake of evangelical unity but also a strong bond with wider alliances. These included, of course, the initially clandestine networks of Reformed Protestant churches as well as the political/military alliances of the Huguenots and Beggars.

---

46. In fact, from Natalie Zemon Davis (1975:esp. chap. 6) to Denis Crouzet (1990), research that focuses specifically on the problem of violence has been among the most fertile and suggestive work on the French Reformation. The same might be said less emphatically for the work on Dutch iconoclasm (see Duke 1990:esp. chap. 6). The difficulty, as I see it, is that by focusing on the ritualized and ideological aspects of many acts of violence, abstracted as a general problem outside the context of specific events whether violent or nonviolent, this research cannot address the obvious question of its variations in time and place. See also Woltjer 1994, which highlights a number of structural and institutional factors that comport well with the more dynamic argument I am making here.

On the other side of this local coin, the strength and character of established ecclesiastical authority also varied considerably. At one extreme, there were thoroughly marginalized ecclesiastical regimes that were beset by an enormous reservoir of anticlericalism yet alienated as well from the local structures of social and political power. In principle, even these marginal regimes were strengthened by the aggressively authoritarian Valois and Habsburg claims for religious uniformity in the name of Catholic orthodoxy, but at the political peripheries of these composite states, such claims were clearly more fictive than real. A truly integrated ecclesiastical regime, by contrast, entailed not only the political support of official repression, whether initiated locally or by the central government, but also a robust Counter-Reformation coalition that tapped the upsurge of popular Catholic piety following the Council of Trent. Even where princely authority was distant and local magistrates were divided, popular support could salvage the authority of the established Church.

At the local level, then, the character and strength of popular mobilizations varied considerably on both dimensions of the cultural/political interaction that is schematized in figure 6, and these variations are certainly salient to our understanding of the widely variable experience of religious contestation within specific communities. In light of the general repression of dissent in the first half of the century, we can safely say that everyone in France and the Low Countries started out in the lower right of the diagram: tiny evangelical communities were barely visible in the midst of the officially *catholic* church that appeared to enjoy the boundless political support of aggressive dynastic princes. The explosion of evangelical dissent in the 1560s changed this equation dramatically, but not all communities set out in the same historical direction. Some communities, like Toulouse, moved quickly from sectarian violence toward civil war and then back toward official repression of dissent; others, like La Rochelle, avoided obvious sectarian violence en route to a temporary accommodation of sectarian differences only to be pushed toward an exclusive reformation by zealous partisans of the Huguenot party; still others, like Leiden, moved via sectarian violence toward civil war and then toward exclusive reformations that eventually yielded, in turn, to an informal accommodation of sectarian differences within the community. For some communities, like Paris or Ghent, situated at the political and geographic center of the ongoing wars, the cycles of violence and temporary resolution must have seemed infinitely various as each successive phase of the civil wars seemed to plunge them into a new round of conflict. Regardless of the specifics of each experience, however, figure 6 suggests how we can transcend the peculiarities of specific cases to include the locally decisive mobilizations of ordinary people in a larger narrative of the Second Reformation.

Revolutionary Reformations and State Power

As we have seen, local contests for control of the religious future were quickly overshadowed and often consumed by political and military conflicts on a grander scale in both France and the Low Countries. As the scale of the conflicts grew, the opportunities for locally independent popular political action certainly declined, but the character of popular mobilization nevertheless remains salient to our understanding of the dynamics of religious contestation and the fate of the larger coalitions of which they were an essential part. For example, truly comprehensive Reformation coalitions on a regional or national scale depended not only on the organization of religious dissenters in worshiping communities but also on their willingness to ally themselves with and commit their collective resources to larger alliances. In short, without ordinary people *national* Reformation coalitions could not be formed. Likewise, a truly integrated ecclesiastical establishment entailed winning not only the military resources of the central state or an ultra-Catholic elite alliance but also the active commitment of those who continued, even on the dismal days, to attend the Mass, to pay the tithe, to join in the sacred processions, and not least of all to pay the extraordinary taxes that the state's defense of the Catholic church required.

Within the same framework provided by figure 6, then, we can also begin to reassess the clearly divergent paths of regional political development that emerged from the religious and political conflicts of the Second Reformation in France and the Low Countries. Let us begin in the north. As noted at the outset, by 1600 the successors of the Dutch Beggars had willy-nilly established an independent republican regime in which the Reformed church enjoyed a privileged position as the "public" church. This was clearly the revolutionary achievement of a comprehensive Reformation coalition that, following the first explosion of evangelical dissent in the 1560s, brought the combined lay and clerical leadership of an extensive network of illegal churches together with the aristocratic leaders of a military resistance to Philip II of Spain and a succession of his governors general in the Low Countries. The public privilege of the Reformed church meant that, besides turning over the best churches to Protestant worship, the new republican regime required that all public officials be at least *liefhebbers* (supporters as opposed to full members) of the Reformed church. Compared to the authoritarian principle (cuius regio eius religio) by which the rulers of Germany claimed the right to determine the religion of their subjects, this strikingly limited privilege for the Reformed church within the territories brought together by the Union of Utrecht mirrors a less than exclusive Protestant reformation at the local level as well.

Although the elaborately articulated structure of the Reformed church polity—consisting of a hierarchy of congregations, classes, and synods in which clergy and laity shared authority—allowed the Reformed communities a disproportionate influence within both the rebel coalition and the new republican regime, the formal membership of local Reformed churches remained in most places small minorities. Indeed, amid a variety of religious "dissenters," they were required to accept variably limited accommodations of their confessional differences on the basis of the Union of Utrecht's prohibition of persecution of individuals with regard to matters of conscience. "Protestantization," to the limited extent that it was successful, was thus a slow process yielding very mixed results, and, not unlike the Lutheran reformations in Germany, the process tended to the gradual estrangement of the clergy from what they considered a generally "ignorant" laity (Kaplan 1989, 1995; Duke 1990:esp. chap. 10). By the same token, the limited success of the orthodox Calvinists in the northern Netherlands is testimony to the dogged determination of countless ordinary people to exercise what was in effect a precious, if limited, freedom to remain "dissenters" in the face of official orthodoxy

In France, by contrast, the Edict of Nantes, which formally ended the last of the sixteenth-century civil wars, established a religious peace that was surely exceptional in Europe at that time: it granted formal toleration to two mutually antagonistic Christian "confessions" within the same polity.[47] Though this was a cultural and political compromise that surely did not please the most zealous on either side of the Catholic/

47. The formal accommodation of religious diversity in France was certainly exceptional but not unique: The kingdom of Poland (and later the combined kingdom of Poland and Lithuania), which had become known as a "refuge of heretics," formally recognized the fact of religious diversity under the Warsaw Confederation of 1573 (see Lecler 1960). It is unclear, however, how much popular support Protestantism involved in this "republic of nobles" (Fedorowicz 1982). See also Christin 1997 on France and Germany.

Reformed divide, it did effectively depoliticize and denationalize the issue of religious reform for critical decades to come. Clearly this was a political victory for the religious Huguenots who had fought so long and hard for an enforceable right to worship in public, though it was, like that of their coreligionists in the northern Netherlands, a limited victory that reflected their inability to institutionalize their voluntary religion as a truly communal church. As most elite-centered accounts insist, this was as well a political victory for the aristocratic politique faction that insisted on religious accommodation as national policy, but it was also an eloquent testimony to the political importance of the massive waves of nonsectarian popular political action in the mid-1590s that had lent such urgency and credibility to their arguments that the wars must stop.

Finally, of course, the success of the Edict of Nantes—in contrast to the failure of earlier compromises, many of which included similar provisions—was a triumph for Henri IV, the formerly Protestant king who became a Catholic to make good his claim to the throne. Though it involved very significant political and military concessions to the Huguenot faction—including a secret subsidy to pay for the fortifications of their self-governing cities—the edict was a political triumph in that it preserved the king's political claim to his whole kingdom. That he was the "patron" of the remnants of the Holy League at the same time as he was the "protector" of the Huguenots reinforced the monarchy's political centrality and thus underwrote the king's implicit claim to cultural and political sovereignty (fig. 2c) even though it would take the doggedly ruthless political efforts of Cardinal Richelieu to subdue and disarm the many Protestant enclaves within the kingdom in the course of the seventeenth century. By the same token, the lingering fear and mutual distrust of Huguenots and Catholics at the local level underscore the important and abiding fact that royal declarations and elite agreements had been incapable of determining the spiritual affections or taming the infrapolitics of religiously divided communities for the better part of a century.

The starkly authoritarian cultural settlement of religious contestation in the southern Netherlands contrasts sharply with the variously successful, if often informal, accommodation of religious difference in France and the northern Low Countries. Although the region's earliest and largest evangelical movements were located in the Walloon and Flemish towns of the south, Philip II and his agents in Brussels were able to deploy overwhelming military force at critical moments to defeat successive waves of religious/political revolt in the 1560s, 1570s, and 1580s.

The Spanish reconquest of the southern provinces reflects, of course, Philip II's determination to defend the Church at all costs, but it also reflects the fragmentation of the Reformation coalition in the south, for by the Union and Treaty of Arras in 1579 the nobility of the Walloon provinces won a guarantee for their political prerogatives—which amounted to a permanent brake on the further consolidation of Spanish authority—in exchange for maintaining the public monopoly of Catholic worship.[48] This defection from the general resistance to Spanish "tyranny" clearly exposed the rebellious Flemish and Walloon towns, along with their sizable Reformed Protestant congregations, to a piecemeal reconquest that, in turn, precipitated a massive stream of more than 100,000 Protestant refugees, many of whom were prosperous merchants and skilled artisans, toward the officially Protestant north. To be sure, this was a relatively unambiguous victory for the central government's authoritarian claim to cultural sovereignty, but it was clearly one that came at enormous political and social cost.

In summary, then, how was it that the generally similar patterns of popular religious contestation in France and the Low Countries had yielded these strikingly different settlements? If the above analysis is correct, we can isolate two broad regional trajectories of religious contestation that need to be understood in terms of the active engagement of ordinary people as both religious laity and political subjects (see fig. 7). Coming out of a common experience of repression in the first half of the century, popular Reformation coalitions had exploded into full public view in the 1560s to expose the essential weaknesses of the established churches in both the Habsburg and the Valois domains. The episodic sectarian violence that characterized this early phase quickly escalated into civil war, however, as organized networks of Reformed Protestant churches joined forces with elite opponents of "princely" tyranny. The variable success of these armed coalitions in the course of intermittent warfare resulted in two divergent regional trajectories within these large composite states. After 1572 the "rebel" territories of both the northern Netherlands and southern France veered sharply in the direction of exclusive reformations on the strength of their military leaders in alliance with the popular network of Reformed Protestants who were now in a position to establish their own public churches. As new republican

---

48. I do not mean to suggest that the political status quo was frozen in place in the southern Netherlands; rather, it is clear that henceforth development was channeled within the narrow confines of aristocratic and provincial "privileges." Cf. De Schepper 1987.

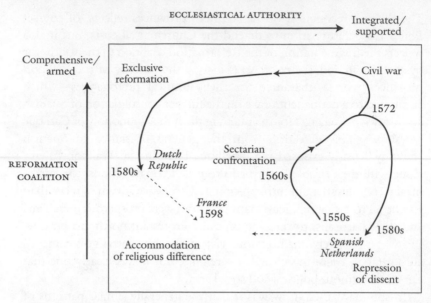

Figure 7. Regional patterns of religious contestation in the Second Reformation

regimes were consolidated in these areas of rebel success, the zealous evangelicals who surely hoped, at one level, for a complete reformation of church *and* society were nevertheless confronted by the reality of both hesitation among their elite protectors and stubborn resistance, whether public and demonstrative or merely passive, among devout Catholics. Consequently the rebel territories veered away from strictly authoritarian reformations toward some form of accommodation, albeit reluctant in many cases, of other religious "dissenters" or Catholics.

Meanwhile, the "obedient" territories of northern France and the southern Low Countries veered, once again, in the direction of repression as locally powerful Reformation coalitions either confronted overwhelming military force from outside their communities, without the benefit of equivalent support from their (erstwhile) allies, or, in some cases, were bested at their own game by robust Counter-Reformation coalitions. As these Counter-Reformation regimes were consolidated, however, they too had to confront the practical limits and the enormous social and economic costs of an uncompromising victory. But for the cultural compromise that a formerly Protestant sovereign was able to sell, with the help of nonsectarian rebellions, to both his Catholic and his

Protestant subjects, France too might have been divided between an oligarchic Protestant republic and a severely limited Catholic "prince."

By comparison with the "official" reformations that had characterized the first phase of the Protestant Reformation, the reformations in France and the Dutch Republic may usefully be considered "revolutionary" reformations. By this I do not mean to suggest that there was an ideological propensity among Calvinists to radical revolution or even democracy, as both their opponents and some later-day scholars have suggested; on the contrary, the literature on confessionalization in Germany suggests that Calvinist theology was perfectly compatible with authoritarian politics (cf. Fulbrook 1983; Hsia 1989; Nischan 1994). Rather, by calling these reformations revolutionary I want to point out that while the Reformation coalitions aimed for the religious transformation of whole communities, like the Lutherans and Zwinglians before them, after decades of struggle they were forced to accept the long-term segmentation of cultural authority among alternative religious groups. Thus by the beginning of the seventeenth century it was clear that in neither France nor the Dutch Republic would the reformation be officially enacted for the whole community and that the authoritarian principle of *cuius regio eius religio* would not be institutionalized. As these contrasting political histories suggest, such a cultural compromise was not the consequence of a particular sort of state formation; indeed, it proved to be variously compatible with both the local consolidation of power that characterized the Dutch Republic (fig. 2a) and the territorial reconstruction of a severely decimated monarchy that occurred in France (fig. 2c). In both cases ordinary people remained important political actors, though in strikingly different ways. By contrast, in the southern Netherlands the political cost of Philip II's refusal to compromise his claim to cultural sovereignty was his long-term acceptance of the consolidation of elite power—at the immediate expense of well-organized popular political actors (fig. 2b). This is, of course, a settlement clearly reminiscent of the one his father had found it necessary to accept in both Catholic Germany and Castile.

In the end, of course, it is true that ordinary people were neither the principal architects nor the primary beneficiaries of these cultural and political settlements. It is equally true, however, that in a variety of ways ordinary people were actively involved in establishing the basic historical trajectories of two of Europe's most "successful" regimes in the early modern period as well as one of its more dismal "failures." Though the traditional, elite-centered histories of the French and Dutch conflicts have tended to separate the combatants into clear winners and losers, from the point of view of ordinary people, the religious wars of the latter part of the sixteenth century were too destructive and their eventual settlements too ambiguous to yield to simple tallies on either side. But having challenged and, in various ways, broken their rulers' unambiguous claims to both cultural and political sovereignty, ordinary political actors may be said to have entered the early modern era with a new array of political and cultural resources with which to exploit the political and cultural opportunities afforded to them by a whole array of strikingly novel regimes.

4

The Political Crisis of
the Seventeenth Century

Firstly, the aforesaid Lord King [Philip IV of Spain] declares and recognizes that the aforesaid Lords States General of the United Netherlands and the respective provinces thereof, with all their associated districts, cities, and dependent lands, are free and sovereign states, provinces, and lands, upon which, together with their associated districts, cities, and lands aforesaid, he, the Lord King, does not now make any claim, and he himself and his successors descendants will in the future never make any claim; and therefore is satisfied to negotiate with these Lords States, as he does by these presents, a perpetual peace, on the conditions hereinafter described and confirmed.

Article 1, Peace of Münster, January 1648

It is obviously difficult for a population as large as that of our city suddenly to unite and arm itself. Good opportunities are rare: therefore when they occur, it is an act of prudence and great magnanimity to accept them. If you only are clear-sighted enough to recognize it, you will see that God has already delivered you into the hands of good fortune. . . .

And have no fear, fellow Neapolitans, of [the Spaniards'] power, for they allowed themselves to be expelled from the seven provinces of Flanders [sic] by Dutch fisherman, and from Portugal on their frontiers; and though on each occasion they were supported by your forces, they were powerless to resist. What, then, can they do without you, against you?

Discorso fatto al popolo napoletano
per eccitarlo alla libertà, 1647

The most common idea that is spreading among the people [of Paris] is that the Neapolitans have acted intelligently, and that in order to

shake off oppression, their example should be followed. It is
understood, however, that allowing the people in the streets to shout
aloud their enthusiasm for the revolt of Naples has caused great
inconvenience. Therefore measures have been taken to prevent
gazettes from reporting further on it.

Battista Nani,Venetian ambassador to Paris,
September 1647

The 1640s were especially trying for the Spanish branch of
the Habsburg dynasty. Aside from the ongoing challenge of ending the
long and costly war with his rebellious provinces in the northern
Netherlands, Philip IV was faced in 1640 with two new revolutions: in
May, the principality of Catalonia, which on the commercial strength of
Barcelona was the most important part of his Aragonese possessions,
rose up in revolt; in December, the kingdom of Portugal, which had
been cobbled into the composite Habsburg state in Iberia and Italy some
sixty years earlier, declared its independence, taking with it a vast array of
colonial interests. After an unsuccessful military campaign to subdue
Barcelona as well as a diplomatic failure to prevent a Catalonian alliance
with France, the Habsburg regime in Madrid appeared to be incapable of
mounting even a token resistance to the Portuguese secession. Meanwhile, although the effective loss of Portugal had simplified some of the
sticking points in negotiating peace with the Dutch, it was not until 1647
that a preliminary treaty, formally recognizing the independence of the
Dutch Republic, was completed in the Westphalian city of Münster.
Thus even before the Peace of Münster could be ratified and officially
promulgated (1648), a spectacular popular revolt in Naples in the summer of 1647, paired with several others in Sicily, threatened even more
serious damage to Philip's dynastic house of cards. Surely all of this
opposition merely confirmed the English ambassador's belief, expressed
as early as 1641, that "the greatness of this monarchy is near to an end."[1]

Yet the tribulations of Philip IV were hardly unique. At the same time
that Philip was being confronted with the obvious limits of his autonomy as the sovereign of a composite monarchy in the Mediterranean, the
Austrian Habsburgs were coming to grips with the limits of their imperial ambitions in Germany. Though imperial forces had enjoyed considerable success and Ferdinand III had entered the initial negotiations to

---

1. Quoted in Elliott 1963:523. The diplomat was Sir Arthur Hopton (1588?–1650); he
returned to England during the civil wars and died not long after the revolution of 1649.
See *Dictionary of National Biography* (1891), 27:345.

end the Thirty Years' War boldly by claiming to speak for the empire as a whole, he had to negotiate alongside and with many of his nominal subordinates and was eventually forced to acknowledge the sovereignty of the constituent units of his empire in the Peace of Westphalia (1648). Meanwhile, the same English ambassador who observed the decline of the Spanish monarchy saw his homeland engulfed in civil war (1642–1649) and his own sovereign executed before the decade was out. And the same French monarchy that had sought to take advantage of Spanish troubles in Barcelona, Lisbon, and Naples found itself under direct attack at home during the so-called Fronde, which began in earnest in 1648 and forced the young king, Louis XIV, to flee Paris. In an imaginary political commodities market around 1650, then, the value of princely futures in general would surely have been depressed; in fact, given the evidence most readily at hand, only the most adventurous of investors were willing to risk a great deal on new investments in the future of monarchical or imperial consolidation.

The simultaneity of so many serious challenges to the sovereign claims of existing regimes has spawned a sizable literature regarding what is usually called the Crisis of the Seventeenth Century. R. B. Merriman ([1938] 1963) first explored the similarities and connections among "six contemporaneous revolutions" at midcentury, but in the 1950s and beyond the "crisis" debate, spawned by Eric Hobsbawm and H. R. Trevor-Roper, paid relatively little attention to these political conflicts, focusing instead on questions relating to the characteristics of a more general social and economic crisis of which Merriman's "revolutions" were said to be symptomatic (Ashton 1965; Parker and Smith 1978). Before long the crisis metaphor itself became the focus of attention as a new generation of scholars found ever more crises to explore, either in other dimensions of the mid-seventeenth-century European experience or in other decades, reaching all the way back to the early sixteenth century. Eventually, T. K. Rabb (1975) suggested that the original crisis of the mid-seventeenth century might most usefully be seen as merely the climax of a much grander social, political, and cultural "struggle for stability" that began in the early sixteenth century and finally gave way to the relative stability of Europe's ancien régime by the 1680s.[2]

2. Recently, Jack A. Goldstone (1991) has chastised the narrowly European vision of most students of early modern revolutions and has, consequently, traced the demographic origins of state breakdowns, not only in western Europe but in the Ottoman Empire and China as well; his analysis of the seventeenth-century crisis is, however, narrowly focused on the English revolution.

For our purposes, it is essential to refocus on the political dimensions of the mid-seventeenth-century crisis and to situate these multiple challenges to Europe's dynastic princes within both the changing spaces of European politics and the larger history of popular political practice. Looking prospectively from the end of the sixteenth century, this chapter examines the constellation of political conflicts that finally yielded to a relatively durable pattern of religious and political settlement in the second half of the seventeenth century. I argue that the political action of ordinary people was instrumental in transforming the composite states created by aggressive princes nearly everywhere in Europe, not just in those areas where a broad-based Reformation coalition had succeeded in implanting Protestant churches in the sixteenth century. This is not to say, of course, that popular political actors were everywhere (or even anywhere unambiguously) triumphant; rather, surveying the revolutionary conflicts that constituted the midcentury crisis, I highlight the variable, transient, and often ambiguous outcomes of the religious and political struggles. My goal, in proceeding from one region to the next, is to describe and account for the complex *interactions* of rulers and subjects in a number of revolutionary situations and to suggest how the outcomes of these struggles structured, in turn, the political opportunities of ordinary people under Europe's new regime.

The End of the Religious Wars?

At the beginning of the seventeenth century there was credible evidence to suggest that the dangerous and destructive cycle of "religious" wars that had attended the reformations of the sixteenth century might actually be coming to an end. The most promising signs of hope first appeared in 1598 with the Edict of Nantes in France and the death of Philip II in Spain. On the face of it, the Edict of Nantes might have been just another in the dismal series of merely temporary truces that had marked the intervals between no less than nine wars in France, but two developments signaled that the depoliticization of the question of religious difference might actually be possible. In the first place, a special system of courts proved to be remarkably effective in limiting the scope of conflicts between Protestants and Catholics regarding the practical implications of the edict's formal recognition of religious difference.[3] But equally important, Henry IV apparently convinced enough of the elite leaders on both sides of the Protestant/Catholic divide, with the help of liberal subsidies and pensions, to accept him as the guarantor of their political interests; consequently, the risk of personal losses in a revived war appeared to be greater than the political costs of continuing an initially unsatisfying peace. By 1610 the peace in France was secure enough to survive even the assassination of Henry IV. Similarly, after so many years of Philip II's stubborn refusal to accept any kind of compromise with Protestantism, the ascension of Philip III to the Castilian throne brought with it the possibility of compromise in the Spanish Habsburgs' very costly war with their rebellious Dutch provinces. Though a permanent peace that resolved the especially thorny issues of colonial competition still proved to be elusive, an armistice in 1607 yielded to the Twelve-Year Truce (1609–1621) by which, for all practical purposes, Spain recognized the sovereignty of the United Provinces.

Subtler, though no less important, signs of hope for an enduring religious peace were also visible within the German-Roman Empire, the heartland of the first phase of the European Reformation (see Munck 1990; Hughes 1992). The significant question there was whether the apparently inflexible and unambiguously authoritarian principle of *cuius regio eius religio,* as articulated in the Peace of Augsburg in 1555, could accommodate either renewed contestation between particular subjects and rulers over matters of religious choice and identity or ongoing changes in the larger confessional map of central and eastern Europe. With regard to the latter, by the turn of the century a series of princely conversions had demonstrated the resilience of the agreement, even when princes like the elector of the Palatinate embraced Calvinism instead of Lutheranism, which was the only officially recognized Protestant sect under the Augsburg settlement.[4] As for ongoing conflicts between subjects and rulers, a combined municipal and ecclesiastical revolution in the East Frisian town of Emden in 1595 preserved the local Calvinist church and liberated the municipal council from an aggressively Lutheran count (Schilling 1991); it demonstrated that broadly popular

---

3. There were of course exceptions like the conflict in Paumier noted in Tilly 1981.
4. The general peace even survived the forcible restoration of Catholicism at Cologne (1582–1587) under one of the most contested principles of the Augsburg settlement, the Ecclesiastical Reservation Clause—that is, the provision that prevented Catholic prelates who became Protestants from converting their sees to secular states (Hughes 1992).

challenges to the territorial prince's exclusive claim to the *ius reformandi* would not necessarily lead to a new cycle of war. Similarly, the successful resistance of the Lutheran city of Lemgo to the count of Lippe's attempt to impose Calvinism in the 1610s highlighted the extent to which the authoritarian claims of Germany's rulers could be openly challenged by determined subjects within the framework of the empire (Schilling 1988). Meanwhile, Protestantism seemed to flourish informally even in the patrimonial lands of the Austrian Habsburgs under both Maximilian II (1564–1576) and Rudolf II (1576–1612). Although the latter successfully expelled Protestant pastors from Vienna, his authority nearly collapsed altogether when he tried unsuccessfully to promote the Counter-Reformation in Hungary; in 1609 he was even forced to grant the Letter of Majesty in Bohemia, which entailed not only important political concessions to the Estates of Bohemia but also religious guarantees to the many Protestant groups that were thriving there (Polisensky 1971; Evans 1979; Eberhard 1995).

If, taken together, these were signs of hope for a general religious peace in Europe, they were equally signs of the fragility of peace. Religion and politics remained thoroughly intertwined, and religious difference retained its potential as a marker of political enmity as long as rulers entertained exclusive claims to cultural sovereignty or significant numbers of their subjects actively sought the exclusive reformation or counterreformation of whole polities. Thus the temporary absence of religious war on a large scale merely suggests the temporary absence of comprehensive Reformation and Counter-Reformation coalitions willing and able to press mutually exclusive claims to religious hegemony (see fig. 6); and, for the time being at least, religious dissent and political conflict on the local or regional scale did not automatically lead to a new round of religious war on a broader scale. More precisely, the relative peace of the early years of the seventeenth century appears to have been predicated on the momentary willingness of Europe's princely rulers—rooted as often as not in political and military necessity—to moderate their attempts to consolidate their power over matters of religious conscience. Indeed, it is telling that when the elector of Brandenburg officially embraced Calvinism in 1613, he restricted the scope of this Second Reformation to the court for the sake of peace with his overwhelmingly Lutheran subjects. But on the other side of the same coin, when the Austrian Habsburgs in alliance with the papacy sought to overturn the political and religious compromises they had been forced to accept in Bohemia in 1609, it was enough to precipitate after 1618 yet another round of religious war. This cluster of extremely destructive conflicts, known retrospectively as the Thirty Years' War, eventually involved all of the great powers of Europe before it was resolved by the relatively durable treaties signed at Münster and Osnabrück in 1648 (see Parker 1984).

What made the Thirty Years' War a "religious" war was hardly the purity of religious motives among the many combatants. Rather, like the religious wars that preceded it—from the Peasants' War and the Schmalkaldic War in Germany through the civil wars in France and the Dutch War of Independence—the Thirty Years' War was specifically religious in at least three ways: (1) it was precipitated by significant challenges to an established ruler's claim to a comprehensive political *and* religious sovereignty over his subjects; (2) it invoked and mobilized large-scale, armed coalitions within the empire that were identified in large measure with the Reformation and Counter-Reformation causes; and (3) an unambiguous military victory for one side or the other potentially promised an equally unambiguous victory for the Protestant or Roman Catholic church in the polities of central and eastern Europe where the battles were principally fought. In this sense, although it is well known that the Thirty Years' War was fought by military alliances in which religious conviction took a back seat to political and strategic calculation, it is equally safe to say that it revived and expanded the truly "confessional" era in European history during which an uncompromising princely claim to cultural and religious sovereignty became the hallmark of what is often called absolutism (cf. Hsia 1989). By the same token, the compromise settlements that finally brought an end to the carnage in 1648 did not bring an end to the era of religious politics or even to the age of religious war on a more limited scale within specific polities.[5] Indeed, as long as Europe's rulers were tempted to use religious beliefs and institutions to extend or consolidate their authority over their subjects, religion and politics would continue to be thoroughly entwined.

For our purposes, however, it is important to realize that, even in the territories most directly affected by the Thirty Years' War, religion remained only one of a very mixed bag of issues that animated popular political action. In the Austrian Erblände,[6] for example, locally mobilized peasant resistance to economic and social subjection at the hands of noble

5. See the section on the British Isles below.
6. "Erblände" refers generally to the core of the Austrian Habsburgs' domain in central

landlords in what is often called the "second serfdom" coalesced into a major peasant uprising (the largest within the empire since 1525) across Upper and Lower Austria between 1594 and 1597 (Evans 1979:85–100; Rebel 1983). Since the areas of the revolt were also areas where a variety of forms of Protestant worship had largely overshadowed a weakened Catholic church, however, the military defeat of the peasants provided a pretext for the vigorous assertion of the Counter-Reformation in the Austrian countryside in the course of the seventeenth century. Even though there was intermittent popular resistance to wartime exactions, the Thirty Years' War, like its sixteenth-century predecessors, quickly and effectively closed down most of the opportunities for independent popular political action in those areas most directly affected by it. Thus the Catholic armies in alliance with an aggressive Counter-Reformation clergy succeeded in enforcing the political sovereignty and cultural politics of Ferdinand II—which boiled down to the equation of Protestantism with all manner of disloyalty and the stern insistence on a single-confession state—in Bohemia and the Austrian Erblände in the 1620s; this, in turn, produced massive flows of Protestant refugees comparable to the flight of Protestants from the southern Netherlands after 1585.[7]

The intermixture of religion and politics remained volatile in France and the Low Countries, too, especially with the coming of the Thirty Years' War, but in both places it failed to reignite the fires of civil or religious war on the scale of the sixteenth century. In France the relative tranquillity of the first two decades of the seventeenth century—retrospectively seen as a "golden age" in French historiography—gave way to more serious political dissension in the 1620s, and once again it invoked elements of the Huguenot alliance. Though the Protestant magnates who led the wars of the sixteenth century had been pacified in 1598, they had certainly not disappeared altogether. Thus when the royal government began seriously to reconstruct the king's authority by undermining the political concessions of the Edict of Nantes, they encountered serious resistance from some of the political elites whose power was most directly threatened in the Protestant strongholds of the south and south-

Europe, principally the "inherited lands" known as Upper, Lower, and Inner Austria, as opposed to Hungary and Bohemia.

7. There are no studies of the Protestant movements in Bohemia and Austria comparable to those for France and the Low Countries, but the available evidence suggests a great deal of diversity and disunity among the Protestant groups, which may account for the relatively rapid disintegration of the Reformation coalition following the bold challenge to Ferdinand in Prague in 1618; See Evans 1979; Eberhard 1995.

west. Following the king's successful attack in 1620 on the county of Béarn, a defiant Protestant stronghold in the Pyrenees, there were a series of piecemeal confrontations in which local Protestant resistance might occasionally hold off the royal offensive, as at Montauban. But the monarchy's determination was amply rewarded by the Treaty of Montpellier (1622), which prescribed the dismantling of virtually all of the Protestants' fortified towns (*places de sureté*). What is remarkable about these encounters is that they failed to invoke or re-create the fully articulated Huguenot alliance of the sixteenth-century civil wars; most Protestant leaders, indeed, seem to have concluded that open rebellion was useless or counterproductive (Briggs 1977:92–94), while those who did revolt enjoyed very little popular support. An ill-conceived commitment of English support to La Rochelle in 1627 finally provided the royal government with a pretext for a direct attack on this last bastion of Huguenot independence. Yet when La Rochelle finally fell after a fourteen-month siege, the Peace of Alais (1629), which forced the Huguenots to give up the last of their fortresses and troops, nevertheless guaranteed their liberty of conscience. Though severely tested, then, the central compromise of the Edict of Nantes granting Protestants a limited freedom of worship held firm; and for the time being the volatile identification of religious difference with political revolt was once again broken along with the independent military strength of the Protestant magnates. But the Protestants were more dependent than ever on the king's "protection."

This is not to say, of course, that the relations between subjects and rulers in France remained tranquil. On the contrary, in 1635 France began a direct and exceedingly costly engagement in the Thirty Years' War that precipitated a widespread series of both urban and rural revolts including two very significant regional rebellions—those of the Croquants in 1636–1637 and the Nu-Pieds in 1639—and culminated in the Fronde at midcentury (Tilly 1986; Briggs 1989; Bercé 1990). Just as the religious peace had brought ordinary people a measure of tax relief after 1598, the king's increasingly aggressive domestic and foreign policies in the 1620s and 1630s brought with them a steep rise in royal taxation—both in the *taille,* the tax on peasant land, and in the *aides,* the urban excises on foodstuffs and other essential commodities (Tilly 1981, 1986). Widespread evasion combined with corruption to produce only an incrementally small yield on these new taxes at the same time that the determination of the state's fiscal agents provided the king's subjects with ready targets for their resentment and opposition. Again the building block of popular political opposition was local mobilization against specific officials and over concrete issues. For their part in confronting these local oppositions, royal officials generally followed a two-pronged strategy of compromise when necessary and violent repression when possible, both of which were intended to limit the scope of popular opposition.

As tax evasion gave way to open resistance, however, and local resistance aggregated into broadly based regional revolts, as it did in 1636 and 1639, the French monarchy was faced with fully articulated opposition coalitions of the sort that had briefly disappeared in the first third of the seventeenth century. What made these opposition coalitions especially frightening and dangerous is that they combined a broad base of popular mobilization with locally significant elite leadership, but what these coalitions generally lacked was the ideological glue, the more experienced mercenaries, and the international networks of support that had sustained both the Reformation and the Counter-Reformation coalitions during the wars of religion. Professing allegiance to the king while attacking "corrupt" officials and "tyrannical" policies, then, the popular armies of regional revolt were in the long run no match for the far more professional and resourceful armies of the king. At this level, too, repression was combined with concession to produce inequalities in taxation that would in turn fuel more and different kinds of opposition another day. Yet in the impressively diverse catalog of "contentious gatherings" that Charles Tilly gives us for five selected regions of France in the 1630s and 1640s, the common denominator remains "the royal effort to raise money for war" (1981:139; see also tables, 140–143).

In the Dutch Republic religious difference also threatened to return as a salient marker of political enmity and opposition, but in a rather different way. To the extent that the Union of Utrecht represented a religious settlement for this new polity, it privileged the Reformed church as the exclusive *public* church, but it forbade the persecution of individuals in matters of religious conscience. What emerged in the northern Netherlands, then, was a pluralistic society that afforded religious "dissenters" locally variable opportunities, not only to survive, but in some places even to flourish.[8] Though the relations among the public church, the dissenting communities, and the local officials (who functioned as

8. On the parallel, though also limited, opportunities for the growth of religious pluralism in Hungary and Poland, see Eberhard 1995. What all these cases have in common is the essential weakness or limitation of the dynast's state's claim to cultural sovereignty.

reluctant referees as much as cultural sovereigns) were often contentious and unstable, it was conflict within the Reformed church—not between confessional groups—that most seriously disrupted Dutch politics on a national scale during the truce with Spain.[9] Two antagonistic factions within the Reformed church, the Gomarists and the Arminians, differed from one another not only in the fine points of Calvinist theology— Gomarus and Arminius were theology professors at Leiden—but also on issues relating to church and state or, as they typically stated it, religion and regime. The Gomarists laid a strong claim to Calvinist "orthodoxy" and favored a "pure" Reformed church with significant disciplinary authority over its members but separate from direct political influence; by contrast, the Arminians espoused a less stringent Calvinism as well as a more open, capacious public church closely allied with and supportive of the republican regime. These issues echoed broadly in the voluminous pamphlet literature of the early republic, and although neither side was connected with a political "party" in any direct way, it was evident already in the negotiations leading up to the truce in 1609 that the orthodox Calvinists—many of them refugees from the southern provinces— favored continuation of the war with Spain with an eye to the "liberation" of all the Low Countries. They accused their more latitudinarian enemies—that is, those who advocated the truce and were a good deal less zealous in the promotion of the "truc" reformation of the Church— of both political and religious lassitude (Harline 1987).

During the truce these latent differences over religion and regime became more dangerous and more manifest as the two sides—now called Remonstrants and Counter-Remonstrants—clashed over both the constitutionality and the political wisdom of a proposed "national" synod of the Reformed church to settle the whole range of theological and ecclesiastical issues.[10] This struggle culminated in 1618 with the calling of the Synod of Dordrecht, in which the orthodox Calvinists established unambiguous control of the principal institutions of the Reformed church; its tragic denouement was the trial and execution in 1619 of Johan van Oldenbarnevelt for treason. Oldenbarnevelt had been one of the principal political architects of the Dutch Republic since the late 1580s and the chief advocate of the truce; the authorities who tried and condemned him

9. For a very recent and up-to-date survey in English of these and related events in the Dutch Republic, see Israel 1995.
10. The term "Remonstrant," not unlike the more general term "Protestant," has an unmistakable political origin in that it refers to a formal protest (Remonstrance) against the authoritarian drift of orthodox preachers in the Reformed church.

were closely allied with Maurits of Nassau, son of William of Orange and the heroic military leader of the fledgling republic. The complexity of this difficult and dangerous struggle not only reflects the ambiguous position of the public Reformed church in a pluralist Dutch society, it underscores the peculiarities of the Dutch republican regime. For our purposes it is important to note that ordinary people were very much involved in religious politics at the local level in the sense that their religious affiliations established important limits on the political options available to local rulers, and when they were organized in conventicles, underground churches, and civic militias, they could be an especially dynamic element in determining both the policy and the personnel of local governments. Local rulers, for their part, were often caught in an untenable position between the insistent demands of well-organized groups at home and the pressures of national claimants to power. Meanwhile, the two principal claimants to national leadership, Oldenbarnevelt and Maurits, were, as political appointees, by no means surrogates for the princely sovereignty that by the 1580s had been abjured and defeated; rather, they were the brokers and national symbols of two different and volatile factions of the "regent" oligarchy who claimed the "sovereignty" of the republic by virtue of their membership in a layered system of corporate ruling bodies—the city councils, variously constituted provincial estates, and the national Estates General, which was composed of "instructed" delegates from the provincial estates (see Price 1994).

In this context issues involving religion and regime could become especially volatile when they linked small but zealous groups of orthodox Calvinists through the factional networks of the ruling oligarchy with the military resources commanded by Maurits, the captain-general of the republic's armies. In many of Holland's very independent cities popular Counter-Remonstrant (i.e., orthodox Calvinist) demonstrations, often reinforced by official visits by Maurits as *stadhouder* (formerly the royal governor, now appointed by the provincial Estates), forced the purge of Arminians from the ruling councils. But in the critical case of Utrecht, Maurits deployed troops under his command to purge its municipal council and to disarm a local military contingent outside his control (Israel 1995; Kaplan 1995). In the face of this formidable coalition, Oldenbarnevelt and his allies proved to be no match even where they had solid support at the community level because direct military intervention by the prince tipped the balance in favor of Oldenbarnevelt's religious and political enemies who eventually dominated the synod of the Reformed church as well as the corporate bodies of the republican regime. In the short term the triumph of the orthodox Calvinists at the Synod of Dordrecht resulted in a purge of the clerical leadership of the Reformed church as well as sporadic persecution of a broad range of religious groups who stubbornly asserted their "dissenting" religious identities through conventicles and underground churches. But as long as the Union of Utrecht remained the touchstone of Dutch politics, the newly purified public church would never be in a position, either ideologically or politically, to enforce an exclusive reformation in the northern Netherlands (cf. Kaplan 1995; Hakkenburg 1996). By the same token, the triumph of Maurits's military leadership virtually ensured both the republic's deep involvement in the Thirty Years' War and the resumption of the war against Spain, but it did not alter the constitutional structure of the Dutch Republic in which Maurits and his successors as captain-general of the union and *stadhouders* of the various provinces remained public appointees (with extensive patronage and indirect "influence" over factions of the regent elite) rather than "sovereigns" in their own right. Before long, then, the issues of religion and regime ceased to be as volatile when the transient coalition of orthodox Calvinists with the republic's military leadership began to dissolve under Frederik Hendrik, Maurits's half-brother and his successor as captain-general of the republic (1625–47).

The Spanish Crisis in Iberia: Catalonia and Portugal

Against the backdrop of the Thirty Years' War in central and eastern Europe and the changing patterns of political contention in France and the Dutch Republic, we are now in a better position to consider the character and significance of the six contemporaneous revolutions that are said to have constituted the original crisis of the midseventeenth century. R. B. Merriman began his survey with the "Revolt in Catalonia" (1640–1652), the "Revolution in Portugal" (1640–1668), and the "Uprising in Naples" (1647–1648), all three within the composite monarchy of the Spanish Habsburgs. To these he added the "Puritan Revolution" in England (1642–1660), the "Fronde" in France (1648–53), and the "Revolution in the Netherlands" (1650). According to Merriman, writing in the 1930s and openly troubled by predictions of "world" revolution, "The causes, courses and results of these six revolutions afford an admirable example of the infinite variety of history. Though contemporaneous, they were curiously little alike; their differences were far more remarkable than their similarities" ([1938] 1963:89). It will be useful for us to be more precise about the variety; indeed, I should like to treat the first three, along with the urban uprisings in Sicily in 1646 and 1647, as constituting a cycle of protest and revolution within a single composite state and the last three, though not unrelated to one another and to the conflicts within the Spanish domain, as relatively discrete political contests within very different states. This distinction is especially evident and useful, I think, when we approach the seventeenth-century crisis from the point of view of popular political practice.

The Catalan Revolt illustrates the essential dynamics of the challenges to Spanish-Habsburg power in the Mediterranean in that it grew out of resistance to the forceful assertion of royal authority within a constitutionally and fiscally peripheral component of the composite Habsburg monarchy (Elliott 1963, 1970). Though Catalonia was both economically and strategically invaluable to the Castilian core of the Habsburg state, it was constitutionally peripheral in the sense that the Habsburg dynastic succession was predicated on the king's solemn pledge to guarantee its historic liberties and exemptions (*fueros*); it was fiscally peripheral in the sense that it contributed nothing directly to the defense budget of the Castilian-dominated composite. Such an arrangement produced obvious frustration at the center of this extensive and very diverse composite; from Madrid it was possible, if not always realistic, to dream of a unified kingdom of Spain to replace the diverse sovereignties that had been accumulated by the dynastic union of Aragon and Castile. In an attempt to move in that direction and to consolidate his extractive authority, Philip IV (or perhaps more accurately his chief minister, the count-duke of Olivares) developed the so-called Union of Arms according to which the royal government in Madrid imposed new obligations on its peripheral provinces in the name of a common defense. Specifically, this entailed the imposition on the Catalans of both new taxes and new obligations to billet the king's infantry regiments (*tercios*) in 1639 and 1640. Amid formal and largely unavailing protests by the principality's indigenous elites, however, a broad-based popular mobilization in the spring of 1640 proved to be the most dynamic element in an otherwise familiar standoff between the central government and its nominal agents of indirect rule on the periphery.

The roots of the popular mobilizations in Catalonia in 1640 were, like popular mobilizations everywhere, locally variable. In the more mountainous and remote parts of the principality where the movement drew its original strength, it was rooted in traditions of peasant mobilization reaching back to the so-called syndicates of the fifteenth-century civil wars and to the networks of rural bandits more recently active in Catalonia (Elliott 1963:421–422). In the first week of May, well-armed and well-organized bands of such rustics, summoned quickly to action by the ringing of church bells, challenged the government's attempts to billet troops in several towns and villages in the provincial interior, forcing the tercios to retreat to the coast. But when the viceroy attempted to punish the rebels by sacking the town of Santa Coloma de Farnes, he not only failed to intimidate them but also effectively transformed a localized resistance into a more generalized uprising. One official captured the seriousness of the political situation in early May just before the sack of Santa Coloma:

All this land, by which I mean the peasantry, is so disaffected that I doubt that there are any who do not feel the same way as those of Santa Coloma. And the common people of this town [Girona] are by no means well-disposed. It is true that the town councillors and the superior classes are showing themselves to be devoted to His Majesty's service, but few of the clergy and members of the religious orders are similarly inclined, and most of them follow the voice of the people. (Quoted in Elliott 1963:422)

When the bishop of Girona excommunicated the entire tercio responsible for the official retribution in Santa Coloma (which included the gratuitous destruction of a church in the village of Riudinarnes), it was relatively easy for the rebels to proclaim that they were fighting for God and their churches; their enemies could quite simply be identified as the hated soldiers, the king's viceroy, and "all the traitors," presumably including the officials and superior classes who had showed themselves to be "devoted to His Majesty's service" as well as those who "gave shelter to the soldiers" (Elliott 1963:431).

The popular initiative is once again evident when the resistance movement spread from the countryside to the cities, where riots in the poorer districts typically combined with incursions of armed rebels from the countryside (ibid., 464–465). Amid rumors that the tercios were about to attack Barcelona, for example, a band of rural rebels entered the city on May 22 and quickly emptied the prison of both its political and its criminal inmates before they were convinced to leave again by the local bishop. On May 26, university students, aided by the armed rustics who once again entered the city, attacked the houses of several officials and wealthy residents, announcing "Death to traitors and bad Christians." Meanwhile, the tercios besieged by armed rebels at Blanes, were forced to retreat to the fortified garrison town of Roses in the neighboring Rosselló (Roussillon). Finally, on June 7 yet another group of rural rebels entered Barcelona and, aided by many of the inhabitants and abetted by the refusal of the guild companies to oppose them, precipitated five days of riots, attacked the so-called traitors, and even killed the viceroy as he attempted to flee the city. With all the king's ministers in flight or in hiding and the central government's authority in collapse, it fell to Barcelona's civic elite to organize civic militias to restore order. By the May 11 it appeared to the syndic of Manresa "that we are in paradise in contrast to the state we were formerly in. . . . It is now considered certain that the soldiers of the king are no longer in Catalonia. There is not much fear that they will come back for the time being, and it is hoped that they will also leave Rosselló, where they are at present." Before long, the king's troops were also under attack at Perpinyà (Perpignon), the capital of Rosselló, but in this case, after an all-night bombardment that left half of the city in ruins, the army prevailed.

In short order, then, the popular rebellion first attacked the troops, then the king's ministers, and finally local officials they saw as traitors. The aggregate of these essentially uncoordinated events spread over some six weeks is what J. H. Elliott has called a "social revolution, beginning in the countryside and spreading to the more discontented elements of the towns" (1963:462). Yet this was only the beginning of the Catalan Revolt. The popular unrest clearly presented the indigenous governing classes with a very difficult choice: they could either seek to negotiate with Philip and Olivares, at the risk of popular attack, or they could try to harness the popular mobilization to a political revolution against Castilian domination. The second phase of the Catalan Revolt began when the Diputats, a council of six Catalan notables that had long symbolized the historic freedoms of the Catalans, chose the latter course and allied themselves with the popular rebellion. Led by Pau Claris, canon of Urgell, the Diputats were able to tap their extensive networks of family and political clientage to sustain an elite resistance to Madrid in the summer and fall. Those more loyal elites who did not quietly leave were forced finally to choose when, in response to a popular revolt in July in Tortosa (the populace seized gunpowder being sent to the local garrison, attacked local "traitors," and subsequently expelled the troops altogether), the central government decided to send an army to pacify Catalonia. While the Catalan towns tried to obtain weapons and ammunition for local defense, the Diputats began, with only mixed results, to levy new taxes and to raise a sizable Catalan army while at the same time solidifying an alliance with France. In October, Olivares summed up the gravity of the situation: "In the midst of all our troubles, the Catalan is the worst we have ever had, and my heart admits of no consolation. . . .Without reason or occasion they have thrown themselves into as complete a rebellion as Holland, for news has today arrived that they have signed an agreement with the French and placed themselves under the protection of that king" (quoted in Elliott 1963:510).

Despite widespread popular opposition to the exactions of the Castilian-dominated state, raising a Catalan army, indeed organizing the military defense of the rebellious principality in general, proved to be far more difficult than the Diputats had anticipated. Thus when the king's troops first moved into Catalonia in late November, proclaiming a peaceful mission, they met with little resistance, moving quickly northward from Tortosa along the coast toward Barcelona. At Cambrils in mid-December, however, some six hundred Catalan defenders, who had surrendered to the invading force, were massacred, and when this news along with news of the peaceful surrender of Tarragona reached Barcelona, there was once again a violent popular reaction against the threat of Castilian domination. On Christmas eve a crowd of insurgents, again including forces from outside the city, attacked and murdered officials accused of being traitors, forced open the prisons, and set fire to a number of houses, both in Barcelona and in surrounding villages. The English ambassador offered the following commentary: "In Barcelona there hath happened a great dissension between the magistrates and officers of justice, who would have come to an agreement with the king, and the people that would not. . . . I do now begin to think that this madness of the common people (who are many, and the nobility and gentry few, not exceeding 600) will throw the Principality into the hands of the French" (quoted in Elliott 1963:521). In fact, the Catalan ruling elite was deeply divided, and once again the demonstrative action of ordinary people tipped the balance in favor of resistance. The Diputats quickly worked out an agreement with the emissary of France by which the Catalans would declare a republic and put themselves under French protection.

The declaration of the Catalan Republic on January 16, 1641, may be said to have been the climax of the second phase of the Catalan Revolt— the political revolution against the Spanish monarchy—but it was hardly the end of the story. Within a week, in the face of French dissatisfaction with the proposed form of the new republican government, Pau Claris proposed that instead of creating an independent republic, the principality should submit itself to the French monarchy "as in the time of Charlemagne, with a contract to observe our constitutions." Thus on January 23 the elite leaders of "revolutionary" Catalonia replaced one aggressive "prince" (Philip IV) with another (Louis XIII) in the fervent hope that this would preserve their historic privileges. On January 26 the French alliance did pay an immediate dividend when a combined Catalan-French force defeated Spanish forces under the marquis of los Vélez, but before long the French armies became an occupying force, both provoking and repressing anti-French riots. The French king also appointed his own viceroy, and the governance of the principality was carefully concentrated in the hands of a small group of French supporters.

In retrospect it is certainly tempting to declare the Catalan Revolt a bitter disappointment, if not a complete failure, especially by the definitional standards of modern social and political revolution. But we will do well to recognize how effectively the Catalans protected their fueros by playing one dynastic state maker off against another. Indeed, even after a very destructive decade at the crossroads of the Spanish-French military rivalry, the Catalans were "reunited" with Spain on October 12, 1652, under the very terms they had demanded at the beginning: Philip IV agreed to a general pardon and promised, as count of Catalonia rather than as king of Spain, to preserve the principality's constitutions. We will also do well to remember that the rebels of Holland, with whom Olivares aptly compared the Catalans, also actively sought a replacement sovereign and toyed with English "protection" under the earl of Leicester before they finally backed into the formation of an independent republic. In fact, from the perspective of early modern popular politics, it is important to recognize how thoroughly familiar the political dynamics and the eventual settlement of the Catalan Revolt actually are even though they do not involve religious allegiance as a critical marker of political enmity.[11]

At bottom, the Catalan Revolt is familiar because it involves so clearly the triangulated set of political actors that was the characteristic legacy of

11. To the extent that religious faith and allegiance were invoked in the course of the Catalan Revolt, it was a contest for who might claim to be more faithful to Catholicism; for its part, the religious establishment was often neutralized by internal divisions with, as many contemporary observers suggested, local clergy supporting the cause of popular rebellion and the bulk of the episcopal hierarchy aligning itself with the claims of the prince.

dynastic or composite state formation (see fig. 2): national or princely claimants to power (plus their agents), indigenous or local ruling elites, and ordinary political subjects. Although political alignments between aggressive princes—with often urgent fiscal and military needs—and local rulers—the jealous guardians of historic privileges that were the basis of their position locally—were nearly always uneasy and contentious, they nevertheless consolidated the power of local elites vis-à-vis their local populations (fig. 2b). This pattern of elite consolidation was clearly ruptured in Catalonia as a result of popular political action that forced the local elites to choose between royal political favors and local solidarities. When an important faction of the Catalan elite openly chose the side of the popular resistance, it opened up a revolutionary situation that entailed the possibility of a local consolidation of power under an independent Catalan republic (fig. 2a). But the urgent need for military protection against the king's armies quickly resulted instead in what might well be called a coup d'état in the sense that one very powerful prince replaced another and quickly consolidated his power in conjunction with a faction of the local elites with whom he had struck an alternative dynastic bargain. As the power of both of the contending princes ebbed in the course of the next decade, however, the "restoration" of 1562 returned Catalonia to a version of the status quo ante.

Clearly the Catalans did not challenge the aggressive claims of their dynastic prince in a vacuum. In fact, neither the vigor of the central government's political provocations nor the relative success of the Catalans' reactions is comprehensible without reference to Spanish-French competition and war making on a European scale. Meanwhile, the Catalan Revolt dovetailed with other challenges to Spanish-Habsburg rule in Portugal, Italy, and even the New World.[12] What made these conflicts similar and bound them together as part of a single crisis was the fact that they were all provoked by the king's attempt to enforce the Union of Arms, which greatly increased the fiscal and military demands of the Castilian core on the composite's peripheral provinces. Yet the differences in their outcomes will help us to understand both the dynamics and the consequences of early modern revolutions.

On the face of it, the revolution in Portugal seems very different from the Catalan Revolt because it resulted in the permanent separation of the kingdom of Portugal from the Habsburg composite state (Elliott 1991).

---

12. When the Spanish viceroy in Peru tried to enforce the new exactions of Philip's Union of Arms, he too was faced with revolts in Potosí, Cuzco, and Abancay (Elliott 1963:514).

But it is important to acknowledge their structural similarities at the outset. Though Portugal had not been part of the Habsburg composite as long as Catalonia, both were, from the perspective of the Castilian core, constitutionally and fiscally peripheral provinces whose advantages were clearly threatened by the proposed Union of Arms. In addition, because of the pattern of elite consolidation that characterized the Habsburg composite in Portugal as well as Catalonia, it should not be surprising that the initial impetus for open resistance to the king's policies came from below. Indeed, as early as 1637 the government's attempts to raise a substantial fixed revenue from Portugal for the defense of the country and the recovery of its overseas possessions awakened serious popular discontent, with riots reported in Évora and other cities. As in Catalonia, too, the popular movement was reportedly abetted by the clergy, and the French government even hoped to take advantage of the unrest by establishing contact with the leaders.

The interaction between the Catalan and Portuguese challenges to Castilian domination became evident in the fall of 1640 when the government in Madrid sought to mobilize for a military offensive against Catalonia. Though the Portuguese elite had appeared to remain loyal to Philip in the face of popular protests, they began to defect when the sizable nobility was called to military service in the campaign to subdue Barcelona. Suddenly the carefully cultivated alignment between the Spanish Crown and the Portuguese elite began to unravel, and with the defection of the duke of Braganza, who was willing to come forward as pretender to the Portuguese throne, it was possible to put together a formidable, if informal, local coalition against Philip IV (Elliott 1963:512–519). On December 1, 1640, Portuguese conspirators broke into the palace of the duchess of Mantua (the official representative of the Spanish monarchy), killed Miguel de Vasconcellos (the hated symbol of Spanish authority), and expelled all Castilians (the principal agents of Spanish control) from Lisbon. Having thus declared their independence from Madrid, the populace of Lisbon jubilantly acclaimed the duke of Braganza as King John IV the next day—this at the same time that the marquis de los Vélez was slowly advancing on Barcelona. Only later, in January 1641, did the Portuguese Cortes formally ratify this popular acclamation and remove the Spanish garrisons from the rest of the kingdom. Distracted by events elsewhere, especially in Catalonia, Philip IV's government did not even undertake a serious effort to regain Portugal until 1643, and the Portuguese, despite a relatively undisciplined and poorly equipped army, easily defeated the Spanish troops at Montijo in May 1644. The war flared up again briefly in the 1650s and 1660s, but it was not until 1668 that Spain recognized Portuguese independence (Merriman [1938] 1963).

Though the relatively bloodless establishment and successful military defense of a new monarchy in Lisbon may seem less than revolutionary today, the revolution of 1640 in Portugal may be considered an especially clear example of "successful" revolution within a late medieval composite monarchy. In the midst of a more general crisis of authority within the Spanish-Habsburg state, popular unrest that implicitly challenged the authority of local elites as well as a distant monarch created an unanticipated opportunity to form a broad-based revolutionary coalition united by its resentment of increased exactions by easily identifiable outsiders. To be sure, the new "revolutionary" government was deliberately modeled on historical precedents, but neither the dynasty nor the popular-based revolutionary coalition that established and sustained it can be considered a simple re-creation of a medieval past. What is more, both the popular and the elite elements of this coalition may be said to have achieved significant and satisfying results—for example, the elimination of the new fiscal demands and the removal of rival Castilian elites—without the long-term sacrifices and setbacks of the Dutch or Catalan wars for independence. Yet in the final analysis, the Portuguese revolution clearly lacks the excitement and narrative drama of the Catalan and southern-Italian revolutions between which it was sandwiched in time.

The Spanish Crisis in Italy: Sicily and Naples

The high drama and political danger of the southern Italian revolutions are due especially to the power and dynamism of popular mobilization that threatened the relatively stable political alignment of local rulers with their distant prince. Though the kingdoms of Sicily and Naples were geographically less proximate to the Castilian core of the Spanish-Habsburg state, they contributed more, fiscally and militarily, to the welfare of the composite than either Catalonia or Portugal. Indeed, by the seventeenth century southern Italy, Naples in particular, had become an especially critical element within the complex system that sustained the Spanish military machine, not only in the Mediterranean but also, via the fabled Spanish Road across the Alps, in Germany and the Low Countries.[13] To be sure, both kingdoms had been cobbled into the Spanish composite in 1504 with constitutional limitations on their distant sovereign, but the consolidation of local elite power that was typical of such bargains had worked especially to the advantage of the landed nobility; not only did the nobility dominate local institutions of government, they were among the principal investors in local government debt that supported Spain's military operations abroad while they were exempt from the excises on basic necessities that were dedicated to the repayment of these government obligations. This meant that the sizable urban populations—Naples at 300,000 and Palermo at 150,000 were among Europe's largest cities—were both vulnerable to fiscal exploitation and politically isolated.

In both Sicily and Naples the revolutions of 1647 grew out of one of the most basic interactions between early modern rulers and their urban subjects: the so-called food riots occasioned by apparently arbitrary or unjust governmental decisions regarding the price of staples like bread. Since the price of basic foodstuffs was directly related to the burdensome excises by which these governments taxed their urban populations, protests over the price and availability of food easily dovetailed with more general attacks on tax collectors or demands for the repeal of burdensome exactions and unjust regulations. Inasmuch as most local rulers had insufficient means to quell such episodic events as food riots and local tax protests, they were often obliged to make temporary concessions such as subsidizing the price of bread in times of dearth or even repealing taxes that were identified as particularly irksome. Repression and exemplary punishment, if it occurred, usually attended the arrival of troops from outside the community (cf. Beik 1997). In both Palermo and Naples, however, these almost routine interactions issued into obviously revolutionary situations that threatened to displace both the local rulers and the larger pattern of elite consolidation of which they were an essential part.

In Sicily the first food riots took place in Messina in the fall of 1646; these were suppressed by Spanish troops and the leaders executed, though the government also supplied more food (Koenigsberger 1971b). In May 1647, however, similar protests over the price of bread in Palermo quickly developed into a massive demonstration at the Spanish viceroy's

13. That the Neapolitans were aware of their importance within the Habsburg composite is suggested by the anonymous pamphleteer quoted at the beginning of this chapter.

palace: "Long live the king and down with taxes and bad Government." The demonstrators also broke open the prisons, freeing some six hundred inmates, burned the gates of the palace, and warned the archbishop not to oppose their movement. Soon this popular mobilization, apparently under the leadership of a miller, focused its attacks on the treasury and tax offices, demanding in particular the abolition of the five *gabelles*, the excises on grain, wine, oil, meat, and cheese. Apparently lacking the means of immediate repression, the viceroy made impressive concessions: he restored the price and quality of bread, abolished the excises, issued an amnesty for the attack on the prison, deposed the local senate, and granted the artisan guilds the right to elect two senators. Soon the guilds were taking over the city's fortifications and restoring order; the leaders of the original food riots were, however, tortured and executed. On May 25 the viceroy tried belatedly and unsuccessfully to introduce Spanish troops into the city, but as H. G. Koenigsberger suggests, "the guilds remained in control of the city, and for the moment the government was too weak to take decisive counteraction. The nobles, solidly behind the government, retired to their country estates" (1971b:260–261).

In the summer of 1647, parallel revolts enjoying varying degrees of support from local clergy and advancing similar demands against Spanish taxation occurred in other smaller cities such as Girgenti, Syracuse, and Cefalù, though Messina, which had earlier seen the repression of popular protest, remained squarely in government hands. Meanwhile, in Palermo, the leaders of the guilds began to press for further constitutional reform; as one contemporary observer reports, "with truly unspeakable audacity they began to treat of the reform of the city, not knowing how to govern their own house," and to formulate new *capitoli* (laws) for the city (ibid., 1971:262). In August, amid reports of the sensational revolt in Naples in July, a new wave of popular mobilization, rooted especially in the large tanners' and fishers' guilds and led by an artisan who had witnessed the revolt in Naples, attempted to establish a revolutionary government in cooperation with the Spanish government. The movement's self-proclaimed and charismatic leader demanded the government's acceptance of forty-nine capitoli, formulated by the guilds, which would abolish the gabelles in the entire kingdom, grant the guilds far greater participation in local government, dismiss most treasury officials, reform legal procedures and codes, and introduce three popularly elected representatives to watch over the work of the local senate. Though the viceroy tried to break the movement by murdering their leader and arresting several guild consuls, he was forced on August 23 to publish the capitoli and release the guild leaders he had arrested. The viceroy was allowed to retain the trappings of his office even though he had obviously lost control of the capital city.

The contemporaneous revolution in Naples was in many ways similar, though more violent and, by extension, more famous. In Naples the popular collective action began with what Peter Burke (1983) has described as a ritualized confrontation, full of religious symbolism, between a more or less spontaneous crowd of protesters and the tax authorities on July 7, 1647. Very quickly, however, the protesters, under the charismatic leadership of a fisherman named Masaniello,[14] confronted the viceroy, reportedly crying "Long live the king" and "Down with taxes." Immediate concessions were followed by an unsuccessful attempt by the viceroy and the archbishop to restore order, and in angry response, Masaniello called out the civic guard, who numbered in the thousands, were well organized in the city's wards and were readily called into action by the ringing of bells. At this point the popular mobilization, a great deal more organized, was directed especially at the wealthy officials who, by profiting from the fiscal exploitation of the city, were seen as traitors of the people. The level of violence—the ritualized degradation of victims as well as the systematic destruction of their homes—clearly separated the revolution in Naples from that in Palermo, yet it did not differ a great deal politically in that the militia-led rebels at first sought to establish a revolutionary government with royal sanction.

Even after Masaniello was assassinated on July 16 the rebels made several overtures to the royal government, although they were repeatedly betrayed by the viceroy. At long last, on October 1, a flotilla of ships carrying some five thousand Spanish troops arrived in support of the viceroy, but when they attacked the city, the rebels, now under the leadership of an illiterate blacksmith, claimed a decisive victory. Thus on October 24, 1647, the Neapolitan rebels formally renounced Spanish rule and declared an independent republic. At this point the Neapolitan revolution came to resemble the Catalan revolution, of which its leaders were very well aware, in that they actively sought French protection against a likely Spanish invasion. When timely French support was not forthcoming, the rebellious city finally fell to the Spanish in February

14. His name was actually Tomaso Aniello, but shortened to Masaniello it became a pointed reference to an earlier popular revolt in Naples against the Inquisition in 1547 in which the leader was named Masaniello.

1648. Meanwhile, the revolution in Palermo faded away more gradually as popular enthusiasm for guild leadership and the requirements of constant political vigilance waned; in July 1648 the guilds finally surrendered the fortifications to Spanish troops and the population was disarmed.

These immediately famous conflicts undoubtedly reflected, in some measure, the extremes of conjunctural social dislocation—bad harvests, artificial scarcity due to corruption, famine, migration of dislocated peasants from the countryside—to which many scholars ascribe their occurrence (see esp. Villari 1993). But from the perspective of popular political practice, they can also usefully be seen as a reflection of both exceptional political opportunities and the formidable capacity of popular political actors in a dense urban setting. The opportunities were clearly afforded by the more general crisis of the Spanish-Habsburg state: (1) the state's fiscal demands combined with its dependence on a privileged rural nobility fractured the critical relations between urban subjects and local rulers; (2) insurrections and war making elsewhere undermined the government's ability to repress popular dissent; and (3) France was willing to profit from Spain's temporary weakness by positioning itself as an ally or protector of revolutionary coalitions. Yet clearly the dynamism, the initiative, and the critical decisions in these remarkable sequences came from the popular political actors. In both Palermo and Naples these popular coalitions were not only numerous but also well organized and armed.

That the revolutionary governments failed to last may be said to reflect two fundamental weaknesses of the revolutionary coalitions. On the one hand, both revolutionary movements failed to work out an alignment, though they appear to have tried, with at least a segment of the local political elite; such an alignment might have resulted more readily in a consolidation of local power of the sort that occurred in the Dutch Revolt. On the other hand, they also failed to make horizontal coalitions with other locally mobilized movements and thereby failed to transcend the jurisdictional boundaries of their familiar urban political spaces. To be sure, the revolutionaries in Palermo benefited from the simultaneous and complementary popular political movements in other Sicilian cities, and the Neapolitans surely drew some of their strength and boldness from the massive insurrections that shook the countryside of the kingdom of Naples in the summer of 1647 (Villari 1993). Yet in the absence of political brokers or preexisting networks of organization and communication, these popular movements failed to find a basis for "national" solidarity within the much larger political spaces that they shared as subjects of a common monarch.[15] That they actually aspired to a political alignment with their distant prince against local political elites, whom they accused of treason, may seem naive and fanciful in retrospect, but had they been able to realize such an alignment, they certainly would have moved their political histories in a dramatically different direction (see fig. 2c).

Leaving such eventualities aside, however, it is possible to combine the revolutions in Palermo and Naples with their counterparts in Portugal and Catalonia in a more focused discussion of the political results or outcomes of revolutionary situations within composite states. It is probably safe to say that given the obvious level of popular discontent in Catalonia in 1640 and Sicily and Naples in 1648, the likelihood of revolution was extremely high, but it is equally safe to say that the likelihood that these revolutions would produce a durable republican form of government to replace the monarchy—something that even by modern definitional standards would qualify as a revolutionary outcome—was always remote. In theory, the simple reason is that the conditions that are conducive to the appearance of revolutionary situations are significantly different from those that are conducive to revolutionary outcomes that entail radical transformations of political power. As we have already seen—from the Comunero Revolt in Castile to the War of Independence in the Low Countries; from the Peasants' War in Germany to the Croquant revolts in France—even transient alignments between popular political actors and a segment of the indigenous ruling elite were enough to produce revolutionary situations within late medieval composite states (cf. Tilly 1993); in exceptional cases, such as we have seen in the large provincial capitals of southern Italy, ordinary political subjects might even be able to precipitate a revolutionary situation on their own. But the closely related cases of Catalonia, Portugal, Sicily, and Naples allow us to discern, more clearly than the sixteenth-century conflicts, the conditions for different kinds of revolutionary outcomes.

As we have seen in the previous chapters, when local revolutions were repeatedly swallowed up by large-scale religious wars on a national and

---

15. In both Catalonia and Portugal it may be said that the regional elites, who were willing to seize the political opportunity afforded by popular opposition to royal exactions, were the political brokers who enabled the establishment of revolutionary governments on the grander scale of a constituent kingdom. Compare the Comunero Revolt in chapter 2, above; there, too, relatively isolated cities failed to build coalitions with the countryside and the various other pieces of a composite monarchy.

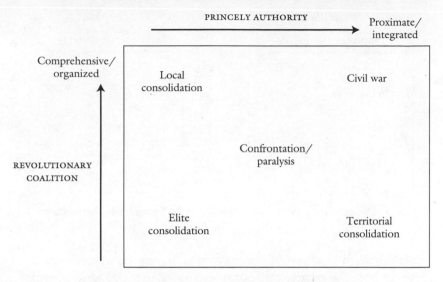

Figure 8. Dynamics of revolutionary conflict in composite states

international scale, the relative proximity and capacity of national claimants (and their armies) are certainly salient factors in determining the outcomes of local revolutionary situations.[16] But the strength of local political alignments was equally important in shaping the historically specific political results. Figure 8 suggests how we might imagine the interaction between the two in accounting for revolutionary outcomes or transfers of power within composite states. In one dimension, with reference to the capacity of princely or central authorities, this figure captures both the structural/geographic variations between different parts of the same composite state—the core as opposed to the periphery—and the more transient variations that occur within them, as when a princely army or flotilla draws near to a regional capital like Barcelona or Naples. In the other dimension, this figure encompasses variations in the social basis of the revolutionary coalition between narrow and disjointed coalitions at either end of the social scale or more comprehensive and organized coalitions within or among communities.

Within this framework, then, one would account for the fairly

16. Recall the difference between Charles V's inability, as Holy Roman Emperor, to reward his supporters or punish his enemies in Germany (chap. 2) and his obvious ability to intervene directly in religious affairs in his patrimonial lands in the Low Countries (chap. 3).

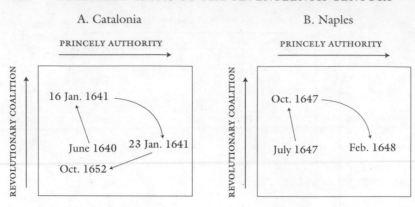

Figure 9. Dynamics of revolutionary conflict in the Spanish Mediterranean

straightforward "success" of the Portuguese separation from Castile in terms of both the relative distance or incapacity of the Madrid government and the durability of the broad cross-class coalition against Castilian domination. By contrast, the Neapolitan and Catalan revolutions are more complicated (and for that reason illuminating) in that they both cycled through a series of transient outcomes.

In the beginning of the story in Catalonia (fig. 9a), a socially limited and essentially uncoordinated popular mobilization in May and June 1640—what J. H. Elliott called the "social revolution"—quickly produced ad hoc concessions to popular demands (plus the hasty retreat of the tercios), which in essence confirmed Catalonia's fiscal and military exemptions. Yet the persistence and spread of popular mobilization forced the defection of an important segment of the Catalan elite and helped to create a truly revolutionary republican government on January 16, 1641. With the rapid approach of two powerful princely armies, however, the Catalan Republic gave way to what might be considered a French coup d'état just a week later. With the gradual disaffection, co-optation, repression, and demobilization of the bulk of the popular political actors under the French regime, Catalonia was finally "reunited" with Spain in 1652 under the specific guarantee of its historic privileges. Against the backdrop of this sequence of transient settlements, even a return to a semblance of the status quo ante may be considered a "revolutionary" outcome in the very real sense that it did not result in the consolidation of absolute princely power in the territorial state that Olivares had in mind; indeed, the defeat of Philip's "Spanish" pretensions was so complete that, as J. H. Elliott observes from the perspective of Catalonia, "the second half of the seventeenth century was . . . for the Spanish monarchy the golden age of provincial autonomy—an age of almost superstitious respect for regional rights and privileges by a Court too weak and too timid to protest" (1963:547; cf. Kamen 1980).

The revolution in Naples (fig. 9b) not only took a different course, but it set the kingdom of Naples on a different historical trajectory after the restoration of the Spanish viceroy. The popular movement, initially an informal coalition based on a common opposition to the hated excises, gained some immediate concessions in July 1647. But over time it tapped the neighborhood networks and organizational strength of the civic militia, it received an assist from simultaneous and widespread peasant attacks on noble landlords in the countryside, and it gained a certain degree of political and military experience. Thus the revolutionary coalition confidently declared its independence from Spain and the creation of a revolutionary republic in October 1647. Still, lacking both elite allies and political connections in the countryside, the municipal revolution disintegrated in the face of superior Spanish force in February 1648. In the process, however, the power of the Madrid government had become a good deal more proximate and directly coercive even though it still depended in practice on some of the traditional forms of indirect rule through a dependent but privileged local elite. Unlike the Catalan experience, then, the kingdom of Naples can hardly be said to have enjoyed a golden age of provincial autonomy in the second half of the seventeenth century.

Multiple Revolutions in the British Isles

When we move from the first cluster of Merriman's "contemporaneous revolutions" in Spain to the "Puritan Revolution" in England, it is clear that we have moved into another historical world. If nothing else, the voluminous historical literature and the lively debates concerning the causes, character, and consequences of the English Revolution are an unmistakable warning against broad generalizations and facile comparisons. Still, the essential political facts with which we are concerned are not in dispute: at the end of 1648 and the beginning of 1649 a faction of the broad parliamentary coalition that had been at war with the English king intermittently for more than six years expelled its enemies from the House of Commons, tried and executed the king,

Charles I, abolished the monarchy and the House of Lords, and established a Puritan commonwealth (Underdown 1971; Manning 1992). To be sure, these events are so dramatic that they have invited comparison with revolutionary challenges in France in 1789 and in Russia in 1917, and in this company, the English Revolution is often considered the first of the "modern" or "great" revolutions that have become the normative baseline for a succession of academic models of revolution in the twentieth century.

For our purposes, however, it is important to locate the political engagement of ordinary people more precisely within early modern composite states and to recognize the role that religious differences played in shaping the multiple conflicts of which the events of 1648–1649 may be considered the climax. It may thus be useful to take as our starting point John Morrill's (1984:178) boldly contentious suggestion that "the English civil war was not the first European revolution: it was the last of the Wars of Religion."[17] Here I should like to argue, more specifically, that although the English civil war, which began in 1642, may usefully be considered a "religious war," it can also usefully be considered a revolutionary situation (cf. Tilly 1993:104–141); its climax in the events of 1648–1649 can, by extension, be considered a singularly "revolutionary" outcome—albeit, like so many others in the seventeenth century, a transient one.[18]

Let us begin with the civil war. Instead of highlighting the nature of social dislocation and the particulars of constitutional crisis within England, Conrad Russell (1987, 1990, 1991) begins his revisionist account of the "causes of the English Civil Wars" by emphasizing the compositeness of the British state.[19] The kings of England had striven for centuries to become masters of all the British Isles—not to mention some major

17. Though Morrill is certainly right to stress the salience of ecclesiastical issues and religious difference in the English civil war, he is wrong to suggest that it was the *last* of the wars of religion. At the very least, Louis XIV's wars against the Protestant Camisards of the Cévennes (1702–1706) following his revocation of the Edict of Nantes belies this English claim to fame.

18. In employing these terms for the sake of a broader comparison, I wish to avoid Morrill's implicit dichotomy between "religious war" and "revolution." At the same time, however, I think my use of the distinction between revolutionary "situations" and revolutionary "outcomes" comports well with Conrad Russell's insistence (1990:esp. chap. 1) that explaining the beginning of the civil war in 1642 is a different task from accounting for the events of 1648–1649.

19. Russell uses the term "multiple kingdom" instead of composite monarchy but seems thereby to underscore the same political and constitutional complexity of dynastic state formation; cf. Elliott 1992. For critiques of this perspective, see Cust and Hughes 1989 and

sections of the Continent—but the composite that the Stuart dynasty ruled in the middle of the seventeenth century was in its specifics of relatively recent date (see chap. 2). Following the loss of England's continental possessions during the fifteenth century and the successful incorporation of Wales within the English monarchy at the beginning of the sixteenth, the Tudor monarchy had once again become a composite with the formal acquisition of the Irish throne in 1543 and the dynastic union, after Elizabeth I, of the thrones of Scotland and England under James Stuart in 1603. Like all early modern composite state makers, James was continually facing fiscal constraints, but having steered clear of direct involvement in the Thirty Years' War, the financial burdens that Charles I inherited from his father in 1625 were not the worst of his problems.[20]

Whereas the top-down reformation of the Church of England had asserted the king's ecclesiastical supremacy from the 1530s onward, the steady growth of "Puritan" dissent within England as well as the addition of Catholic Ireland and Presbyterian Scotland presented the new Stuart dynasty with a minefield of ecclesiastical politics. Under James, the Church of England proved to be a remarkably capacious institution, accommodating a variety of religious sensibilities and theological tendencies (Collinson 1982, 1991). But in the 1630s Charles—not unlike his continental counterparts prior to the outbreak of "religious wars" in France, the Low Countries, and Bohemia—began ever more insistently to demand religious conformity from all of his subjects. In England Charles's particular brand of high church Arminianism brought him face-to-face with a parliamentary opposition that eventually included a broad spectrum of Presbyterians and Independents. Though the often-debated motives and social interests of the leaders on all sides in this escalating conflict were undoubtedly mixed, the factions in this thoroughly divided political elite were increasingly identified, in word as well as parliamentary deed, in terms of their ecclesiastical politics (Morrill 1984). Yet rather than two clearly defined parties, the Long Parliament, which began its fateful sitting in 1640, was composed of a cacophony of political and religious voices. And the political dynamics that transformed a sufficient number of the parliamentary elite of England into "Puritan" revolutionaries—albeit by most accounts reluc-

---

Hughes 1991. In what follows, I will use Britain and British to refer to the composite kingdom and England, Scotland, and Ireland to refer to its constituent parts.

20. Charles created significant fiscal and, by extension, political problems for himself by making war on Spain and France between 1626 and 1629, but he was quickly forced to retreat from this aggressive foreign policy.

tant ones—were neither exclusively ecclesiastical, nor narrowly aristocratic, nor parochially English.

From the broader point of view of the composite monarchy, the British crisis of the mid-seventeenth century clearly began in earnest in Scotland (Stevenson 1973, 1977). There had been periodic friction between Charles and the local aristocratic rulers of Scotland throughout the 1630s, but as Keith Brown (1992:107) argues, "it was his religious policy which caused most controversy and which provided the popular support for aristocratic action against the king." Specifically, the forceful introduction in 1637 of a new liturgy (in the form of an Anglican prayer book) as the exclusive basis for Protestant worship was greeted with both a howl of official Presbyterian protest and popular demonstrations in Edinburgh and Glasgow. The adamant refusal of the royal government to compromise in the face of local opposition led in February 1638 to the signing of a national "covenant," which took the apparently conservative form of a traditional bond expressing loyalty to the king but nevertheless implied a "radical agenda aimed at the destruction of Charles's authoritarian, imperial monarchy and the episcopal church" (Brown 1992:112). Though it started in aristocratic circles, the national covenant was popularized by evangelical preaching and found a popular organizational base in conventicles and private churches (Morrill 1990). This growing popular movement eventually forced the uncompromising king to call a general assembly of the Scottish church in November 1638, and dominated by "covenanters," the general assembly directly challenged the king's claim to ecclesiastical authority, abolishing the episcopal structure and undoing his liturgical reforms.

As military confrontation loomed in 1639, the covenanters consolidated their control within local parishes and presbyteries—creating rival institutions when they could not control the existing structures—and established a national military apparatus rooted in organizations and mobilization at the local level; a national army, 18,000 strong, was led by soldiers with mercenary experience on the Continent. Eventually, the Scottish parliament also met, without royal permission, in June 1640 and within a matter of days fashioned a new constitutional structure to sustain itself as an independent political force. "The covenanters refashioned government entirely," Keith Brown writes, "replacing the old model with one based on committees in parliament and the general assembly, and locally in the shire committees of war and the presbyteries" (1992:119; see also Macinnes 1990). Anticipating attack by royal armies, the Scottish army boldly crossed the English border at the end of August

1640, emphatically defeating the king's hastily assembled and poorly equipped army.

To this point, then, the Scottish Covenanter Revolution appears to be a particularly illuminating case of a well-organized political alignment between local rulers and popular political actors yielding quickly to a revolutionary government and a local consolidation of power vis-à-vis a nonresident composite monarch (see fig. 2a). But the Scottish covenanters were hardly acting in a political vacuum. Indeed, their success in challenging Charles in Scotland forced Charles to call the Long Parliament that would directly challenge him "at home" in England. What is more, by 1641, when there appeared to be little basis for a peaceful restoration of royal authority in Scotland except on decidedly Scottish terms, Ireland had begun to follow a similar path, though with decidedly Irish variations on the theme. The destruction of the records of the Irish rebellion prevents us from seeing as clearly the internal organization of the revolutionary coalition, but in broad outline the dynamics appear to be familiar.

Both the politicization of Irish religious identities and the transformation of Irish society under British rule help to account for the distinctiveness of the Irish case (see Dunlop [1906] 1934; Clarke 1984; Fitzpatrick 1988; Russell 1988). Though the historical background of Irish/English relations is complicated and deeply conflicted, the heart of the matter in the first half of the seventeenth century can be stated briefly: having utterly failed to convert the Irish to Protestantism in the sixteenth century, the agents of British rule initiated a policy of radical social transformation that involved "planting" Protestantism on Irish soil through the confiscation of Catholic land, the removal of the Catholic population to the western periphery, and the importation of Protestant settlers (mostly Scots) to fill the demographic void. The project was begun with considerable vigor in Ulster, but before it could be expanded it began to founder on growing divisions within the local ruling elite. Historians often refer to the earliest English elites in Ireland, those who predated the Reformation and remained to a great extent Catholic, as the "old English," as distinct from the "new English" who were the Protestant beneficiaries of the plantation scheme. In the 1630s the British government effectively played these factions of the local elite off against one another to extract the fiscal and military resources it wanted, but as the old English became increasingly fearful of the anti-Catholicism of the British system, they came to feel like the "new Irish." These divisions within the aristocracy, combined with the example of the Scottish covenanters, set the stage for an Irish uprising, supported by a comprehensive coalition of all Catholics in Ireland.

The Irish Revolution of 1641 appears to have been deliberately planned: a coup d'état by well-connected and well-armed elites at Dublin was to be paired with popular uprisings, especially in Ulster, where the Catholic population had been effectively marginalized but not removed. The coup at Dublin failed, but the popular uprising, led by a group of sworn "confederates," proved to be a surprising success. That this Confederate Revolution fed on local Catholic solidarity in the face of official anti-Catholicism is obvious; that it was nurtured and sustained both by the local Catholic clergy and the Counter-Reformation church in Rome is also evident. What is especially ironic is that in the confusion of British politics in the early 1640s, the Irish rebels continued to profess (not unlike popular revolutionaries in Naples and Sicily in 1647) support and loyalty to their distant monarch (in his ongoing battle with the Puritans in the Long Parliament) while their actions on the ground effectively dismantled his sovereignty as well as his social and religious policies (cf. Canny 1994). In contrast to the apparent "national" solidarity of covenanter Scotland, however, confederate Ireland was more clearly divided between a Catholic majority and a small but resourceful Protestant minority.

The political chaos of the composite British state in the early 1640s—occasioned by the Covenanter and Confederate revolutions on the periphery as much as parliamentary opposition at the core—certainly helps us to understand the depths of the crisis of the English monarchy well before the trial and execution of the king in 1649. To this we should also add a growing tide of popular protest in many parts of England—protest that variously attacked enclosures, defied taxes, and destroyed the symbols of the new Anglican liturgy while precipitating a kind of "moral panic" among those in the parliamentary elite who were particularly fearful of the "many-headed monster" of popular insurrection (Morrill and Walter 1985). But the severity of this crisis should also serve to underscore more precisely what was distinctive about the English Revolution. For while the king's enemies in the peripheral kingdoms moved quickly and decisively to establish "revolutionary" governments that they would be forced to defend against various "British" enemies in the course of the Wars of the Three Kingdoms (1643–1648), his enemies "at home" in England were thrust immediately into a civil war that, their leaders claimed loudly and eloquently, was not revolutionary at all but a morally justifiable defense of the established political order. Despite their defensive claims, of course, those who took up arms against Charles within England were, in the terms we have employed above, no less revolutionary than their rebellious counterparts in Scotland and Ireland. That their efforts to press political claims unacceptable to their immediate sovereign resulted in a long and difficult war is a reflection not only of Charles's dogged determination to have his own way but also of the immense difficulty of displacing a composite monarch at the territorially consolidated core of his state where his power is necessarily more proximate and usually more integrated through alignments with local elites.

While the crisis of the composite state helps us to understand the origins of the revolutionary situation, then, it does not go very far in illuminating the dynamics of revolutionary conflict within England during and after the civil war. Indeed, that the English monarchy actually survived as long as it did in the face of such seemingly universal opposition to its authoritarian policies may be a useful perspective from which to focus on the role of popular politics in the English Revolution. Despite a good deal of controversy on other matters, especially the nature and significance of divisions among the aristocracy, British historians seem generally to agree that the people of England were deeply divided by the political crisis of the British monarchy, and in the midst of that division there was a significant and sustained level of popular support for the king.[21] That this popular royalism was regionally differentiated, that it was in many ways equivalent to the level of popular support for the king's parliamentary enemies, and that in the long run the majority of the population of England and Wales preferred to remain politically independent or as unengaged as possible with either side seems, by all accounts, to be generally accepted as well. Indeed, though historians continue to debate the social, political, and religious motives that underlay it, the thoroughgoing political division of English society, at all levels, would seem to be the most obvious reason why England, like France in the second half of the sixteenth century, was plunged into a prolonged and costly civil war between two uncompromising and comprehensive coalitions contending for national power.[22] Quite unlike the French

21. See especially "Introduction to the Second Edition" in Manning 1991 and the literature cited there.
22. At the center of a composite state, the distinction between local rulers and national claimants to power breaks down quite easily. The political leverage that local people might have over "merely" local rulers diminishes when these local rulers form national coalitions that are dependent on popular support but are not as vulnerable to popular influence as they compete for control of the national political space.

civil wars, however, the climax of the English civil wars was the total defeat of the king.

Not surprisingly, the civil war opened up unprecedented political opportunities for a broad range of ordinary political subjects in England. On the parliamentary side especially, the ongoing war effort afforded the "middle sort" of independent craftsmen and yeoman farmers the possibility of direct engagement in political activities that were normally reserved for the established elite (Underdown 1971:chap. 2). The collapse in many parts of the country of the authority of the established Church also gave birth to a variety of new religious groups and allowed others, who had in the past lived a shadowy, underground existence in conventicles or private churches, to thrive as never before in full public view. And in the military reforms that the parliamentary armies instituted to shore up their effectiveness in the field, ordinary soldiers, who were often religious sectarians, were brought into new, more politicized relationship to the new brand of military officers who led the New Model Army to victory in the first of the civil wars by 1646 (Gentles 1992). Clearly not everyone was inclined or able to exploit such opportunities, but in the context of the enduring polarization of the political elite, it was a small but well-organized "Puritan" minority rooted in the sectarian or "gathered" churches and well represented in the rank and file of the New Model Army that repeatedly seized the political initiative from more reluctant allies within the political elite, prevented a compromise between the king and his enemies in parliament, and engineered the "radical" revolution of 1648–1649.

To execute the king, to disestablish the Church that he had attempted to use as an instrument of his power, and to abolish the nobility who had been among his most stalwart defenders—all of this was, of course, no mean achievement for the narrow but disciplined and militarily resourceful faction that boldly seized what it considered a providential opportunity to establish a "godly commonwealth." Today, however, historians are generally inclined to regard the revolutionary climax of 1649 as a military coup d'état—this in implicit opposition to the earlier designation of these events as a modern or social revolution with great significance for the future. To be sure, the revolution of 1649 did in many ways boil down to a military coup, but demystifying the revolution in this way ought not blind us to its political significance. According to Brian Manning, "1649 was the climax of the revolution, but it was also the watershed. Within the first few months of that year, in a series of conflicts, the limits were established beyond which the revolution would not go" (1992:10). Later, having focused on a series of army mutinies in the course of 1649, Manning concludes, "Military force triumphed over the more radical and populist wing of the revolution. In the late 1640s the army was a revolutionary force, in the 1650s it became a force for order and stability, inhibiting or repressing radical dissent and suppressing popular resistance" (ibid., 215). The defeat, in particular, of the Levellers—the radical or populist wing of the revolutionary coalition of 1649 which had promoted a dramatic displacement of power from the traditional elite at the center to the "middle sort of people" at the community level, not unlike the "republicans" of Naples in 1647—is what makes the English Revolution seem more like a failure than a success when judged by the standards of "modern" revolutions. But the Levellers, or for that matter the religious radicals who did prevail, it must be remembered, represented only a small part of the history of popular political engagement in this complex historical process.[23]

So what political course *did* the coup of 1649 chart for the English Revolution? With regard to the core issue of ecclesiastical politics, the Puritans of 1649 did move radically toward the displacement or diffusion of cultural sovereignty by guaranteeing the liberty of religious conscience and treating the "true" Church as a gathering of the "saints" rather than a universal institution embodying the king's claim to cultural sovereignty. Unfortunately, this very "modern" and tolerant stance earned the leaders of the republican Commonwealth few significant allies; it clearly satisfied no one in the English religious establishment, alienating Episcopalians and Presbyterians alike, plus a goodly number of so-called Independents who nevertheless sought a total reformation of English society. Ironically, then, the English revolutionaries of 1649 appear to have succeeded primarily in charting a constitutional or political course

---

23. The parallel here with the "Revolution of the Common Man" in sixteenth-century Germany and Switzerland is instructive (Blickle 1981). There, too, the actions and aspirations of the most radical and well-organized elements of a larger revolutionary coalition have dominated the discussions of the revolutionary explosion of 1525, and 1525 has, in turn, dominated our understanding of larger political processes of the early Reformation, in the sense that many scholars still use 1525 to date the end of the "popular" phase of the Reformation and thus to signal the beginning of its "magisterial" phase. While the radicals of 1525 and 1649 were, briefly, the most dynamic elements of a highly charged revolutionary situation, they did not by any means drown out all other popular political voices, nor should they occupy a privileged position in our understanding of popular politics within the larger historical processes under consideration here.

toward an unprecedented degree of territorial state consolidation during the 1650s.[24] Indeed, one of Oliver Cromwell's most important successes was the sequential military subjugation of the separatist Confederate and Covenanter regimes in Ireland (1649–1650) and Scotland (1650–1651). Cromwell's conquest of Ireland is notorious, of course, for its brutality, but his less brutal triumph in Scotland was just as unambiguous a testimony to his determination, not to dismantle, but to reconstruct and even extend the territorial sovereignty that he and his allies had seized from Charles in 1649.

But if 1649 was the climax and the watershed of the English Revolution, it was no more than the declaration of republican regimes in Catalonia and Naples the end of the story of revolutionary conflict in England. By 1653 the so-called Rump Parliament, which had created the republican Commonwealth in 1649, was replaced by the so-called Barebones Parliament, which in the same year was replaced by the Protectorate under the leadership of Oliver Cromwell. The Instrument of Government, the unprecedented written constitution that established the Protectorate, called for a single parliament elected by reformed constituencies throughout England, Scotland, and Ireland, but Cromwell, who was named protector for life, and the parliament never established a modus vivendi that could ensure the stability of a uniform republican government of the entire composite after Cromwell's death in 1657. By 1659 the leaderless regime was collapsing of its own weight—especially the weight of the large standing army—and in 1660 the Stuart dynasty was restored to the throne within a *composite* British state.

Though their opportunities were much diminished following the revolution of 1649, ordinary people in England nevertheless continued to be important political actors right up to the Restoration. David Underdown writes, for example, that "in every crisis of the Interregnum—in the winter of 1648–9, in 1653, and again in 1659—the revolutionary pressure was generated in the Army, in London and a few other towns, and in the congregations of the gathered churches" (1971:354). But by the same token, the revolution awakened popular opposition to the Puritan Commonwealth just as parliamentary opposition during the 1640s had served to awaken popular support for the king (Underdown 1985, 1996; Manning 1991). Not surprisingly, throughout the Interregnum the ordinary polit-

24. On the incremental reforms that tended toward the consolidation of state power at the local level during and after 1649, see especially Underdown 1971:chap. 10.

ical subjects of England remained deeply divided on a whole range of political issues, not least of which was the way in which the success of the revolutionaries had seemed to "turn the world upside down"—that is, to invert the most basic assumptions of this deeply partriarchal society. Indeed, Underdown (1996:chap. 5) argues, without a base of both popular and elite royalism, there would have been no Restoration.

On the face of it, then, it was to an elite condominium of power over a relatively consolidated territorial monarchy that England returned in 1660: "The gentry came round to monarchy again because it alone could complete the reunion of the [aristocratic] political nation. . . . And monarchy alone could guarantee their own kind of liberty: liberty to rule the nation without interference from the Saints, and the counties without interference from Westminster" (Underdown 1971:359). But the institutional familiarity of the king's return to power only masks a more fundamental sea change in political culture that entailed not only a growing suspicion among the gentry of independent popular political engagement but also a variety of deep and enduring religious and political divisions among the whole of the political nation that would continue to roil English politics for decades to come (Harris 1987; Harris, Seaward, and Goldie 1990; Underdown 1996). That an analogous form of institutional restoration occurred in Scotland should not be surprising because it is there that Charles II first attempted to restore, by means of compromises his father found unacceptable, his claim to the various pieces of the composite British throne; in Scotland, however, the experience and the memory of the revolutionary years constituted a different political-cultural legacy rooted in a significant degree of local self-regulation especially in matters of religion. By contrast with both England and Scotland, there appears to have been little of the old regime to restore in Ireland in the wake of Cromwell's conquest; on the contrary, Ireland had effectively become a colony ruled from London through the agency of a dependent new English aristocracy on the ground while the process of Protestant plantation that Cromwell had revived continued apace.[25]

Returning finally to the broad comparative context of R. B. Merriman's "contemporaneous revolutions," we can usefully make two more additions to Merriman's list: the revolutions in Ireland and Scotland.

---

25. Whereas Catholics still owned nearly 60 percent of the land in Ireland in 1641—i.e., at the beginning of their revolution—by 1688 they owned but 22 percent (see the maps in Clarke 1984:200).

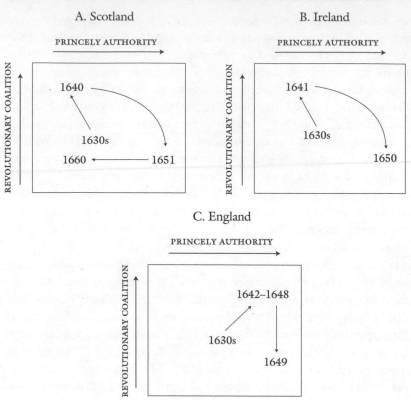

Figure 10. Dynamics of revolutionary conflict in the British Isles

Though they may be said to be part, along with the much more famous English Revolution, of a larger composite revolution within a composite state, each had its own distinctive dynamics. To highlight their similarities as well as their differences, it may be useful to chart their courses in the same schematic terms we used to compare the cluster of revolutions within the Spanish Habsburg domain (see fig. 10). Two points of convergence stand out: at the point of origin in the late 1630s when escalating conflict between local rulers and princely authorities threatened governmental paralysis in all three kingdoms; and in the period 1649–1651 when the new "Puritan" regime achieved an unprecedented degree of territorial consolidation across the three kingdoms. Their points of divergence are equally visible: in the period 1640–1642, revolutionary coalitions in Scotland and Ireland effectively established independent regimes on the periphery while the revolutionary coalition in England was plunged into a civil war with a remarkably resilient princely core;[26] by 1660 both England and Scotland had not only restored their monarch but also reinstituted relatively mediated forms of rule in a familiar pattern of elite consolidation while in Ireland local rulers looked ever more like the agents rather than the competitors of a consolidated princely regime. More broadly, however, it seems obvious from the composite experience of these closely related revolutions that, despite the salience of ecclesiastical issues and the importance of religious affiliation as a marker of political difference, the dynamics of revolutionary conflict in the British Isles were comparable to those in the Habsburg Mediterranean where the politics of religious authority were not explicitly at stake.

Revolution and Civil War in the French Fronde

Following the trail of R. B. Merriman's six contemporaneous revolutions, we have—with the additions of Sicily, Scotland, and Ireland—thus far reviewed seven revolutionary conflicts, divided clearly into two discrete clusters within two of Europe's most prominent composite states. Though we have observed some important structural similarities in the dynamics of revolutionary conflict, especially on the peripheries of the Spanish-Habsburg and Stuart composites, it is clear that popular political actors enjoyed extremely variable opportunities to exploit the latent tensions between local rulers and their princely overlords, even within the same composite state. Nevertheless popular political action, with or without strong support from dissident elites, was critical in initiating and sustaining revolutionary political challenges to both the cultural and the fiscal demands of aggressive princes. In the long run the challengers failed to maintain their revolutionary regimes except in Portugal, but even political and military defeat came in different guises, ranging from Catalonia's golden age of provincial autonomy to Ireland's direct colonization. Turning our attention, finally, to the Fronde in

26. With the collapse of the king's sovereignty, there clearly was the opportunity for local consolidations of power at the expense of the center. That this did not occur is a testimony to the fact that the parliamentary coalition represented an alternative form of territorial consolidation rather than a drive toward local rule.

France, we will find still more variations on these now-familiar revolutionary themes.

Historians have, for good reason, had considerable difficulty constructing coherent narratives of the French conflicts between 1648 and 1653: "Virtually every kind of protest and disobedience," Robin Briggs suggests, "occurred simultaneously during the Fronde, only to demonstrate once again that they were incapable of coalescing into a real challenge to the government" (1989:176–177). If we recall, however, the origins of the French monarchy as a dynastic construction from a variety of preexisting pieces of political sovereignty and its even more recent disintegration during the civil wars, the lack of coalescence may not seem so surprising. On the contrary, the very different conflicts that together made up the crisis of the Fronde serve to underscore the important sense in which Henry IV's reconstruction of the French monarchy had by no means obliterated its compositeness. To be sure, his skillful alignment with the former Huguenot rebels as their protector and with the remnants of the Catholic League as their patron established the basis for a new kind of territorial consolidation in the seventeenth century, but at bottom the France whose princely sovereignty Louis XIV inherited in 1643 was still a patchwork quilt of jurisdictions overlaid by the fundamental distinction between the pays d'état, which enjoyed a good deal of provincial self-government through their estates, and the pays d'élection, which were more directly under the fiscal administration of the king. Thus, although the kingdom of France was a different sort of composite state than the "multiple kingdoms" of Iberia and the British Isles, it is important to situate the various conflicts, and in particular the popular interventions that were an essential part of the Fronde, in appropriate political arenas and within them to discern both the political alignments and the (transient) outcomes that they entailed. Here, I use the revolutionary conflict in Paris and Bordeaux to illustrate both the complexities and the peculiarities of the Fronde from the perspective of popular political actors.

Although it is conventional to suggest that the Fronde—the name derives from the playful but destructive slingshots of young boys—began in Paris and spread to the provinces, James B. Collins (1995:68) argues that it was more clearly "a case of the discontent of the provinces spreading at last to Paris." Indeed, as we saw earlier, French involvement in the Thirty Years' War had occasioned a rising tide of political discontent over the rapidly escalating demands of the royal government—both for more money and for more direct control of the extractive apparatus.

In the provinces these oppositions, as the regional revolts of the late 1630s demonstrated, could result in politically potent alignments between ordinary people, concerned especially with rising taxes, and local rulers, whose authority was being compromised by the king's attempts to create new *élections* (tax districts controlled by royal officials called *élus*) in the pays d'état and to send intendants to oversee the process.[27] The essential fragility of royal authority was only exacerbated by the nearly simultaneous deaths of Louis XIII (May 1643) and his dedicated minister, Cardinal Richelieu (December 1642); predictably, the regency of Anne of Austria, mother of the young Louis XIV, was immediately beset by a host of grandees competing for control of national policy during the interregnum. Amid popular protest and increasing political uncertainty, then, even royal tax officials began exhibiting what Orest Ranum describes as a "lack of zeal" in prosecuting lawbreakers:

Tax officials reported to Paris that peasants simply would not pay taxes, and that in many instances they could not do so. Occasional reports of peasants breaking into tax offices and destroying records, setting fire to houses in which tax officials lived, or physically intimidating or accosting those officials were all part of the routine of seventeenth-century government. Without a company or two of soldiers to support his efforts to raise taxes by confiscating property for non-payment, the tax collector could do little but wring his hands and inform Paris that tax revenues in his district had dried up. (1993:6)

It was in this general atmosphere of crisis and uncertainty that the Fronde finally spread to Paris as the officers of the "sovereign" royal courts,[28] led by the Parlement of Paris, broke with the government of the regent and her chief adviser, Cardinal Mazarin, in early 1648.

The officers of the sovereign royal courts were especially concerned to protect the noble privileges that attached to their offices as well as to ensure the security of their heavy investments in government obligations. But when they boldly squared off against the Council of State, domi-

27. Historians of France often assume that imposing élections on the more self-regulatory pays d'état would have produced more effective taxation for the central government; Collins 1995 points out, however, that the most reliable flows of revenue for the monarchy came from the pays d'état, not the pays d'élection, and that realizing both the political and fiscal costs of direct control, the royal government quietly gave up the attempt during and after the upheavals of midcentury.

28. These courts were sovereign in the sense that they rendered final judgments in the name of the king. For a useful introduction to the very complex French judiciary, see Collins 1995:4–14.

nated by Mazarin, they began deliberately to champion a whole range of popular grievances as well. Thus, meeting in a special combined session called the Chambre St. Louis, they drew up a list of twenty-nine specific grievances that included firmer controls on tax farming (the system by which private entrepreneurs collected taxes in return for a negotiated payment to the royal fisc), a 25 percent reduction in direct taxes, the abolition of the intendants, and the release of political prisoners. At first the Council of State temporized, but when it arrested leaders of the Parlement of Paris, massive popular mobilizations in defense of the defiant officials including the systematic erection of barricades to prevent armed repression—the Day of the Barricades, August 26, 1648—forced the royal council to accede to the judges' demands. In October another round of confrontation again forced the government to accept all of the opposition's demands, but in January 1649 the situation in Paris was still so volatile that the king, his regent mother, and Mazarin actually fled the city, and civil war broke out between the city of Paris and the regency government. As royal mercenaries encircled the city in an attempt to cut off its food supply, a heroic popular mobilization in the winter months of 1649 proved to be largely ineffectual militarily, but the tenacity of the rebels was nevertheless rewarded by a "compromise" in March by which the royal council formally confirmed the concessions they had made in earlier rounds in this "negotiation."[29]

In this way the people of Paris, like the people of London at almost the same time, became directly involved in a struggle for control of a national political space. Theirs was very much a classic local mobilization within and in defense of their urban community, and much of the discipline and determination that characterized their actions at critical moments like the Day of the Barricades was due to the organizational framework of the civic militia, which could bring thousands of bourgeois—well-integrated members of the urban community such as merchants and artisans—into collective action through district- and ward-level structures. Though the scale and character of popular political action might not be appreciably different from what occurred in other French cities—or, for that matter, in Naples or Palermo—its location at the core of a large composite monarchy gave it special significance.

29. The royal council's willingness to compromise for the sake of peace with its rebellious capital may have been related, as some historians have suggested, to the defeat and execution of the English king, Charles I, whose queen, the sister of Louis XIII, was living in exile in France; by this reckoning, the dangers of stubborn intransigence in the face of generalized opposition had become all too apparent.

Indeed, where there is no clear distinction between local rulers and national claimants to power as in both London and Paris—where the consolidation of territorial sovereignty had gone a long way toward replacing local self-regulation with direction from the center—temporary coalitions between elite political factions and massively mobilized political subjects are often said, in retrospect, to have had a "national" significance even though the claims of the transient victors were not necessarily enforceable on a national scale. Such coalitions could appear to be so dramatic and decisive in the resolution of short-term "national" crises that during the Fronde political elites frequently sought to create the illusion of crisis and thus to appeal for popular political intervention to seek short-term advantage against their opponents (Descimon and Jouhaud 1985; Ranum 1993). That many more of these apparently cynical attempts to exploit—and on occasion to buy—popular political activism failed than succeeded in the seemingly endless conflicts following the Day of the Barricades in 1648 belies the assumption of these factional leaders—and in many cases, their retrospective claims—that popular political action could be easily or simply manipulated by political elites. For their part, most of the citizens of Paris, having achieved significant (though in retrospect, short-term) concessions from the Council of State in 1648 and 1649, were apparently reluctant to identify their long-term collective interests with the ever-changing and obviously self-promoting factions that characterized elite struggles for control of the monarchy throughout the king's minority.

In the French southwest, the port city of Bordeaux and the province of Guyenne, of which Bordeaux was the political center, had a long and more continuous history of opposition to the exactions of outsiders, especially royal tax officials and marauding armies.[30] In 1528, for example, the citizens of Bordeaux had revolted against a new excise tax on wine, and in 1548 the city had joined major portions of the province in revolt against the gabelle, the royal tax on salt (cf. Heller 1991:42–44). During the sixteenth-century civil wars Bordeaux was neither a center of Huguenot dissent nor a stronghold of the Catholic League, but Guyenne more generally was at the heart of the massive rural mobilizations of the Tard-Avisés or Croquants who opposed equally the plunder and pillage of all the warring parties and helped to bring the factional leaders in the con-

30. The specialized literature on the Fronde in Bordeaux includes Westrich 1972, Kötting 1983, and Birnstiel 1985; see also Beik 1997 who considers Bordeaux in a broader (non-Parisian) seventeenth-century urban context.

test for national power to the peace table (see chap. 3 above). Under Henry IV, Guyenne lost a measure of its provincial self-regulation and was forced to accept the more direct administration of élus and intendants as agents of the royal government,[31] but this did little to temper its opposition to the new forms of taxation that were required to sustain the war against Spain after 1635. In fact, Bordeaux led a new series of very explosive demonstrations and tax protests that virtually halted the flow of royal tax revenues altogether. As Robin Briggs suggests, "this was a fiscal débâcle on a disastrous scale, and the rebels had achieved a great deal at relatively little cost to themselves. The weakness of the authorities had been starkly revealed, together with the unwillingness of the local élites, nobles and bourgeois alike, to protect the tax officials and agents, widely seen as traitors to their region" (1989:136). Thus, as in many other parts of rural France, tax collection in Guyenne was, on the eve of the Fronde, an increasingly difficult, even risky venture amid an entirely predictable tide of noncompliance and popular protest.

As for Bordeaux, the city retained most of its traditional self-government—its historic "privileges"—and despite a number of extraordinary exactions in the 1630s and 1640s remained one of the most lightly taxed jurisdictions in the realm. As was so often the case in early modern cities, these political and fiscal privileges can be seen as the fruit of an informal, almost natural alliance between the local magistracy—the *jurade*—and the bourgeois, or propertied, citizens. Though the magistrates routinely pledged their allegiance to the king, they also routinely opposed new royal taxation on behalf of their subjects, whose support and approval made daily governance possible. When their appeals to abolish new taxes altogether were unsuccessful, the jurade typically bought out the new tax with a negotiated lump-sum payment, thereby acceding to intermittent royal extortions rather than putting themselves in the position of having to collect unpopular royal taxes on a regular basis (Ranum 1993). In short, on the southwestern periphery of France local rulers in informal alliance with popular political actors proved to be a remarkably successful brake on the extension of royal administration and taxation. This put the privileged officers of the Parlement of Bordeaux—a sovereign royal court with jurisdiction in much of southwestern France—in a particu-

31. Major 1966. Guyenne may have been particularly vulnerable to the Crown's introduction of élus because it did not have provincial estates; rather it had ten local assemblies. The attempt to introduce élus in the pays d'état more generally, both under Henry IV and Louis XIII, was largely unsuccessful; see Briggs 1989.

larly awkward position: they were at once the most prominent members of the local political elite and obliged officially to enforce royal edicts and protect tax collectors, the hated *gabelleurs*. But when push came to shove repeatedly in the 1630s and 1640s, the *parlementaires* generally sided with the local coalition rather than with the king's tax agents by refusing to register new tax edicts and by failing to prosecute tax resisters. During the regency, however, the duke of Épernon—royal governor of Guyenne, a staunch ally of Mazarin, and a personal enemy of many parlementaires—gladly exploited the Parlement's failure to stem (much less to quell) the rising tide of popular tax protests in his own attempt to gain more direct control of Bordeaux's local administration.

The predictable consequence of this complex interaction among local rulers, ordinary political subjects, and national claimants to power was a classic and largely successful coalition in defense of the local community during the initial phase of the Fronde. This took especially the form of a massive armed mobilization of the city's population—an expansion of the number of militia companies from twelve to thirty-six—in the face of a military buildup and an attempted blockade of the city by the royal governor in 1648. The general armament of the populace was controversial because it threatened to dilute the political elite's control of the civic militia, but it appeared dramatically to bear fruit when, in 1649, the militia attacked and dismantled one of the governor's most important fortifications within the city, the Château Trompette. Thus the alliance of municipal authorities and parlementaires with popular political actors in Bordeaux produced a compromise agreement—the rebels were granted an amnesty and promised the destruction of the royal governor's fortification at Libourne—that could be interpreted as an important victory. In this case it was not a "national" victory over arbitrary government and excessive taxation as the Frondeurs in Paris might claim but a decidedly local victory in defense of a privileged, self-regulating urban community.

There are some similarities or parallels between the early phases of the Fronde in Paris and in Bordeaux. The most obvious is a coalition between the privileged officers of sovereign royal courts—led by the parlements—and massive mobilizations of ordinary people—led by civic militias—in defense of the local community and in opposition to the regency government (or its agents). Indeed, in both cases this formidable alliance, which emerged full-blown in the course of 1648, forced the Council of State to make significant concessions in the course of 1649, and their coincidence in time surely underscored the fragility of the regency government. Still, it is clear that these conflicts were moving in different directions that reflected structural differences relating to the geography of power within composite states and the correspondingly variable opportunities open to popular political actors. Whereas elite factionalism and the collapse of royal authority afforded popular political actors in Paris the unique opportunity to affect short-term "national" crises directly and immediately, popular political actors in Bordeaux were given the opportunity to chart a far more independent course of action that culminated in the revolutionary regime of the Ormée in 1652.

Besides offering liberal pensions to former or potential competitors in the political elite, the Council of State set about reconstructing royal power on behalf of the young king Louis XIV by formally visiting some of the centers of the rebellion. The king's return to Paris and official visits to Rouen and Dijon appeared to be quite successful as elaborate displays of royal authority and popular affection, but the city of Bordeaux refused at first to give him entrance in August 1650 amid a new round of open warfare between Governor Épernon and his many enemies in the region. Many members of the Parlement wanted to open the city's gates to the king, but the leaders of the popular movement, especially those who had assumed new positions of militia leadership, were deeply suspicious of this kind of formal and ostentatious display of the king's claims to sovereign authority *within* their community. As the grape harvest neared in September, they reluctantly agreed to the king's visit, but instead of being allowed to arrive by land at the head of his army like a conqueror, Louis XIV arrived via the Garonne on board a magnificent, but militarily insignificant, galley. By the summer of 1651 the magistrates of Bordeaux found themselves under renewed popular pressure to shore up the city's defenses against royal encroachment, and when the jurade excluded this collection of merchants and artisans from official meetings, the leaders of the popular movement began holding their own meetings outside under a magnificent grove of elm trees, from which they adopted the name for their movement: the Ormée.

The extralegal meetings of the Ormée to discuss political issues normally reserved for the officers of the municipality opened up a second phase of the Fronde in Bordeaux that exposed deep rifts within the local political elite. Though the Parlement strictly forbade the extraordinary political meetings, the merchants and artisans of the Ormée were still allied with a significant segment of the deeply divided local political elite. The Ormée nevertheless began making fundamentally revolutionary demands—one of their manifestos even announced that they had constituted themselves as a "republic"—that would have radically transformed the political position of both the local magistrates and the royal government.[32] By the summer of 1652, the Ormée had invaded the Hôtel de Ville and effectively taken over the administration of local affairs, and to shore up their position they began forcibly exiling leaders of the old political elite who had not already fled. In this new round of struggle with many of their former allies within the local political establishment, the leaders of the Ormée found willing allies among the agents of the Prince of Condé, who in 1649 had saved the monarchy from its enemies but had subsequently been arrested under order from Mazarin. The city of Bordeaux's formal protection of the Princess of Condé had been an essential part of its ongoing defiance in 1650, and having finally been released from prison, Condé was now openly waging a military campaign against Mazarin and the Council of State. When this national struggle for power ended in the defeat of Condé's armies, the rebels of Bordeaux saw little chance for survival and eventually surrendered the city with relatively little resistance in 1653. In the aftermath the authority and privileges of the Parlement of Bordeaux were restored along with the king's sovereignty, but the leaders of the Ormée were tried and executed.

Though they were thus defeated militarily, the Ormée had nevertheless transformed the political landscape of the city of Bordeaux and, by extension, the kingdom of France. In the course of several years of escalating struggle, the leaders of the Ormée, an amalgam of fringe members of the local political elite, merchants, and artisans, demonstrated that they could use existing organizations like guilds and the expanded militia units to mobilize a broad base of political support and to dominate the local political arena; at the same time they showed considerable political independence by rejecting their erstwhile allies at home (see fig. 2a) in favor of an alliance with the Prince of Condé, a formidable claimant to national power (see fig. 2c). How well this new coalition might have held up in the event of a rebel victory against Mazarin is difficult to say, but it surely would have resulted in a very different path of political development, not only for Bordeaux, but possibly for the whole of the kingdom. As it happened, the numerical strength and stubborn tenacity of the Ormée—the very qualities that allowed them to

32. Their political priorities, according to Ranum (1993:252), were: "(1) the right to meet, debate, and in a sense legislate on affairs in Bordeaux; (2) the recruitment of a citizen army and the building of fortifications; and (3) the exclusion from the city of any Bordelais who was suspected of sympathizing with Governor Épernon, even if he were a parlementaire."

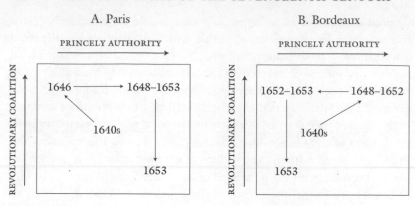

Figure 11. Dynamics of revolutionary conflict in the French Fronde

dominate the municipal arena—had the unintended consequence of driving the local political elite into the direction of the king who, in exchange for their loyalty, guaranteed their offices and their privileges against attack from below. In this sense, the political outcome of the Fronde in Bordeaux is an especially vivid illustration of the political consequences that Charles Tilly describes for France as a whole: "Quelling the Fronde did not eliminate resistance to royal demands; it displaced and fragmented that resistance. Alliances between ordinary people (typically aggrieved by taxation or other forms of extraction) and important nobles (typically aggrieved by checks to their power) became both less likely and less effective" (1986:242).

In other words, the monarchy's ability variously to defeat, to co-opt, or to bribe its many enemies, one by one, entailed a significant political realignment and underwrote a pattern of political development that belies the inflated rhetorical claims of all parties during the conflict: a general consolidation of elite power in terms of noble privilege vis-à-vis both ordinary political subjects and the "sovereign" prince (see fig. 2b). This thoroughly unintended and ambiguous outcome, which became deeply embedded in the political culture of the resurgent French regime of the 1660s, would remain an important brake on future attempts to "reform" French politics and to assert a more uniform and unlimited territorial sovereignty in the kingdom as a whole.

Yet the diminished likelihood of a comprehensive opposition had different political implications under different circumstances. Using the analytic framework of our more general comparisons of composite revolutions, it is also important to underscore more specific differences in both the dynamic process of revolutionary conflict and its long-term political consequences in Paris and Bordeaux. Figure 11 suggests how we might describe and account for these differences in terms of the proximity/integration of princely authority and the changing character of the local revolutionary coalitions.

At the core of the reconstructed French monarchy, the ordinary political subjects of Paris quickly discovered that the political confrontation and paralysis of the 1640s led not only to what Orest Ranum (1993) describes as the heady albeit transient "joy of revolution" in 1648 but also to the ongoing depredations of a five-year civil war. The tax relief they had demanded and actually been promised proved to be short-lived while the outcome of the civil wars—the survival of both the dynastic prince and his somewhat chastened sovereign courts—was predicated on the king's ability to reestablish unmediated administrative control of his capital, even though for the bulk of his long reign Louis XIV, having fled the symbolic center of his kingdom during the Fronde, chose to reside elsewhere. By contrast, on the southwestern periphery of the same monarchy, the ordinary people of Bordeaux discovered that the political confrontation and paralysis of the 1640s led directly to intermittent civil war and only indirectly to the heady but equally transient experience of revolution. The local self-regulation that they championed turned out to be more contentious and divisive than they imagined while the "survival" of royal sovereignty over their city was predicated on the destruction of their long-standing and largely successful alliance with local rulers in opposition to the exactions of a distant monarch. In short, the microgeography of composite state formation remained a salient feature of the political experience of the ordinary political subjects of Paris and Bordeaux, not only in terms of the taxes they paid but also in the political experiences they remembered and the reconfigured range of opportunities available to them.

Composite Revolutions and State Power

In the context of the French Fronde and the multiple revolutions in Iberia and the British Isles, R. B. Merriman's inclusion of the "Revolution" in the northern Netherlands in his list of contemporaneous revolutions may seem curious, if not fundamentally mistaken. In fact, Herbert H. Rowen (1972) has aptly termed it "the revolution that wasn't."[33] For our purposes, Merriman's apparent mistake may be a particularly creative one because it encourages us to clarify what was distinctive—or at least not revolutionary—about political conflict in the Dutch Republic at the end of its long war of independence. This will allow us, in turn, a useful perspective from which to reflect more generally on the nature of composite revolutions and their relationship to the consolidation of sovereign authority over ordinary political subjects.

For the Dutch Republic the ratification of a permanent peace with Spain in 1648 was a moment of general relief and celebration, but it also opened up many of the political wounds that had been so inflamed during the temporary truce with Spain some forty years earlier. As in 1609, the political leaders of the province of Holland, and the city of Amsterdam in particular, had been the most forceful advocates of peace negotiations, while the Prince of Orange, William II, who succeeded Frederik Hendrik in 1647, was intent on pursuing the war with Spain in concert with France and with an eye toward the division of the southern Netherlands between the republic and France. After he failed to sidetrack the peace, William's conflict with the powerful regents of Holland only escalated as the regents pushed hard to scale back the size of the army— their specific proposal was to eliminate the foreign contingents most loyal to the prince—and by extension to reduce the burdensome taxes that were required to support a large standing army.[34] In 1650 this fundamental disagreement over defense policy, which was pregnant with constitutional implications for the republic as a whole, culminated in an attempted coup d'état by William II, which proved, in the end, to be "the revolution that wasn't."

For young William II, who was deeply concerned about establishing his "glory" as a military leader, peace with Spain came at an inopportune time, and his attempted coup was in many ways a defensive move to prevent further erosion of his leadership position (Rowen 1988). As political appointees, the princes of Orange had only indirect "influence" in the formal structures of republican governance: as captains-general, they commanded the Union's army and dispensed commissions to subordi-

33. In addition to Rowen 1972, the literature on the Dutch crisis includes Kernkamp 1943, Groenveld 1967, and Poelhekke 1973.
34. As recently as 1642 the Dutch Republic had had a standing army of more than 70,000, but by 1650 it had been pared to less than 30,000. The regents of Holland were proposing to reduce it further to 26,000.

nate officers; as members of the Council of State, which advised the Estates General, they influenced defense and foreign policy; as provincial stadhouders, they mediated internal disputes and presided over a political patronage network that had been expanded by Maurits and Frederik Hendrik.[35] In the Dutch republican system, then, the princes of Orange were generals, advisers, and patrons, but not sovereigns; they may be considered national claimants to power only to the extent that they were the brokers of broader political alliances, which might include both regents and ordinary political subjects. More obviously resourceful militarily than politically, William undertook a series of extraordinary moves in the early summer of 1650 that appear to have been carefully planned some time in advance and were intended not simply to resolve the immediate issue of troop levels in his favor but to wrest decision-making authority over defense and foreign policy away from the individually "sovereign" provinces.[36] First he used the failure of negotiations with the province of Holland over troop levels as the occasion to undertake a series of official visits to the most intransigent cities in Holland—whose narrow majority in the Estates of Holland stood in the way of compromise—to compel them to change their positions. Then, when these well-orchestrated confrontations produced no significant result and the province of Holland took unilateral action to dismiss troops in its pay, he openly countermanded their orders and obtained a vague instruction from the Estates General, over Holland's objection, to take unspecified measures to ensure public order. Finally, armed with this mandate, at the end of July he simultaneously arrested six prominent regents from the cities of Holland and secretly deployed more than ten thousand troops to the gates of Amsterdam.

Thus the disagreement over troop levels quickly escalated into a military confrontation with Amsterdam, the symbolic center of political opposition to the stadhouder/captain-general. Given the numbers and the apparent loyalty of the troops at his disposal, it is perhaps surprising

---

35. In most places, the stadhouder was granted the right to approve municipal elections— that is, lifetime appointments to municipal councils (generally known as the "regents") and term appointments to the corps of ruling magistrates (*burgemeesters*); in this sense, they controlled access to political office but little more.

36. Since William deliberately masked his intentions in public (and he did not live long enough to offer us a retrospective clarification), his ultimate goals are not entirely clear; in all likelihood, however, he aimed for a dominant position within a Council of State with real discretion over foreign and defense policy. Though in some sense a modest goal, this would clearly have altered the political balance between the institutions of central government and the provincial Estates.

that William's bold actions—the combination of symbolic visitations, arrests, and military confrontations are clearly reminiscent of the tactics that Maurits used so successfully against Oldenbarnevelt in the 1610s—produced so little result. When the city mobilized massively in its own defense, William agreed to further negotiations and settled for the resignation of two powerful Amsterdam regents and a vague promise to work out the policy issues peacefully. Though it is conventional to suggest that William's political failure was accidental—first, because the troops he secretly sent to Amsterdam were reported to the authorities by a post courier who happened to witness their movement, thereby compromising the element of surprise; second, because of the accident of his untimely death a few months later—William more fundamentally failed to re-create the political coalition that his uncle, Maurits, had used to such great advantage.

To be sure, on the policy issues William appears to have enjoyed a fairly solid base of support among the regent elite of all the provinces except Holland, but even in Holland he was supported by nearly half of the enfranchised towns. Rather, the principal difference was his own lack of popular support, which stands in sharp contrast to the robust popular defense of Amsterdam in the face of William's military challenge. By comparison with Maurits, who built on the prior politicization and mobilization of orthodox Calvinists within religiously divided communities to make "extraordinary" changes in municipal councils (*wetsverzettingen*), William was unable to generate the kind of popular support necessary to dislodge his opponents at the municipal level—this despite his strenuous assertion that he, too, was defending both the Union and the "true religion." Thus his monthlong series of theatrical official visits to the most recalcitrant cities of Holland failed to turn any votes in his favor at the provincial Estates, and lacking the authority to make decisions in his own name or to force majority decisions at the Estates General over the objections of Holland especially, he could do little in the face of Amsterdam's apparently four-square defense but return to the bargaining table.

When the immediate crisis had passed and the troops had been sent away from Amsterdam, William did enjoy some modest success in the promised negotiations over military policy. But his more fundamental inability to transform the structures of sovereign decision-making authority in the Dutch republican state was obvious. Thus, immediately following William's death from smallpox in October, the regents of Holland summoned an extraordinary Grand Assembly of all the provincial Estates to take measures to prevent similar political crises in the future. Though the Grand Assembly did not agree to Holland's proposal that henceforth the offices of stadhouder and captain-general should not be united in a single person, it did unequivocally affirm the sovereignty of the constituent provinces—even with regard to troops in their employ—and inaugurate the first stadhouderless period in Dutch republican history.[37] In this sense, the nonrevolution in the northern Netherlands both highlighted and reinforced the general direction of Dutch political development since the 1580s: the *permanent* elimination of the dynastic prince and the consequent consolidation of alternative sovereignties, at the provincial and even the municipal level.

All in all, the distinctiveness of the political and constitutional crisis in the Dutch Republic does appear to defy R. B. Merriman's inclusion of it in his list of contemporaneous revolutions. Still, it can be useful in our broader assessment of the political dynamics of seventeenth-century revolutions. First, it underscores obliquely the sense in which the mid-seventeenth-century political crisis was a crisis of princely power, a crisis brought on by concerted attempts to consolidate the authority—especially fiscal and cultural authority—of dynastic princes within composite states. If nothing else, the crisis in the Dutch Republic, where the dynastic prince had been replaced by a loose condominium of oligarchic regents, suggests a simple proposition: no princely consolidation, no composite revolution.[38] This is not to say, of course, that in the absence of aggressive princes there will be no political conflict; on the contrary, I want only to suggest that where the dynastic prince had actually been eliminated, where the princely authority had previously been limited, or where the prince had merely been chastened by previous experience, we should expect that political conflict will take different form from that which we have called composite or multiple revolutions. At the same time, to the extent that the Dutch Republic remained a composite of previously constituted political units, William's failed coup underscores a more general observation that in a composite state military intimidation alone was more likely to awaken local alliances in defense of the self-reg-

---

37. Actually, William's cousin was stadhouder in the provinces of Friesland and Groningen, and there was a continuous succession of stadhouders of the Frisian line throughout the history of the republic. The critical point is, of course, that the majority of the seven constituent provinces left the office of stadhouder vacant.

38. In this regard, Merriman's "mistake" was to imagine that the Prince of Orange was, in some sense, a "sovereign" in the Dutch Republic and that his antagonists, the regents, were challengers; from that perspective, of course, the work of the Grand Assembly would indeed seem to be the climax of a revolutionary movement.

ulation of the local community than to encourage massive shifts of popular allegiance in favor of a territorial consolidation of power.[39] In addition, this account of the Dutch crisis reinforces the more general argument of this book that in early modern composite states, popular political actors are essential to any attempt to describe and account for the divergent paths of European political development over the longue durée; the specific corollary suggested by the Dutch "revolution that wasn't" might read: no popular mobilization, no revolutionary seizure of power.

To return finally to the cluster of composite revolutions we have examined here, we can say once again that ordinary political subjects—far from being hapless victims or passive observers—were active participants in the creation of the new complex of European states that emerged from the Crisis of the Seventeenth Century. At the beginning of these revolutionary processes, the stubborn resistance, defiant demonstrations, and occasionally violent insurrections of ordinary political subjects invariably disrupted the relations between local rulers and national claimants to power and thereby occasioned a variety of more general crises of state power. In the middle of these processes, their more massive mobilization through community networks and militia companies, often (though not always) in alliance with a segment of the political elite, opened up a variety of revolutionary situations in which the dynastic prince's claim to sovereignty was fundamentally shaken—by the threat of either secession at the periphery or replacement by alternative claimants to national power at the center. And at the end of these revolutionary processes, even when the dynastic princes eventually prevailed or their authority was later revived, it was invariably under informal conditions and/or constitutional regulations that betrayed the potency of the comprehensive revolutionary coalitions that were rooted in the intentional engagement and deliberate mobilization of ordinary political subjects.

As in the clusters of Reformation era contention for power we examined in previous chapters, these composite revolutions were far too complex and their outcomes far too ambiguous and transient to be susceptible to a simple tabulation of winners and losers. It is especially important to recognize, however, that the variations we have attempted to describe and account for were not only those that obviously distinguished the composites from one another but also those that were evident within

---

39. Israel 1995:607–608 even notes opposition in otherwise Orangist and orthodox Zutphen to William's military confrontation with Amsterdam.

these larger constructs. Indeed, the microgeography of composite state formation remained a defining feature of the new European political landscape for the simple reason that the most obvious cost of princely "survival"—not only in the German-Roman Empire in central Europe but also in the resurgent kingdoms in the west—was some form of agreement on the part of the dynastic prince to accept or even to guarantee the internal boundaries of their composite states. This meant that both the proximity of princely power and the viability of broad political alliances in opposition to them varied considerably while ordinary political subjects remained a salient feature of the complex political relations between local rulers and national claimants to power. In the concluding chapter we will turn our attention to a more global comparison of the variant trajectories of state formation that were the accumulated residue of some one hundred fifty years of religious and political struggle in Europe.

5

Popular Politics and the Geography of State Formation

When states newly acquired . . . have been accustomed to living freely under their own laws, there are three ways to hold them securely: first, by devastating them; next, by going and living there in person; thirdly, by letting them keep their own laws, exacting tribute, and setting up an oligarchy which will keep the state friendly to you. In the last case, the government will know that it cannot endure without the friendship and power of the prince who created it, and so it has to exert itself to maintain its authority. A city used to freedom can be more easily ruled through its own citizens, provided you do not wish to destroy it, than in any other way.

Niccolò Machiavelli, *The Prince*, 1514

Majesty or Sovereignty is the most high, absolute, and perpetual power over the citizens and subjects in a Commonwealth: . . . that is to say, the greatest power to command.

Jean Bodin, *The Six Books of a Commonweale*, 1576

I have attributed the rights of sovereignty . . . not to the supreme magistrate, but to the commonwealth or universal associations. Many jurists and political scientists assign them as proper only to the prince and supreme magistrate to the extent that if these rights are granted and communicated to the people or commonwealth, they thereby perish and are no more. . . . A few others and I hold the con-

trary. . . . I recognize the prince as the administrator, overseer and governor of these rights of sovereignty. But the owner and usufructuary of sovereignty is none other than the total people associated in one symbiotic body from many smaller associations.

Johannes Althusius, *Politics*, 1614

At the beginning of the sixteenth century the famous Italian humanist Niccolò Machiavelli wrote a brief tract that was intended specifically for the edification of the rulers of what I have called composite states. Though *The Prince* is viewed by some as a timeless handbook for amoral political behavior, it can also be regarded as a well-informed and insightful distillation of the lessons of late medieval statecraft.[1] Particularly interesting for our purposes is Machiavelli's cautionary message regarding the rule of newly acquired states or cities that "are accustomed to living under their own laws" (bk. 5). In such cases, Machiavelli argued, the ruler could expect to be able to consolidate his power through new legislation only under very limited conditions— namely, by first going there to live or, at great cost, nothing less than the destruction of the acquisition! The obvious alternative, he insisted, was to "let them keep their own laws." Now, the princes that Machiavelli had most clearly in mind were the Visconti, the Borgias, and the Medicis who had dominated the late medieval politics of northern Italy. A century and a half later, however, he would certainly have been justified in declaring an emphatic "I told you so" to the descendants of the dynastic princes of transalpine Europe whose attempts to accumulate new power in northern Italy had, during the Italian Wars (1494–1559), destroyed Machiavelli's fervent hopes for the preservation of Italian independence. In fact, as Machiavelli might have predicted, the stubborn attempts by Habsburg, Valois/Bourbon, and Tudor/Stuart "princes" to consolidate their power within territories that had long been accustomed to living under their own laws had plunged them into decades of very destructive civil and religious strife. As we have seen, it was especially the prince's claim to an unprecedented cultural sovereignty in response to the challenges of Protestant reform that called forth the most unified and potent oppositions, but even in situations in which the issue of religious "liberty" was not explicitly or primarily at stake, princely attempts to strengthen their fiscal administrations at the expense of local self-regula-

---

1. What has made Machiavelli's work seem controversial is not that he sought to understand the limits of princely power but that he defined those limits exclusively in terms of utility and historical precedent rather than Christian moralism.

tion and thus to augment their tax revenues could awaken very dangerous domestic opposition.[2]

But what were the alternatives to the territorial consolidation of
princely power? If the princes of Europe were not Machiavellian in the
narrow sense that they heeded his caution regarding the rule of composite states, what were they? Theoretically, the alternatives were clear:
Machiavelli seemed generally to be counseling princes to accept and
work within the compositeness of their states, to follow the tried-and-
true method of aligning selectively with indigenous elites to establish an
orderly if limited and indirect rule, what I have termed elite consolidation (fig. 2b); the obvious alternative, which Machiavelli apparently
feared as much as princely tyranny and violence (fig. 2c), was the dissolution of the composite and local consolidation of power, in which case
the constituent parts would once again be vulnerable to "foreign" intervention in a disorderly and chaotic political environment (fig. 2a).

To judge by the subsequent history of princely politics and political
thought during the early modern period, Europe's most ambitious rulers
generally preferred the kind of political thinking that more conveniently
juxtaposed the consolidation of princely "sovereignty" with chaos, disorder, and anarchy. Thus from Jean Bodin in the sixteenth century to
Thomas Hobbes and Jacques-Benigne Bossuet in the seventeenth, the
principal theorists of political consolidation within territorial states
denied the viability of composite states and emphasized, instead, the
indivisibility and even the absolute qualities of sovereign political authority—that is, the ruler's ability to make enforceable decisions in matters of
concern for all his subjects. Consequently, the dynastic prince was transformed, in theory at least, into the territorial monarch whose absolute
sovereignty was said to be divinely ordained and whose behavior was
subject only to God's judgment. Though Machiavelli's other alternatives—what I have called elite consolidation and local consolidation—
were thus marginalized or eliminated in theories of monarchical "absolutism" within idealized territorial states, they hardly disappeared
altogether. On the contrary, the political geography of Europe in the second half of the seventeenth century indicates that various forms of elite

2. See also book 20 in which Machiavelli underscores the dangers of incurring the enmity
of a subject population: "If you have fortresses and yet the people hate you they [the
fortresses] will not save you; once the people have taken up arms they will never lack outside help." Then, citing the contemporary example of the countess of Forlí, he concludes,
"So then as before it would have been safer for her to have avoided the enmity of the people than to have had fortresses" ([1514] 1961:119).

and local consolidation were the most common outcomes of the myriad domestic and international conflicts during Europe's age of religious wars. To be sure, the resisters of princely "tyranny" were not without their theoretical defenders, from the French Monarchomachs (roughly, "fighters of kings") in the sixteenth century to Johannes Althusius and the English "radicals" in the seventeenth century (cf. Van Gelderen 1992), but it is on the practical and often unintended consequences of concerted popular political action vis-à-vis aggressive and consolidating princes that I should like to focus here.

In fact, a number of difficulties arise when historians use political theorists as guides for the description of actual political relations in the sixteenth and seventeenth centuries. The most obvious is the theorists' normative, as opposed to merely descriptive, intent even when, in good humanist fashion, they follow the rhetorically inductive strategy of building larger generalizations from a series of historical examples. A more fundamental problem is that, having been trained in the common Latin-based curricula of Western educational institutions, the theorists of the sixteenth and seventeenth centuries (and, by extension, their intellectual descendants) almost always betray a loyalty to the two standard classification systems that derive from the Hellenistic learning of late antiquity. When they were not emphasizing some version the Aristotelian triad of monarchy/aristocracy/democracy, political theorists of the time typically distinguished between absolute monarchies and constitutional republics, by which they sometimes meant to underscore the difference between states with singular/unlimited and multiple/limited "sovereigns."[3] Neither of these categorical systems is a particularly useful starting point if our intent is to describe and account for the variety of states-in-formation across the whole of Europe in the course of the sixteenth and seventeenth centuries. In the final analysis, however, the greatest difficulty in taking any of the early modern theorists as our guide is that ideological legitimations of a coercive religious or political sovereignty—whether vested in princes or lesser magistrates—usually presuppose some kind of idealized community of interest regardless of the scale and internal composition of the preferred political unit. The evidence of deep and enduring political and religious divisions among both rulers and their subjects and

---

3. Since in Anglo-American history the monarchy-republic distinction took on heavy ideological baggage in the contest between Whigs and Tories, it often clouds the very important fact that both Whigs and Tories were fighting for control of a relatively unitary "national" political space within England and Wales.

the often reluctant acceptance of variously segmented and divided sovereignties within the closely linked structures and political cultures of all of Europe's *new* regimes, I suggest, belie that most fundamental of assumptions.

Here we will take as our point of departure the empirical observation with which we began this book: at the beginning of the sixteenth century virtually all Europeans lived within composite states, which is to say, they were variously subject to the claims of a dynastic prince. As we have seen, however, a century and a half of political and religious struggle overwhelmed, at one time or another, virtually all of these late medieval composites, and the cumulative effect was nothing less than the creation of a new European regime—or, rather, a motley collection of regimes—that entailed a new set of relations between ordinary Europeans and their rulers. The purpose of this chapter is to take stock of this new regime, to underscore the role of ordinary people in the making of the European political landscape, and in general to assess the place of ordinary people in European politics at the end of the seventeenth century. This will necessarily require an interruption of the standard procedure by which, in previous chapters, we have moved from one region to another examining the contemporaneous patterns of political contention among the principal actors within composite states. Here we will explore the broad range of variation evident in early modern European state formations in the age of religious wars as a whole, paying particular attention to the variably successful alternatives to the political consolidation of dynastic princes within territorial states. Let us begin, then, with the two most famous cases of successful revolt: the Swiss Confederation and the Dutch Republic. For in the constitutions and the routine politics of the Swiss and the Dutch it was especially clear that "sovereignty" was both divisible and less than absolute.

Turning Swiss and Going Dutch

Though our standard histories of the early modern period rarely mention the political history of what today is called Switzerland, the Swiss were certainly a prominent feature of European politics and political culture in this period—and not merely as the purveyors of high-quality mercenary soldiers. As I noted in chapter 2, the Swiss Confederation (Eidgenossenschaft) had defeated the formidable armies of

Emperor Maximilian I in 1499 and thereby seemed to secure their de facto independence and the principle of communal self-governance for the foreseeable future (Bonjour, Offler, and Potter 1952; Peyer 1978). It was against the backdrop of this relatively recent history, then, that the idea or threat of "turning Swiss" became an important element of south German affairs prior to and during the Revolution of 1525. Though in retrospect it seems as if the possibility of a thoroughgoing "Swissification" of southern Germany or the Austrian Tyrol was quite remote—Swabian cities were deeply frightened by the rural revolution of 1525—"the Confederation nonetheless continued to play the role of countermodel, a standing reminder to the lords of why they supported the king or the prince and to the subjects that lordship was not necessarily God's eternal ordinance for the world" (Brady 1985:42).

Swiss history could be interpreted in different ways, not only because of the differing perspectives of subjects and rulers, but because there were clearly different ways of "turning Swiss." At the beginning of the sixteenth century the Confederation itself was a composite of twelve distinctive units (the thirteenth and last of the early modern cantons, Appenzell, was added in 1512) ranging from the original forest cantons of Uri, Schwytz, and Unterwalden to powerful city-states like Bern and Zürich. In addition, in the late fifteenth century and the early part of the sixteenth century, a broad stretch of mostly rural Alpine communes to the southeast of the Confederation successfully resisted their feudal overlords and coalesced into the Freestate of the Three Leagues, or Graubünden (Grisons). Often allied with the Confederation but politically separate from it, Graubünden not only represented a different form of confederation—that is, a varied set of communal leagues within a league—it retained remarkably direct forms of popular political participation and an often vengeful popular "justice" for allegedly corrupt officials, which is what many of Europe's rulers may have feared most when they worried that their subjects might turn Swiss.[4] In the 1520s, moreover, the prince-bishopric of Geneva shed itself of its feudal overlord as a preliminary to reforming its religious institutions; henceforth, the Republic of Geneva depended on external protection, especially from Bern, but nevertheless managed to go it alone as a self-governing

4. Jean Bodin, in the Six Books of a Commonweale, not only highlights the extent of popular sovereignty in Graubünden (Grisons) but also contrasts its politics with the more oligarchical confederation. See Head 1995 for an account of the evolution of politics and political culture in Graubünden, from medieval lordships to self-governing and eventually oligarchical communal leagues.

city-state with enormous influence in the cultural politics of the Second Reformation (Monter 1967; Kingdon 1974).

It is thus not immediately clear which political model the judges of the Parlement of Aix-en-Provence had in mind in the 1540s when they ordered the destruction of "Waldensian" villages under their jurisdiction for fear that they might "turn Swiss" (Cameron 1984); nor is it obvious what the peasant leagues of Dauphiné and Guyenne intended when they threatened to "turn Swiss" in the course of the French wars of religion (Hickey 1986; Bercé 1990). At the very least, turning Swiss meant the rejection or expulsion of feudal or dynastic overlordship and, consequently, the local consolidation of political authority or sovereignty.[5] The precise character of this local consolidation of power varied considerably both across the territory of modern-day Switzerland and over time. Yet we can safely assume that except for the Alpine communes where there was at least transient evidence of "popular sovereignty" that might serve as an inspiration, if not a model, for rebellious subjects elsewhere in Europe, the most obvious political models that were reflected in the constituent cantons of the Swiss Confederation and the independent city-state of Geneva were oligarchic rather than democratic.

In the second half of the sixteenth century the United Provinces of the Northern Netherlands emerged alongside the Swiss Confederation as another well-known example of the successful rejection of dynastic overlordship. It is unlikely that anyone in the early modern period ever used the opprobrious English colloquialism "going Dutch" (or "Dutch treat," to which it is closely related) to conjure up the political lessons of the Dutch example. Still, this expression does suggest, with its emphasis on individual self-sufficiency in the context of collective effort, some of the import of Dutch political experience. The independence of the United Provinces, as we have seen in chapter 3, was the initially unintended consequence of the long struggle between the kings of Spain and their rebellious Netherlandic subjects in the peculiar context of the Second Reformation. Eventually, the Union of Utrecht, which bound its signatories to a permanent defensive alliance, served as the principal constitution of this new polity and set the framework for political and economic

---

5. It is perhaps important to note that the forceful rejection of feudal overlordship was not peculiar to the Swiss alps; see Te Brake 1993 and Urban 1991 for the coastal examples of Flanders and Dithmarschen in the late Middle Ages. What still distinguishes the Swiss in this company is their ability to remain independent in the long term.

interaction among provinces, and within them cities, that were largely self-governing (Te Brake 1992; 't Hart 1993).

Dutch history could also be read in a variety of ways reflecting not only the different perspectives of subjects and rulers but also the variant forms of political organization that were preserved within the constituent parts of the larger confederation. Despite enormous variations in the structures of provincial power, outside observers frequently confused the important province of Holland with the whole of the United Provinces and were thus generally impressed with the power of its urban magistrates or "regents" (see, e.g., Temple 1972). In doing so they overlooked the entrenched power of the local nobility in the eastern provinces and the remarkably participatory politics of rural smallholders in the northeast (Te Brake 1992). Still they rarely mistook the general lessons of the Dutch Revolt. According to J. V. Polisensky (1971), at the turn of the seventeenth century the "Dutch question" divided the whole of Christian Europe between the resurgent and increasingly confident forces of Catholic counterreform and a complex network of Protestant polities; indeed, to the Bohemians on the eve of the Thirty Years' War, Polisensky suggests, the "liberated Netherlands" was already the international symbol of opposition to the Habsburgs in general and to the "universal monarchy" that Spain in particular seemed to represent. Even the anonymous pamphleteer in Naples in 1647, who spoke mistakenly of the "provinces of Flanders," understood that the cutting edge of the history of the Dutch Revolt was the expulsion of its feudal overlord or "prince" (see chap. 4).

Taken together, then, "turning Swiss" and "going Dutch" may be said to have symbolized the local consolidation of power at the expense of feudal overlords. As we have seen throughout this work, the formation of leagues or confederations in defense of common political interests vis-à-vis aggressive princes was characteristic of large-scale conflicts in very diverse settings, from the urban Comuneros of Castile to the peasant leagues of rural Germany and France, from the League of Schmalkalden in Germany and the Huguenot and Catholic leagues in France to the Covenanters of Scotland and the Confederates of Ireland. Such leagues or alliances were typically brokered by the local leaders of insurrectionary movements within previously constituted political units with long histories of self-regulation—units that were capable not only of local self-government but also of mobilizing at the local level the wherewithal of a collective defense. Of course, most of these largely defensive unions did not survive in the long run, but when they did, the Dutch and Swiss cases suggest, the historical experience of often "heroic" collective efforts became deeply embedded in the political culture of the resulting confederations. Thus, even though the most obvious principle of political organization implied by "turning Swiss" and "going Dutch" was local self-government or the local consolidation of power, the confederations continued to exist not merely as defensive alliances but as the arbiters of local conflict when the failure of local self-regulation might threaten the perceived interests of the whole.

It is nevertheless important to recognize differences between the Swiss and Dutch confederations as regards their role in European affairs more generally. In the Swiss Confederation a defensive alliance against a variety of feudal overlords obviously preserved the self-regulation of previously and distinctly constituted cantons, but during the sixteenth century the confederation as a whole was too riven by religious and political differences (Gordon 1992; Greyerz 1994) to be able to participate fully in European affairs, especially as a war-making power. The most obvious difficulty was that, having agreed to accept religious differences between the cantons, the leaders of the confederation found it virtually impossible to formulate a common foreign policy in a religiously polarized Europe. Likewise, the Republic of Geneva was too dependent on external protection and the Graubünden were too much the object of diplomatic intrigue and too vulnerable to official corruption and bribes to be a potent force in European affairs. By contrast, the defensive alliance of the Union of Utrecht, which prescribed a "national" accommodation of religious difference while preserving the "sovereignty" of its signatories, proved to be an effective and fairly reliable vehicle for the protection and advancement of Dutch commercial interests on a worldwide scale.[6] Indeed, the Dutch Republic emerged as one of Europe's most bellicose polities in the second half of the seventeenth century while the Swiss retreated from direct involvement in European affairs (Tilly 1990).

Inasmuch as the resisters of princely "tyranny" typically claimed only to be defending traditional political practices, we should perhaps regard the negotiation of formal limitations on the prince's sovereignty—as opposed to his elimination altogether—as the more logical outcome of a

---

6. See 't Hart 1993. The most obvious exception to this rule was the political crisis that erupted during the truce with Spain (1609–1621); in this case, Prince Maurits, who opposed the commercial interests in Holland that had supported the truce, exploited religious divisions within the Reformed church to defeat his political enemies and restart the war.

"successful" opposition to princely consolidation. It was, in any case, the more common outcome, although this, too, took a variety of forms. The fundamental limitation of the prince's sovereignty as a consequence of local and regional resistance was especially evident in the principality of Catalonia in the second half of the seventeenth century. There, the king of Spain was forced, after years of costly struggle that included the temporary loss of Catalonia to France, to reaffirm the long-standing privileges of this essentially peripheral province, treating it by decidedly different rules than its Castilian core. Indeed, the status of Catalonia may be considered analogous to that of the provinces of the southern Netherlands, which continued to enjoy a separate status guaranteed to them since the Treaty of Arras (1579) in return for their loyalty to the king of Spain in his war against the north and for their acceptance of the religious monopoly of the Catholic church. In cases like these the prince's sovereignty was profoundly limited by local legal jurisdictions, traditions of self-regulation, and the ongoing obligation to negotiate with local rulers all contributions to the general fisc, especially those contributions to underwrite the escalating cost of military operations. This formal consolidation of elite power in terms of the confirmation of geographically segmented provincial privileges implied the multiplication of political spaces to match the complex multiplication of distinctive and often competitive rulers; in fact, this constellation of power often consolidated the authority of both municipal (or communal) and provincial "sovereigns" vis-à-vis their local subjects as well as the distant overlord, who served as the guarantors of their local authority in return for the payment of tribute.

In the end the most obvious and significant case of the formal limitation of the putative sovereign was the German-Roman Empire because of its broad implications for virtually all of central Europe. Despite his best efforts from the Diet of Worms onward, Charles V was not able to enforce his claim to religious sovereignty within the empire either by persuasion or by war; indeed, the alternative claim to cultural sovereignty by his nominal subordinates in the newly Protestant principalities and free cities of the empire was institutionalized by the Peace of Augsburg (1555) when the principle of *cuius regio eius religio* was applied to the constituent parts of the empire rather than to the empire as a whole. Even so, the question of political and cultural sovereignty within the empire was highly contested through the end of the Thirty Years' War, both from below—as territorial cities claimed the right of reformation at the expense of *their* immediate overlords—and from above—as the emperor demanded the restoration of land seized from the Catholic church or claimed the right to negotiate an end to the Thirty Years' War in the name of the empire as a whole (cf. Hughes 1992). In the end, however, the imperial claims were simply unenforceable, and in 1648 the Peace of Westphalia permanently divided and layered the sovereignty of the empire.

A comprehensive peace conference among the great powers of Europe to bring an end to the Thirty Years' War had first been proposed in 1641, but by the time the negotiations were concluded, representatives from approximately one hundred fifty interested parties, not all of them great powers, had sent official emissaries to take part in the negotiations. Not surprisingly, a peace settlement involving that many parties necessitated more than one treaty: besides the separate treaty ending the Eighty Years' War between Spain and the Dutch Republic, there were two different treaties between the emperor and the estates of the empire with France (signed at the Catholic city of Münster) and with Sweden (signed at the Protestant city of Osnabrück). Except for some relatively minor boundary adjustments, this comprehensive agreement served primarily to consolidate political transformations within central Europe that had been forged in the course of nearly one hundred fifty years of intermittent struggle. As Richard Bonney sums it up,

The Peace clarified the relative positions of the participants in the Imperial constitution, and removed the pre-eminence of the Habsburg dynasty in Germany. Henceforth, it would be possible to view the Emperor as acting against as well as for the interests of the Empire, which was taken to be synonymous with the "Imperial Estates"—that is to say, the electors, princes and free cities represented in the diet. All princes were accorded "territorial superiority" (but not sovereignty, an important distinction) "in matters ecclesiastical as well as political." (1991:200–201)

Not only did the princes of Germany gain the right to conduct their own foreign policies, provided these were not directed against the empire, but the emperor had to cede to the Imperial Diet the right of declaring war and negotiating peace.

Although the Peace of Westphalia virtually eliminated the empire as a war-making power because of the requirement of consensus within the Imperial Diet for the declaration of war,[7] it nevertheless confirmed the important judicial functions—especially those regarding the mediation

7. This is not to say, of course, that the Austrian Habsburgs were no longer involved in

of internal conflict within the constituent units of the empire—that had accrued to a variety of imperial institutions since the late Middle Ages (Hughes 1992). The result, as many German scholars suggest, was an "open constitution" of government in which the general "juridification" of political conflicts within the empire both guaranteed the self-regulation and channeled the subsequent development of its constituent parts (Walker 1971; Vann 1986; Mörke 1995). Not unlike the Dutch and the Swiss, then, the ordinary political actors of the German-Roman Empire inhabited variously constituted political spaces as subjects of both local rulers and imperial powerholders, but in configurations and under constitutional limitations that were decidedly new.

Altogether, the two branches of the Habsburg family—the most successful of late medieval dynasties, whose composite state at its height under Charles V stretched from the Baltic and North seas to the Mediterranean and Atlantic—had by the middle of the seventeenth century suffered a remarkable series of political setbacks and been forced to accept a broad range of initially unacceptable compromises of their claims to sovereign authority. It was not their dynasticism, as such, that brought these princes to grief but more specifically their aggressive attempts to consolidate new kinds of sovereign authority within their existing domains—especially with regard to religion, public welfare, and taxation—that occasioned the most comprehensive and potent alliances in opposition to them. The political action of ordinary people, I have argued, is critical to our understanding of these political developments even when the prince's long-term survival entailed an accommodation with local rulers at the apparent expense of popular political actors. The simple reason is that the most forceful resistance to princely consolidation inevitably came from informal and often transient alliances that brought local rulers together with popular mobilizations in a common defense of the "privileges" of the local polity. What is more, in all the cases we have examined here—from the imperial cities of Germany to the provincial capitals of the Spanish Mediterranean—it took popular initiative at the local level to overcome the initial hesitation of local rulers to oppose their princely overlords, and it required popular mobilization in defense of local self-determination to mount a challenge serious enough to force aggressive princes to compromise with local rulers and to accept constitutional limitations as the price of their survival.

---

military affairs of Europe; rather, it was as kings of Austria and Hungary, not as emperors, that they declared war or concluded peace and extracted the means of making war.

The Ongoing Formation of Composite States

There is, of course, a very real danger in overstating the case. By focusing on the relative success of local oppositions to princely consolidation, rooted in popular political action, we might well overlook or underestimate the relative success of territorial consolidation in other parts of Europe. To be sure, in this context and from the perspective of popular political action, even the classic cases of England and France seem like less than ideal examples of the "absolute" sovereignty of political theory or the paradigmatic and unilinear "state formation" of traditional historiography. In the British Isles, as we have seen, the Restoration had by 1660 brought back the distinctive features of a composite state in which the same monarch claimed a variously limited sovereignty over three previously constituted kingdoms, while in France, in the wake of the Fronde, the reconstruction of the monarchy under Louis XIV was clearly predicated on a whole series of piecemeal bargains that variously confirmed the distinctive "privileges" of local elites in many parts of the realm. The most obvious result was that even the most powerful survivors of the seventeenth-century crisis of princely power still betrayed their origins as composite states. For our purposes in describing and accounting for the whole range of states-in-formation within the new European regime, however, it is just as important to describe and account for the limited success of territorial state makers as it is to understand the principal alternatives to consolidation of territorial sovereignties.

To begin, it is important to distinguish the two dimensions of early modern state formation: the accumulation of power through the acquisition of new territory as opposed to the consolidation of power through the appropriation of new authority (see fig. 1). In at least two prominent cases the clusters of conflict we have studied involved the dismantling rather than the extension of composite states: in the north, the Union of Scandinavian Kingdoms disappeared altogether during the early years of the Reformation, and the Spanish Habsburg domain was seriously scaled back with the loss of both the northern Netherlands and the kingdom of Portugal. Still, the process of dynastic state formation continued to add new territories to existing domains, especially on the eastern frontiers of Latin Christendom. In 1569, for example, the Union of Lublin formalized the voluntary conjunction of the kingdoms of Poland and Lithuania to create one of Europe's most extensive polities (Dembkowski 1982;

Fedorowics 1982). Meanwhile, a more coercive dynasticism was evident in the intermittent expansions of Muscovy and the Ottoman Empire throughout this period (Tilly 1990). But even in western and central Europe there were still limited opportunities for territorial expansion. In the course of the sixteenth century, for example, the kings of England finally made good their claims over the kingdom of Ireland, and at the beginning of the seventeenth century the Stuart kings of Scotland laid claim to the royal succession in England. Across the North Sea, Charles V significantly expanded his Low Countries domain—he added seven provinces between 1521 and 1543—before his successors lost most of these new acquisitions during the Eighty Years' War (Parker 1985). South of the Alps, foreign intervention during the Italian Wars incorporated Savoy, Piedmont, and Milan into the larger French and Spanish composites. At the same time, however, the larger regional powers of northern Italy—especially Florence (Tuscany), Venice, and Rome (the papacy)—also grew at the expense of their smaller neighbors (Guarini 1995), and in the later stages of the Dutch Revolt, the Dutch Republic added sections of Flanders, Brabant, and Limburg to its domain (Israel 1995). Finally, at the end of the Thirty Years' War, Sweden and France are often said to have been the principal beneficiaries of the Peace of Westphalia inasmuch as they augmented their authority in western Pomerania and the bishoprics of Bremen and Verden and in Alsace and Lorraine, respectively, but in light of the massive cost and destructiveness of this war, these seem like relatively minor adjustments.

In other words, it may even be said that Europe's most successful state makers continued to increase their power the old-fashioned "dynastic" way: by adding new territory to their existing domains. Although the pace of acquisition was not as fast and as furious as it had been during the fourteenth and fifteenth centuries, it is clear that the augmentation of existing composites states remained an important feature of European politics. Two new dimensions of the process during the early modern period stand out, however. First, as the expansion of the Dutch and Venetian republics suggests, with the formal elimination of feudal over-lords in some parts of Europe, the makers of composite states were not necessarily dynastic princes or their agents.[8] Second, as increasingly stable and defensible boundaries within Europe offered greatly diminished

---

8. Just as the Dutch provinces ruled their Generality Lands collectively through the Estates General, so too did the Swiss cantons rule collectively over the Mandated Territories and the Graubünden over the Valtellina; see Peyer 1978; Price 1994; Head 1995.

opportunities for territorial expansion, Europe's most ambitious state makers clearly exported their competition for power, in the form of colonization and monopolized trade, to Asia and the New World. Even with these innovations, those who augmented their power by adding new territories to their composite states—whether they were princes or not—appear to have been most successful when they were old-fashioned and Machiavellian in the very specific sense that they resisted the temptation to consolidate their direct control over populations that "have been accustomed to living under their own laws"; rather, in the short term at least, they generally aligned themselves selectively with indigenous elites and accepted a variety of forms of indirect rule.

Since such limited bargains among different kinds of rulers rarely awakened either popular opposition or popular approval, this dimension of the process of composite state formation has been largely invisible in our focus on the interactions of subjects and rulers within specific political spaces. This important dimension of ongoing transformation of composite states is nevertheless relevant to our analysis for at least two reasons. First, when it was successful, territorial expansion might serve to stabilize or even reduce the ruler's claims on the resources of his subjects in other parts of the composite; by the same token, of course, failure to make significant territorial gains in the course of increasingly expensive and destructive war making repeatedly troubled the relations between the rulers of composite states and virtually all of their very diverse subjects.[9] In addition, in augmenting their power through territorial (including colonial) acquisitions, Europe's composite state makers were willy-nilly increasing the difficulties of their rule and complicating the microgeography of their composites. This is particularly important for our analysis because, as we have seen throughout this work, instability, protest, and crisis in one part of a composite state necessarily alter the structures of political opportunity, often in favor of popular political actors, in the rest of the domain. In short, the benefits of new resources that might result from territorial acquisitions could easily be offset by an increased vulnerability to political challenge.

Against the backdrop of this ongoing, if limited, "dynasticism" within western and central Europe, we are now in a position to formulate a broadly comparative answer to the more specific problem of the consol-

---

9. In the long run what might be most troubling is the fact that the costs of dynastic aggression and empire building could easily outstrip the benefits.

idation of power within territorial states.[10] Using the terminology suggested by figure 2, we need to ask more precisely where, and under what conditions, national claimants to power were able to appropriate new (and more direct) forms of sovereign authority at the expense of local rulers. In the first phase of the Reformation, we saw that ambitious princes were able to enforce their unprecedented claims to a *national* cultural sovereignty primarily in Denmark, Sweden, and England and under two important but relatively unusual conditions. In all three cases the putative sovereigns were bold enough to align themselves selectively with the zealous proponents of religious reform, even though they might as a consequence be confronted with equally zealous opponents of Protestant reform. But at the same time they had the peculiar, if transient and unintended, fortune of ruling relatively small or compact domains by comparison with both their predecessors and their more powerful Habsburg and Valois counterparts. Neither Frederick I, Gustav Vasa, and Henry VIII nor their immediate successors would succeed in establishing *national* religious monopolies without a complex and truly dangerous struggle, but the struggle itself served to confirm the notion that in these places problems of religious division and conflict were susceptible of, indeed required, comprehensive national solutions. By comparison, neither Charles V nor Francis I, who chose instead to defend Catholic orthodoxy, was able to stem a rising tide of Protestant dissent even at the centers of their more extensive domains.

During the second phase of the Protestant Reformation, we saw that in the face of an ongoing and violent repression of religious dissent, secret networks of underground churches, nourished by international leadership and support, seized on transient political uncertainties in both France and the Low Countries and joined with dissident elites to make forceful claims to both political and religious sovereignty on a *national* scale. Subsequently, in the course of very costly and often traumatic civil wars, Henry IV of France and Philip II of Spain were able to make good their claims to cultural sovereignty only under two somewhat different conditions. In France reconstruction of the territorial state after the depredations of the civil wars was predicated on Henry IV's willingness and abil-

10. Unfortunately, this comparatively narrow perspective and theoretically limited question, which masks the teleology of "modern" or "national" state formation, is still the exclusive focus of social scientific debates on European political development; see, e.g., Ertman 1997.

ity to tap the resurgent and well-organized popular piety of Counter-Reformation Catholicism at the core of his domain and to accept profound limitations on both his political and cultural sovereignty in the Huguenot strongholds on the southern and western peripheries of his extensive domain. In the Low Countries, by contrast, Philip II's adamant refusal to accept any compromises of his claim to cultural sovereignty cost him the permanent political separation of the rebellious provinces of the northern periphery and even the formal limitation of his political sovereignty in the southern core provinces of his now-restricted domain.

During the escalating political Crisis of the Seventeenth Century we saw that the eventual survival of the embattled princes of western and central Europe generally came at the expense of their most aggressive claims to cultural and political sovereignty on a *national* scale. In Spain the king's attempts to extract more resources to support his far-flung war-making efforts precipitated a series of locally potent revolutions in peripheral provinces in both Iberia and Italy which, taken together, soundly defeated the king's claims to a new kind of territorial sovereignty. But in France and Britain locally powerful opposition to the extension of the king's fiscal or cultural sovereignty that began on the peripheries helped to precipitate direct challenges at the center of these composites as well. In France the regency government alternately deflected and compromised with its myriad enemies until the crisis had passed, but in Britain a less compromising monarch enjoyed sufficient popular support at the core of his domain in England to dare to attempt to defeat his enemies altogether. When Charles was himself defeated, however, the victorious Oliver Cromwell skillfully used his selective alignment with zealous and well-organized "Puritans," not to dismantle, but to consolidate the political authority of the territorial state first within England and then more generally in Ireland and Scotland. Meanwhile, amid the anarchy and massive destruction of the Thirty Years' War, the Austrian Habsburgs were forced to accept the virtual extinction of their sovereign authority as emperors, but on a much more modest scale in their patrimonial lands and in Bohemia—that is, at the core of their domain—they were able to align themselves with the resurgent forces of Counter-Reformation Catholicism to enforce their previously unenforceable claim to cultural sovereignty over religiously divided territories. By contrast, William II failed to win even a modest share of formal authority within the Dutch Republic when he failed to win popular support in his effort to unseat his opponents in local and provincial government.

In short, I have argued that popular political action, in particular at the core of a more extensive composite state, was a critical element—the sine qua non of princely success—in each of these specific cases where "princes" were able to enforce or consolidate new claims to territorial power at the expense of local rulers. Both the spatial and the cultural dimensions of this argument are critical. On the one hand, within the microgeography of composite states, popular political engagement away from the centers of territorial power generally tended toward local consolidations of power even if the leaders of such movements aspired to national power. On the other hand, such alignments between national claimants and ordinary people at the core of composite states were relatively rare for perhaps self-evident cultural reasons: on the side of the rulers, many claimants to national power were reluctant to admit, if not viscerally opposed to, such radical realignments of their political attitudes toward their subjects; on the side of their subjects, it was inevitably a hard sell to champion a dramatic increase in the authority of territorial rulers, especially among those who would be most directly subject to that authority.[11] Not surprisingly, however, in this age of religious wars, it was the common bond of religious ideology and the institutionalized solidarity of underground churches and religious confraternities that facilitated and sustained the most successful of these relatively rare political coalitions and thus laid the foundations of enforceable territorial sovereignties, albeit within relatively circumscribed domains.

Ordinary People in European Politics (ca. 1700)

In the second half of the seventeenth century, then, one can safely say that while all of the polities that constituted the new European regime still betrayed their late medieval origins as or within composite states, they were nevertheless moving in fundamentally different directions. Going beyond teleological accounts of "national" state formation, which often boil down to retrospective institutional

11. Once this alignment had been realized at the core of a composite state, it may be that national claimants could more easily invoke it vis-à-vis challengers or "rebels" on the periphery. Though this may very well have been the case under Oliver Cromwell in England, it is more commonly evident after the 1650s than it was before.

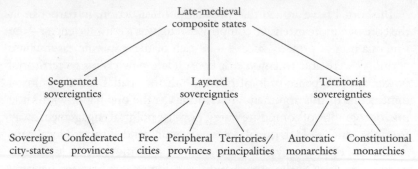

Figure 12. Trajectories of political change in Europe (1500–1700)

analyses of the most militarily competitive states, my purpose has been to describe and account for the broad variety of interactions of subjects and rulers over relatively long stretches of time. Consequently I have tried to comprehend as well the consolidation of political and cultural sovereignty in the hands of rulers who did not necessarily claim the authority to mobilize armies, declare war, or negotiate peace.[12] In conclusion, figure 12 presents a visual summary of this account of the divergent paths of political development in early modern Europe. In its general outline, this figure suggests not only a common point of origin in the composite states of late medieval Europe but also simultaneous movement in three different directions; moreover, it describes the political outcomes in terms of the principal arenas for interaction between rulers and subjects rather than as idealized Weberian states.

On the left side, figure 12 suggests that in those places where the composite state maker was eliminated altogether, we can clearly see the consolidation of geographically segmented local sovereignties as a consequence of political alignments between local rulers and ordinary political subjects (fig. 2a). These segmented sovereignties might take the form of either city-states like Venice or Geneva (with or without extensive hinterlands) or confederated provinces like the Swiss Confederation and the Dutch Republic (with or without conquered territories or colonies ruled collectively by the confederation). These may usefully be considered seg-

12. While it was often true that war making and state making went hand in hand in the very real sense that the conflicts we have studied here were adjudicated by force of arms, the failure of princely war makers to enforce their most aggressive claims for cultural and political sovereignty—including the authority to make war—should not be taken to imply the absence of historically significant state and political-cultural formation.

mented states in the very real sense that the heroic defense of local self-regulation in the face of princely "tyranny" imposed significant polit-ical-cultural limits on the legitimacy of rulers in these polities and ensured the primacy of relatively small political spaces like provinces and cantons or even, within them, autonomous cities and communes. To the extent that war making remained a significant activity of segmented states, the authority to declare war and ratify peace treaties was shared by a relatively large number of essentially local rulers.

At the other extreme, figure 12 suggests that where "princes" suc-ceeded in subordinating cities and constituent territories to more or less direct forms of political and cultural authority (usually at the core of their patrimonial lands), we can discern the consolidation of territorial sover-eignties as a consequence of alignments between national claimants to power and ordinary political subjects (fig. 2c). These territorial sover-eignties might take the form of either autocratic monarchies, as in the core provinces of France and Spain (in which elite competitors for power were co-opted by guarantees of elite privilege), or constitutional monar-chies, like England and Sweden (in which political competitors bar-gained for an active stake in the exercise of the territorial sovereignty). These may be considered territorial states in the sense that decision mak-ing at the center affected the entire territory even though the bureaucratic ideal of uniform execution might in practice be mediated and deflected by elite patronage, local advocacy, and the expedients of indirect rule. Within these territorial states, princes invariably claimed "absolute" sov-ereignty with regard to their war-making activities, but the specific con-ditions under which these princes might mobilize the resources for mak-ing war were generally the cutting edge of the political difference between autocratic and constitutional regimes.

Between these two poles, figure 12 suggests that where dynastic princes were neither eliminated nor triumphant, we can discern the con-solidation of formally layered sovereignties in which the powerful rulers of free cities, peripheral provinces, and subordinate territories or princi-palities stood in a variety of complex juxtapositions with imperial or monarchical authorities as a consequence of political alignments between local rulers and national claimants to power. In these political forma-tions, which included long-standing peripheral provinces like Catalonia or the provinces of the southern Netherlands as well as newly acquired colonies and the constituent parts of the German Empire, locally seg-mented jurisdictions remained the primary arena for political interaction between subjects and rulers, but the formal, if distant, retention of royal or imperial sovereignty both opened up opportunities and imposed significant limits on all political actors and thus routinely shaped the relationships between local rulers and their subjects. On the face of it, these formally layered sovereignties might bear the closest constitutional resemblance to the dynastic configurations of old, but the historical experience of often violent conflict over the allocation of political and cultural sovereignty within them had resulted in a new level of political-cultural precision regarding the limits of legitimate rule and popular political action.

Since the primary purpose of figure 12 is to encompass the wide variety of arenas within which ordinary people engaged in politics, it does not serve well as a catalog of Europe's most influential rulers or of the "states" they ruled. In fact, given the complexity of composite state formation, some of Europe's most prominent individual rulers were deeply frustrated by the multiplicity of the political roles they were required to play. Thus, in the 1660s, Charles II ruled England and Wales, Scotland, Ireland, and his newly chartered North American colonies under decidedly different rules, and Louis XIV not only agreed to respect the differences between pays d'état and pays d'élection but also accepted even greater limitations on his political and cultural sovereignty in newly acquired territories like Alsace and Lorraine where he might not even be identified as king. Likewise, both branches of the Habsburg dynasty ruled far more directly over their patrimonial domains or core principalities than their much more extensive empires. By contrast, the most effective *national* leaders of segmented states, such as the Dutch Republic, were not "sovereigns" in their own right but political brokers whose leadership depended on their ability to form and manipulate informal patronage networks and alliances among fundamentally local sovereigns.

Altogether, then, the various political configurations listed at the bottom of figure 12 may be considered the residue of some one hundred fifty years of often violent political interaction between subjects and rulers; at the same time they set the parameters of political development under the new regime. For the next century or more—from the 1660s to the 1790s—the international boundaries of Europe's principal states remained remarkably stable despite the prevalence of war among the "great" powers of Europe. Indeed, the aggregate stability of the political boundaries established by the Peace of Westphalia, more than anything else, is what lends a retrospective credibility to the notion that this had become, by the end of the eighteenth century, an ancien régime. This is not to say that the new European regime was the final outcome of a century and a half of crisis. On the contrary, what is important to remember about the political configurations at the bottom of figure 12 is that none was at some point in time a fait accompli; each represents, instead, a transient outcome within an ongoing political process—for us, an indicator of a trajectory of political change that was continually subject to bargaining between rulers and subjects with regard to both governmental policy and the general rules of political interaction (see fig. 3).

Consequently, the history of the second half of the seventeenth century is replete with conflicts and struggles that suggest Europe's new regime was no more than a new set of parameters within which subjects and rulers would continue to negotiate not only the particulars of governmental policy but also the very definition of political and cultural sovereignty. Consider the following, for example. In Switzerland in 1653, amid the collapse of the wartime economy that had been stimulated by the profitable transit trade across the Alps, a massive peasant revolt in the geographic heartland of confederation temporarily displaced local rulers in large areas of the countryside and required an equally massive collaboration among the Swiss cantons to restore the ruling oligarchies (Suter 1995, 1997). In the Dutch Republic in 1672, amid the general crisis occasioned by simultaneous military offensives by France, England, Münster, and Cologne, ordinary people in the cities of Holland and Zeeland took forceful, sometimes gruesome, action to "restore" the House of Orange to its important leadership role and to secure the simultaneous appointment of William III as provincial stadhouder and as captain-general of the republic's armed forces (Roorda 1978; Israel 1995). In France in 1685, Louis XIV, having deliberately aligned himself with the popular piety and official orthodoxy of the Counter-Reformation church to put increased pressure on the stubbornly independent Huguenot minority, boldly reasserted the French monarchy's claim to territorial sovereignty over matters of religious conscience by revoking the Edict of Nantes, thereby precipitating yet another massive flow of Protestant refugees and eventually the last of Europe's major religious wars against the Camisards of the Cévennes (Garrisson 1985; Joutard 1994; Collins 1995). In Great Britain in 1688, amid the political confusion created by the stubborn Catholicism of James II, a parliamentary faction joined forces with William III of Orange and Mary, James's daughter, to drive yet another Stuart king from power in England and, in the process of defeating him militarily, not only consolidated more direct English control over Ireland but also called into being a new kind of "Jacobite" political opposition (Clifton 1984; McLynn 1985; Grell, Israel, and Tyacke 1991).

These episodes are only some of the more dramatic pieces of evidence that the shape of political authority was still very much subject to negotiation in post-Westphalian Europe. Each of them deserves careful historical reconstruction in its own right, and, in fact, each has received the kind of special treatment that is given to pivotal events in a particular *national* history. But it is also important to locate them, alongside the countless other interactions of a less spectacular nature or in more peripheral locations, in the broader comparative context of clearly divergent paths of state formation that we have identified here as the touchstone of European political development in the early modern period. For from this broader comparative perspective, it is especially clear that, having variously challenged the claims and broken open the exclusive political domains of their rulers, ordinary political subjects across the length and breadth of Europe had entered into the political process that continued to shape Europe's peculiar system of militarily competitive states.

Of course, there is so much more that can be said about this political process and about the history of popular politics in particular. In fact, some readers may be frustrated that this book has done little to illustrate how specific changes in the trajectories of state and political-cultural development influenced the broad environmental conditions that, as figure 3 suggests, helped to configure political interaction in other times and places. Or how in specific polities, all political actors, rulers and subjects alike, were forced to adapt to changing circumstances and thus, through the intangibles of creative invention and trial and error, learn how to do politics in new ways. Or how these changes in the repertoires of political interaction might be said to have transcended the boundaries of particular political spaces and constituted regional or even continental changes in the patterns of political contention as such. These are, indeed, questions that may be considered particularly salient to the understanding of the history of European politics as a consequence of the work that I have tried to synthesize here. My more specific goal in this work has been to demonstrate that by focusing on the interactions of rulers and subjects as the heart of political history, we will finally be able to move beyond both elite-centered and structurally determined accounts of European political development. If I have succeeded in that task, it may be that ordinary people will have finally broken through the barriers of traditional scholarship and entered, once and for all, our understanding of the mainstream of political history.

References

Abray, L. J.
   1985.   *The People's Reformation: Magistrates, Clergy and Commons in Stras-bourg, 1500–1598.* Ithaca: Cornell University Press.
Althusius, Johannes.
   [1614]   *The Politics of Johannes Althusius.* Trans. and ed. Frederick S.
   1964.   Carney. London: Eyre & Spottiswoode.
Ashton, T., ed.
   1965.   *Crisis in Europe, 1560–1660.* New York: Basic Books.
Audisio, Gabriel.
   1984.   *Les Vaudois de Luberon: Une minorité de Provence, 1460–1560.* Gap: Mérindol.
Aya, Rod.
   1990.   *Rethinking Revolutions and Collective Violence: Studies on Concept, Theory, and Method.* Amsterdam: Het Spinhuis.
Bak, Janos, ed.
   1975.   *The German Peasant War of 1525.* London: F. Cass.
Bak, Janos M., and Gerhard Benecke, eds.
   1984.   *Religion and Rural Revolt: Papers Presented to the Fourth Interdisci-plinary Workshop on Peasant Studies, University of British Columbia, 1982.* Manchester: University of Manchester Press.
Beik, William.
   1997.   *Urban Protest in Seventeenth-Century France: The Culture of Retri-bution.* Cambridge: Cambridge University Press.
Benedict, Philip.
   1978.   "The Saint Bartholemew's Massacres in the Provinces." *Historical Journal* 21:205–225.
——.
   1979.   "The Catholic Response to Protestantism: Church Activity and Popular Piety in Rouen, 1560–1600." *In Religion and the People,*

189

800–1700, ed. James Obelkevich, 168–190. Chapel Hill: University of North Carolina Press.

———.

1981.   *Rouen during the Wars of Religion.* Cambridge: Cambridge University Press.

Bercé, Yves-Marie.

1987.   *Revolt and Revolution in Early Modern Europe: An Essay on the History of Political Violence.* New York: St. Martin's Press.

———.

1990.   *History of Peasant Revolts.* Trans. Amanda Whitmore. Ithaca: Cornell University Press.

Birnstiel, Eckart.

1985.   *Die Fronde in Bordeaux, 1648–1653.* Frankfurt am Main: P. Lang.

Blickle, Peter.

1979.   "Peasant Revolts in the German Empire in the Late Middle Ages." *Social History* 4:223–239.

———.

1981.   *The Revolution of 1525: The German Peasants' War from a New Perspective.* Trans. Thomas A. Brady and H.C. Erik Midelfort. Baltimore: Johns Hopkins University Press.

———.

1986.   "Communalism, Parliamentarism, Republicanism." *Parliaments, Estates and Representation* 6:1–13.

———.

1992.   *Communal Reformation: The Quest for Salvation in Sixteenth-Century Germany.* Trans. Thomas Dunlap. Atlantic Highlands, N.J.: Humanities Press.

Blockmans, Wim P.

1988.   "Alternatives to Monarchical Centralisation: The Great Tradition of Revolt in Flanders and Brabant." *In Republiken und Republikanismus im Europa der frühen Neuzeit,* ed. Helmut G. Koenigsberger, 145–154. München: R. Oldenbourg Verlag.

———.

1989.   "Economische systemen en staatsvorming in pre-industrieel Europa." *NEHA Bulletin* 3:7–19.

Bodin, Jean.

[1576,   *The Six Books of a Commonweale.* Ed. and trans. Kenneth Douglas
1606]   McRae. Cambridge, Mass.: Harvard University Press.
1962.

Bonjour, E., H.S. Offler, and G.R. Potter.

1952.   *A Short History of Switzerland.* Oxford: Oxford University Press.

Bonney, Richard.

1991.   *The European Dynastic States, 1494–1660. The Short Oxford History of the Modern World.* Oxford: Oxford University Press.

Boogman, J.C.

1942.   "De overgang van Gouda, Dordrecht, Leiden en Delft in de zomer van het jaar 1572." *Tijdschrift Voor Geschiedenis* 57:81–112.

Boom, H. ten.
1987.   *De Reformatie in Rotterdam, 1530–1585.* Hollandse Historische
            Reeks, 7. N.p.: De Bataafsche Leeuw.
Boone, Marc, and Maarten Prak.
1995.   "Rulers, Patricians and Burghers: The Great and Little Traditions
            of Urban Revolt in the Low Countries." In *A Miracle Mirrored:
            The Dutch Republic in European Perspective,* ed. Karel Davids and
            Jan Lucassen, 99–134. Cambridge: Cambridge University Press.
Brady, Thomas A.
1978.   *Ruling Class, Regime and Reformation at Strasbourg, 1520–1555.* Lei-
            den: Brill.
———.
1985.   *Turning Swiss: Cities and Empire, 1450–1550.* Cambridge: Cambridge
            University Press.
———.
1991.   "Peoples' Religions in Reformation Europe." *Historical Journal*
            34:173–182.
Brandi, Karl.
[1939]   *The Emperor Charles V: The Growth and Destiny of a Man and of a*
1980.   *World-Empire.* Trans. C.V. Wedgewood. Atlantic Highlands, N.J.:
            Humanities Press.
Briggs, Robin.
1977.   *Early Modern France, 1560–1715.* Oxford: Oxford University Press.
———.
1989.   "Popular Revolt in Its Social Context." In *Communities of Belief:
            Cultural and Social Tension in Early Modern France,* 106–177.
            Oxford: Clarendon Press.
Broadhead, P.
1979.   "Popular Pressure for Reform in Augsburg, 1524–1534." In
            Stadtbürgertum und Adel in der Reformation, ed. W.J. Mommsen,
            P. Alter, and R.W. Scribner, 80–87. Stuttgart: Klett-Cotta.
———.
1980.   "Politics and Expediency in the Augsburg Reformation." In *Refor-
            mation Principle and Practice: Essays in Honour of A.G. Dickens,* ed.
            P.N. Brooks. London: Scolar Press.
———.
1984.   "Rural Revolt and Urban Betrayal in Reformation Switzerland:
            The Peasants of St. Gallen and Zwinglian Zurich." In *Religion and
            Rural Revolt: Papers Presented to the Fourth Interdisciplinary Work-
            shop on Peasant Studies, University of British Columbia, 1982,* ed.
            Janos M. Bak and Gerhard Benecke, 161–172. Manchester: Univer-
            sity of Manchester Press.
Brown, Keith M.
1992.   *Kingdom or Province? Scotland and the Regal Union, 1603–1715.*
            British History in Perspective. Houndsmills (U.K.): Macmillan.

Burke, Peter.
    1983.   "The Virgin of the Carmine and the Revolt of Masaniello." *Past and Present* 99:3–21.

    ———.

    1987.   *The Historical Anthropology of Early Modern Italy: Essays on Perception and Communication.* Cambridge: Cambridge University Press.

Cameron, Euan.
    1984.   *The Reformation of the Heretics: The Waldenes of the Alps, 1480–1580.* Oxford: Clarendon Press.

    ———.

    1991.   *The European Reformation.* Oxford: Clarendon Press.

Canny, Nicholas.
    1994.   "Irish Resistance to Empire? 1641, 1690 and 1798." In *An Imperial State at War: Britain from 1689 to 1815,* ed. Lawrence Stone, 288–321. London: Routledge.

Christin, Olivier.
    1991.   *Une révolution symbolique: l'Iconoclasm huguenot et la reconstruction catholique.* Paris: Éditions de Minuit.

    ———.

    1995.   "La coexistence confessionelle 1563–1567." *Bulletin de la Société d'histoire du Protestantisme* 141:483–504.

    ———.

    1997.   La paix de religion: L'Autonomisation de la raison politique au XVie Siècle. Collection Liber. Paris: Éditions du Seuil.

Clark, Geoffrey Whitman.
    1972.   "An Urban Study during the Revolt of the Netherlands: Valenciennes 1540–1570." Ph.D. dissertation, Columbia University.

Clarke, Aidan.
    1984.   "The Colonization of Ulster and the Rebellion of 1641 (1603–60)." In *The Course of Irish History,* ed. T.W. Moody and F.X. Martin, 189–203. Cork: Mercer Press.

Clifton, Robin.
    1984.   *The Last Popular Rebellion: The Western Rising of 1685.* New York: St. Martin's Press.

Collins, James B.
    1995.   *The State in Early Modern France. New Approaches to European History.* Cambridge: Cambridge University Press.

Collinson, Patrick.
    1982.   *The Religion of Protestants: The Church in English Society 1559–1625.* The Ford Lectures 1979. Oxford: Clarendon Press.

    ———.

    1991.   "The Cohabitation of the Faithful with the Unfaithful." In *From Persecution to Toleration: The Glorious Revolution in England,* ed. Ole Peter Grell, Jonathan Israel, and Nicholas Tyacke, 51–76. Oxford: Clarendon Press.

Cornwall, Julian.
    1977.   *Revolt of the Peasantry 1549.* London: Routledge and Kegan Paul.

Coudy, Julien, ed.
1969.   *The Huguenot Wars.* Trans. Julie Kernan. Philadelphia: Chilton.
Crew, Phyllis Mack.
1978.   *Calvinist Preaching and Iconoclasm in the Netherlands, 1544–1569.*
Cambridge: Cambridge University Press.

———.
1979.   "The Wonderyear: Reformed Preaching and Iconoclasm in the
Netherlands." In *Religion and the People, 800–1700,* ed. James
Obelkevich, 191–220. Chapel Hill: University of North Carolina
Press.
Crouzet, Denis.
1990.   *Les guerriers de Dieu: La violence au temps des troubles de religion (vers
1525–vers 1610).* 2 vols. Seyssel: Champ Vallon.
Cust, Richard, and Ann Hughes.
1989.   "Introduction: After Revisionism." In *Conflict in Early Stuart Eng-
land: Studies in Religion and Politics, 1603–1642,* ed. Richard Cust
and Ann Hughes, 1–46. London: Longman.
Davies, C.S.L.
1984.   "The Pilgrimage of Grace Reconsidered." In *Popular Protest and the
Social Order in Early Modern England,* 16–38. Cambridge:
Cambridge University Press.

———.
1985.   "Popular Religion and the Pilgrimage of Grace." In *Order and Dis-
order in Early Modern England,* ed. Anthony Fletcher and John
Stevenson, 58–91. Cambridge: Cambridge University Press.
Davies, Joan.
1979.   "Persecution and Protestantism: Toulouse, 1562–1575." *Historical
Journal* 22:31–51.
Davis, Natalie Zemon.
1975.   *Society and Culture in Early Modern France.* Stanford: Stanford
University Press.

———.
1981.   "The Sacred and the Body Social in Sixteenth-Century Lyons."
Past and Present 90:40–70.
Decavele, Johan.
1975.   *De dageraad van de Reformatie in Vlaanderen (1520–1565).*
Verhandelingen, Klasse der Letteren, 76. Brussels: Koninklijke
Academie voor Wetenschappen, Letteren en Schone Kunsten van
België.

———.
1984.   "De mislukking van Oranjes 'democratische' politiek in
Vlaanderen." *Bijdragen en Mededelingen Betreffende de Geschiedenis
der Nederlanden* 99:626–650.
———, ed.
n.d.   *Keizer tussen stropdragers: Karel V, 1500–1558.* Leuven: Davidsfonds.

Dekker, Rudolf.
  1982.   *Holland in beroering: Oproeren in de 17e en 18e eeuw.* Baarn: Amboboeken.

Delumeau, Jean.
  1977.   *Catholicism between Luther and Voltaire: A New View of the Counter-Reformation.* Philadelphia: Westminster Press.

Dembkowski, Harry E.
  1982.   *The Union of Lublin: Polish Federalism in the Golden Age.* Boulder, Colo: Eastern European Monographs.

Denis, Philippe.
  1984.   *Les églises d'étrangers en pays rhénans (1534–1564).* Bibliothèque de la Faculté de Philosophie et Lettres de l'Université de Liège, 242. Paris.

Desan, Suzanne.
  1989.   "Crowds, Community, and Ritual in the Work of E.P. Thompson and Natalie Davis." In *The New Cultural History,* ed. Lynn Hunt, 47–71. Berkeley: University of California Press.

Descimon, Robert, and Christian Jouhaud.
  1985.   "De Paris à Bordeaux: Pour qui court le peuple pendant la Fronde [1652]." In *Mouvrements populaires et conscience sociale, XVIê–XIXê Siècles,* ed. Jean Nicholas, 31–42. Paris: Maloine.

Dickens, A.G.
  1964.   *The English Reformation.* New York: Schocken Books.

Diefendorf, Barbara B.
  1985.   "Prologue to a Massacre: Popular Unrest in Paris, 1557–1572." *American Historical Review* 90:1067–1091.

———.
  1991.   *Beneath the Cross: Catholics and Huguenots in Sixteenth-Century Paris.* New York: Oxford University Press.

Downing, Brian M.
  1992.   *The Military Revolution and Political Change: Origins of Democracy and Autocracy in Early Modern Europe.* Princeton: Princeton University Press.

Duke, Alastair.
  1990.   *Reformation and Revolt in the Low Countries.* London: Hambledon Press.

Duke, Alastair, Gillian Lewis, and Andrew Pettegree, eds.
  1992.   *Calvinism in Europe, 1540–1610: A Collection of Documents.* Manchester: Manchester University Press.

Dunlop, R.
  [1906]
  1934.   "Ireland, from the Plantation of Ultster to the Cromwellian Settlement (1611–59)." In *The Cambridge Modern History,* 4:513–538. Cambridge: Cambridge University Press.

DuPlessis, Robert S.
  1991.   *Lille and the Dutch Revolt: Urban Stability in an Era of Revolution, 1500–1582.* Cambridge Studies in Early Modern History. Cambridge: Cambridge University Press.

Eberhard, Winfried.
1995.   "Reformation and Counter-Reformation in East Central Europe."
In *Handbook of European History, 1400–1600*, ed. Thomas A. Brady,
Heiko A. Oberman, and James D. Tracy. Vol. 2: *Visions, Programs
and Outcomes*, 551–605. Leiden: E.J. Brill.
Elliott, J.H.
1963.   *The Revolt of the Catalans: A Study in the Decline of Spain, 1598–1640*.
Cambridge: Cambridge University Press.

———.
1970.   "Revolts in the Spanish Monarchy." In *Preconditions of Revolution
in Early Modern Europe*, ed. Robert Forster and Jack P. Greene,
109–130. Baltimore: Johns Hopkins University Press.

———.
1991.   "The Spanish Monarchy and the Kingdom of Portugal,
1580–1640." In *Conquest and Coalescence: The Shaping of the State in
Early Modern Europe*, ed. Mark Greengrass, 48–67. London:
Edward Arnold.

———.
1992.   "A Europe of Composite Monarchies." *Past and Present* 137:48–71.
Elliott, John Paul.
1990.   "Protestantization in the Northern Netherlands: A Case Study:
The Classis of Dordrecht, 1572–1640." Ph.D. dissertation, Colum-
bia University.
Elton, G.R.
1980.   "Politics and the Pilgrimage of Grace." In *After the Reformation:
Essays in Honor of J.H. Hexter*, ed. B. Malament, 25–56.
Philadelphia: University of Pennsylvania Press.
Ertman, Thomas.
1997.   *Birth of the Leviathan: Building States and Regimes in Medieval and
Early Modern Europe.* Cambridge: Cambridge University Press.
Evans, R.J.W.
1979.   *The Making of the Habsburg Monarchy, 1500–1700: An Interpretation.*
Oxford: Oxford University Press.
Fedorowicz, J.K., ed.
1982.   *A Republic of Nobles: Studies in Polish History to 1864.* Cambridge:
Cambridge University Press.
Finlay, Robert.
1980.   *Politics in Renaissance Venice.* New Brunswick, N.J.: Rutgers University Press.
Fischer, P. Rainhald, Walter Schläpfer, and Franz Stark.
1964.   *Appenzeller Geschichte.* Vol. 1: *Das ungeteilte Land (Von der Urzeit
bis 1597).* Appenzell: Regierungen der Beiden Halbkantone Appenzell.
Fitzpatrick, B.
1988.   *Seventeenth-Century Ireland: The Wars of Religion.* Totoa, N.J.:
Barnes and Noble Books.

Fletcher, Anthony.
   1983.   *Tudor Rebellions.* 3d ed. London: Longman.
Friedrichs, C.R.
   1978.   "Citizens or Subjects? Urban Conflict in Early Modern Germany."
            In *Social Groups and Religious Ideas in the Sixteenth Century,* ed.
            M.U. Chrisman and O. Grundler, 46–58. Kalamazoo: Medieval
            Institute, Western Michigan University.
Fulbrook, Mary.
   1983.   *Piety and Politics: Religion and the Rise of Absolutism in England,*
            Württemburg and Prussia. Cambridge: Cambridge University
            Press.
Garrisson, Janine.
   1980.   *Les Protestants du Midi, 1559–98.* Toulouse: Privat.
———.
   1985.   *L'Edit de Nantes et sa révocation: Histoire d'une intolerance.* Paris:
            Éditions du Seuil.
Gelder, H.A. Enno van.
   1930.   "Een historise vergelijking: De Nederlandse opstand en de Franse
            godsdiensttoorlogen." *Verslag van de Algemeene Vergadering der*
            leden van het Historisch Genootschap: 21–42.
———.
   1943.   *Revolutionarie Reformatie: De vestiging van de Gereformeerde Kerk in*
            de Nederlandse gewesten, gedurende de eerste jaren van de Opstand
            tegen Filips II, 1575–1585. Patria Reeks, 31. Amsterdam: P.N. Van
            Kampen & Zoon.
Gelderen, Martin van.
   1992.   *The Political Thought of the Dutch Revolt 1555–1590.* Ideas in Context,
            23. Cambridge: Cambridge University Press.
———, ed. and trans.
   1993.   *The Dutch Revolt.* Cambridge Texts in the History of Political
            Thought. Cambridge: Cambridge University Press.
Gentles, Ian.
   1992.   *The New Model Army in England, Ireland, and Scotland, 1645–1653.*
            Oxford: Blackwell.
Geyl, Pieter.
   1958.   *The Revolt of the Netherlands (1555–1609).* 2d ed. London: Ernest
            Benn.
Giugni, Marco G.
   1992.   "The Role of Diffusion Processes in New Social Movements: Some
            Conceptual Clarifications." Working Paper no. 143, July. Center for
            Studies of Social Change, New School for Social Research.
Goldstone, Jack A.
   1991.   *Revolution and Rebellion in the Early Modern World.* Berkeley: Uni-
            versity of California Press.
Gordon, David.
   1992.   "Switzerland." In *The Early Reformation in Europe,* ed. Andrew Pet-
            tegree, 70–93. Cambridge: Cambridge University Press.

Gray, Janet G.
　1983.　"The Origin of the Word Huguenot." *Sixteenth-Century Journal*
　　　　14:349–359.
Greengrass, Mark.
　1983a.　"The Anatomy of a Religious Riot in Toulouse in May 1562." *Journal of Ecclesiastical History* 34:367–391.
　———.
　1983b.　"The Sainte Union in the Provinces: The Case of Toulouse."
　　　　Sixteenth-Century Journal 14:469–496.
　———.
　1987.　*The French Reformation*. Historical Association Studies. Oxford:
　　　　Blackwell.
　———, ed.
　1991.　*Conquest and Coalescence: The Shaping of the State in Early Modern
　　　　Europe*. London: Edward Arnold.
　———.
　1994.　"France." In *The Reformation in National Context*, ed. Bob Scribner
　　　　et al., 47–66. Cambridge: Cambridge University Press.
Grell, Ole Peter.
　1988.　"The City of Malmo and the Danish Reformation." *Archiv für
　　　　Reformationsgeschichte* 79:311–339.
　———.
　1990.　"The Emergence of Two Cities: The Reformation in Malmo and
　　　　Copenhagen." In *Die dänische Reformation vor ihrem internationalen
　　　　Hintergrund*, ed. Leif Grane and Horby Kai, 129–145. Göttingen:
　　　　Vandenhoeck and Ruprecht.
　———.
　1992.　"Scandinavia." In *The Early Reformation in Europe*, ed. Andrew Pettegree, 94–119. Cambridge: Cambridge University Press.
　———.
　1995.　"The Catholic Church and Its Leadership." In *The Scandinavian
　　　　Reformation: From Evangelical Movement to Institutionalization of
　　　　Reform*, ed. Ole Peter Grell, 70–113. Cambridge: Cambridge University Press.
Grell, Ole Peter, Jonathan Israel, and Nicholas Tyacke, eds.
　1991.　*From Persecution to Toleration: The Glorious Revolution in England*.
　　　　Oxford: Clarendon Press.
Greyerz, Kaspar von.
　1980.　*The Late City Reformation in Germany: The Case of Colmar,
　　　　1522–1628*. Wiesbaden: Steiner.
　———, ed.
　1984.　*Religion, Politics and Social Protest: Three Studies on Early Modern
　　　　Germany*. London: George Allen and Unwin.
　———.
　1994.　"Switzerland." In *The Reformation in National Context*, ed. Bob
　　　　Scribner et al., 30–46. Cambridge: Cambridge University Press.

Groenveld, S.
  1967.   *De Prins voor Amsterdam*. Bussum: Fibula-Van Dishoeck.
Guarini, Elena Fasano.
  1995.   "Center and Periphery." *Journal of Modern History* 67:S74–96.
Guggisberg, Hans R.
  1987.   "The Problem of the 'Failure' of the Swiss Reformation: Some
            Preliminary Reflections." In *Politics and Society in Reformation
            Europe: Essays for Sir Geoffrey Elton on His Sixty-fifth Birthday*, ed.
            E.I. Kouri and Tom Scott, 188–209. London: Macmillan.
Haigh, Christopher, ed.
  1987.   *The English Reformation Revised*. Cambridge: Cambridge Univer-
            sity Press.

———.
  1993.   *English Reformations: Religion, Politics, and Society under the Tudors*.
            Oxford: Clarendon Press.
Hakkenberg, Michael.
  1996.   "Religious Conflict in the Early Dutch Republic: The Case of Rot-
            terdam." Unpublished paper.
Haliczer, S. L.
  1981.   *The Comuneros of Castile: The Forging of a Revolution, 1475–1521*.
            Madison: University of Wisconsin Press.
Harding, Robert R.
  1980.   "The Mobilization of Confraternities against the Reformation in
            France." *Sixteenth-Century Journal* 10(2):85–107.

———.
  1981.   "Revolution and Reform in the Holy League: Angers, Rennes,
            Nantes." *Journal of Modern History* 53:379–416.
Harline, Craig E.
  1987.   *Pamphlets, Printing, and Political Culture in the Early Dutch Repub-
            lic*. International Archives of the History of Ideas, 116. Dordrecht:
            Martinus Nijhoff.
Harris, Tim.
  1987.   *London Crowds in the Reign of Charles II: Propaganda and Politics
            from the Restoration until the Exclusion Crisis*. Cambridge:
            Cambridge University Press.
Harris, Tim, Paul Seaward, and Mark Goldie, eds.
  1990.   *The Politics of Religion in Restoration England*. Oxford: Basil Black-
            well.
Hart, Marjolein 't.
  1989.   "Cities and Statemaking in the Dutch Republic, 1580–1680." *Theory
            and Society* 18:663–687.

———.
  1993.   *The Making of a Bourgeois State: War, Politics, and Finance during
            the Dutch Revolt*. Manchester: Manchester University Press.
Head, Randolph C.
  1995.   *Early Modern Democracy in the Grisons: Social Order and Political
            Language in a Swiss Mountain Canton, 1470–1620*. Cambridge Stud-

ies in Early Modern History. Cambridge: Cambridge University Press.

———.

1997.   "Religious Coexistence and Confessional Conflict in the Vier Dörfer: Practices of Toleration in Eastern Switzerland, 1525–1615." In *Beyond the Persecuting Society: Religious Toleration before the Enlightenment,* ed. John Christian Laursen and Cary J. Nederman. Philadelphia: University of Pennsylvania Press.

Heller, Henry.

1986.   *The Conquest of Poverty: The Calvinist Revolt in Sixteenth-Century France.* Leiden: E.J. Brill.

———.

1991.   *Iron and Blood: Civil Wars in Sixteenth-Century France.* Montreal: McGill-Queens University Press.

Henshall, Nicholas.

1992.   *The Myth of Absolutism: Change and Continuity in Early Modern European Monarchy.* London: Longman.

Hibben, C.C.

1983.   *Gouda in Revolt: Particularism and Pacifism in the Revolt of the Netherlands, 1572–1588.* Utrecht: HES.

Hickey, Daniel.

1986.   *The Coming of French Absolutism: The Struggle for Tax Reform in the Province of Dauphiné, 1540–1640.* Toronto: University of Toronto Press.

Holt, Mack P.

1986.   *The Duke of Anjou and the Politique Struggle during the Wars of Religion.* Cambridge: Cambridge University Press.

———.

1993.   "Wine, Community and Reformation in Sixteenth-Century Burgundy." *Past and Present* 138:58–93.

———.

1995.   *The French Wars of Religion, 1562–1629.* New Approaches to European History. Cambridge: Cambridge University Press.

Hsia, R. Po-Chia, ed.

1988a. *The German People and the Reformation.* Ithaca: Cornell University Press.

———.

1988b. "Münster and the Anabaptists." In *The German People and the Reformation,* ed. R. Po-Chia Hsia, 51–69. Ithaca: Cornell University Press.

———.

1989.   *Social Discipline in the Reformation: Central Europe, 1550–1750.* London: Routledge.

Hughes, Ann.

1991.   *The Causes of the English Civil War.* British History in Perspective. Houndsmills (U.K.): Macmillan.

Hughes, Michael.
  1992.   *Early Modern Germany, 1477–1806*. Philadelphia: University of
           Pennsylvania Press.
Hunt, Lynn, ed.
  1989.   *The New Cultural History*. Berkeley: University of California Press.
Isaac, Rhys.
  1982.   *The Transformation of Virginia, 1740–1790*. Chapel Hill: University
           of North Carolina Press.
Israel, Jonathan I.
  1995.   *The Dutch Republic: Its Rise, Greatness, and Fall, 1477–1806*. The
           Oxford History of Early Modern Europe. Oxford: Clarendon
           Press.
Joutard, Philippe, ed.
  1994.   *Les Camisards*. Collection Folio/Histoire. Paris: Editions
           Gallimard/Julliard.
Justice, Steven.
  1994.   *Writing and Rebellion: England in 1381*. Berkeley: University of Cal-
           ifornia Press.
Kamen, Henry.
  1980.   *Spain in the Later Seventeenth Century, 1665–1700*. London:
           Longman.

——.
  1994.   "Spain." In *The Reformation in National Context*, ed. Bob Scribner
           et al., 202–214. Cambridge: Cambridge University Press.
Kaplan, Benjamin J.
  1989.   "Calvinists and Libertines: The Reformation in Utrecht,
           1578–1618." Ph.D. dissertation, Harvard University.

——.
  1991.   "Dutch Particularism and the Calvinst Quest for 'Holy
           Uniformity.'" *Archiv für Reformationsgeschichte* 82:239–255.

——.
  1995.   *Calvinists and Libertines: Confession and Community in Utrecht,
           1578–1620*. Oxford: Clarendon Press.
Karant-Nunn, S.C.
  1987.   *Zwickau in Transition, 1500–1547: The Reformation as an Agent of
           Change*. Columbus: Ohio State University Press.
Kernkamp, G.W.
  1943.   *Prins Willem II*. Amsterdam: P.N. Van Kampen & Zoon.
Kingdon, Robert M.
  1974.   "Was the Protestant Reformation a Revolution? The Case of
           Geneva." In *Transition and Revolution: Problems and Issues of Euro-
           pean Renaissance and Reformation History*, ed. Robert M. Kingdon,
           53–107. Minneapolis: Burgess.
Kirby, David.
  1990.   *Northern Europe in the Early Modern Period: The Baltic World,
           1492–1772*. London: Longman.

Knecht, R.J.
   1989.   *The French Wars of Religion, 1559–1598.* Seminar Studies in History.
            London: Longman.
Koenigsberger, H.G.
   1971a.   *The Habsburgs and Europe, 1516–1660.* Ithaca: Cornell University
            Press.
———.
   1971b.   "The Revolt of Palermo in 1647." In *Estates and Revolutions: Essays
            in Early Modern European History,* 253–277. Ithaca: Cornell Univer-
            sity Press.
———.
   1986.   "'Dominiium regale' or 'Dominium politicum et regale': Monar-
            chies and Parliaments in Early Modern Europe." In *Politicians and
            Virtuosi: Essays in Early Modern History,* 1–25. London: Hambledon
            Press.
———.
   1989.   "Composite States, Representative Institutions and the American
            Revolution." *Historical Research* 62:135–153.
Kooi, Christine J.
   1993.   "The Reformed Community of Leiden, 1572–1620." Ph.D. disserta-
            tion, Yale University.
Kossman, E.H., and A.F. Mellink, eds.
   1974.   *Texts Concerning the Revolt of the Netherlands.* Cambridge:
            Cambridge University Press.
Kötting, Helmut.
   1983.   *Die Ormée (1651–1653): Gesteiterde Kräfte und Personenverbindungen
            der Bordelaiser Fronde.* Münster: Aschendorff.
Kouri, E.I.
   1995.   "The Early Reformation in Sweden and Finland, c. 1520–1560." In
            *The Scandinavian Reformation: From Evangelical Movement to Insti-
            tutionalization of Reform,* ed. Ole Peter Grell, 42–69. Cambridge:
            Cambridge University Press.
Kouri, E.I., and Tom Scott.
   1987.   *Politics and Society in Reformation Europe: Essays for Sir Geoffrey
            Elton on His Sixty-fifth Birthday.* London: Macmillan.
Lausten, Martin Schwarz.
   1995.   "The Early Reformation in Denmark and Norway, 1520–1559." In
            *The Scandinavian Reformation: From Evangelical Movement to Insti-
            tutionalization of Reform,* ed. Ole Peter Grell, 12–41. Cambridge:
            Cambridge University Press.
Le Barre, Pasquier de.
   1989.   *The Time of Troubles in the Low Countries: The Chronicles and Mem-
            oirs of Pasquier de Le Barre of Tournai, 1559–1567.* Ed. and trans. Char-
            lie R. Steen. Renaissance and Baroque, Studies and Texts, vol. 1.
            New York: Peter Lang.
Le Roy Ladurie, E.
   1979.   *Carnival in Romans.* Trans. Mary Feency. New York: G. Brazillier.

Lecler, Joseph.
    1960.   *Toleration and the Reformation.* 2 vols. New York: Association
          Press.
Levi, Giovanni.
    1988.   *Inheriting Power: The Story of an Exorcist.* Trans. Lydia G.
          Cochrane. Chicago: University of Chicago Press.
Limm, Peter.
    1989.   *The Dutch Revolt 1559–1648.* Seminar Studies in History. London:
          Longman.
Lottes, Günther.
    1984.   "Popular Culture and the Early Modern State in 16th-Century
          Germany." In *Understanding Popular Culture: Europe from the Mid-*
          dle Ages to the 19th Century, ed. Steven L. Kaplan, 142–188. Berlin:
          Mouton.
Luck, J. Murray.
    1985.   *A History of Switzerland.* Palo Alto, Calif.: Society for the Promo-
          tion of Science and Scholarship.
Lynch, John.
    1991.   *Spain, 1516–1598: From Nation-State to World Empire.* A History of
          Spain. Oxford: Blackwell.
Machiavelli, Niccolò.
    [1514]   *The Prince.* Trans. and Intro. George Bull. Harmondsworth:
    1961.   Penguin Books.
Macinnes, Allan J.
    1990.   "The Scottish Constitution, 1638–1651: The Rise and Fall of
          Oligarchic Centralism." In *The Scottish National Covenant in Its*
          British Context, 1638–1651, ed. J.S. Morrill, 106–133. Edinburgh:
          Edinburgh University Press.
McLynn, Frank.
    1985.   *The Jacobites.* London: Routledge and Kegan Paul.
Major, J. Russell.
    1966.   "Henry VI and Guyenne: A Study Concerning the Origins of
          Royal Absolutism." *French Historical Studies* 4:363–383.
Mandrou, Robert.
    1977.   *Introduction to Early Modern France, 1500–1640.* New York: Harper
          and Row.
Manning, Brian.
    1991.   *The English People and the English Revolution, 1640–1649.* 2d ed. Lon-
          don: Bookmarks.
    1992.   *1649: The Crisis of the English Revolution.* London: Bookmarks.
Marnef, G.
    1986.   "Het Protestantisme te Brussel onder de 'Calvinistische Republiek'
          ca. 1577–1585." In *Staat en religie in de 15e en 16e eeuw: Handelingen*
          van het colloquium te Brussel van 9 tot 12 oktober 1984, ed. W.P. Block-
          mans and H. van Nuffel, 231–299. Brussels: H. Van Nuffel.

———.
1987. *Het Calvinistisch bewind te Mechelen, 1580–1585.* Kortrijk-Heule: UGA.

———.
1994. "The Changing Face of Calvinism in Antwerp, 1555–1585." In *Calvinism in Europe, 1540–1620,* ed. Andrew Pettegree, Alastair Duke, and Gillian Lewis, 143–159. Cambridge: Cambridge University Press.

———.
1996. *Antwerp in the Age of Reformation: Underground Protestantism in a Commercial Metropolis, 1550–1577.* Baltimore: Johns Hopkins University Press.

Merriman, Roger Bigelow.
[1938] *Six Contemporaneous Revolutions.* Hamden, Conn.: Archon Books.
1963.

Metcalf, Michael F.
1995. "Settlements: Scandinavia." In *Handbook of European History, 1400–1600,* ed. Thomas A. Brady, Heiko A. Oberman, and James D. Tracy. Vol. 2: *Visions, Programs and Outcomes,* 523–550. Leiden: E.J. Brill.

Meyer, J.C. Pugh.
1977. "Reformation in La Rochelle: Religious Change, Social Stability and Political Crisis, 1500–1568." Ph.D. dissertation, University of Iowa.

———.
1984. "La Rochelle and the Failure of the French Reformation." *Sixteenth-Century Journal* 15:169–183.

Moeller, Bernd.
1972. *Imperial Cities and the Reformation: Three Essays.* Ed. H.C.E. Midelfort and M.U. Edwards. Philadelphia: Fortress Press.

Molinier, Alain.
1984. "Aux originies de la réformation cévenole." *Annales: Economies, Sociétés, Civilisations* 39:240–264.

Monter, E. William.
1967. *Calvin's Geneva.* New York: John Wiley & Sons.

Morgan, Edmund S.
1988. *Inventing the People: The Rise of Popular Sovereignty in England and America.* New York: W.W. Norton.

Mörke, O.
1983. *Rat und Bürger in der Reformation: Sozialen Gruppen und kirchlicher Wandel in den welfischen Hansestädten Lüneburg, Braunschweig und Göttingen.* Hildesheim: August Lax.

———.
1991. *Die Ruhe im Sturm: Die katholische Landstadt Mindelheim unter der Herrschaft der Frundsberg im Zeitalter der Reformation.* Augsburg: Schwäbische Forschungsgemeinschaft.

——.

1995. "The Political Culture of Germany and the Dutch Republic: Similar Roots and Different Results." In *A Miracle Mirrored: The Dutch Republic in European Perspective*, ed. Karel Davids and Jan Lucassen, 135–172. Cambridge: Cambridge University Press.

Morrill, John.

1984. "The Religious Context of the English Civil War." *Transactions of the Royal Historical Society* 34:155–178.

——, ed.

1990. *The Scottish National Covenant in Its British Context, 1638–1651*. Edinburgh: Edinburgh University Press.

Morrill, J.S., and J.D. Walter.

1985. "Order and Disorder in the English Revolution." In *Order and Disorder in Early Modern England*, ed. A.J. Fletcher and J. Stevenson, 137–165. Cambridge: Cambridge University Press.

Muir, Edward.

1993. *Mad Blood Stirring: Vendetta and Factions in Friuli during the Renaissance*. Baltimore: Johns Hopkins University Press.

Muir, Edward, and Guido Ruggiero, eds.

1991. *Microhistory and the Lost Peoples of Europe*. Trans. Eren Branch. Baltimore: Johns Hopkins University Press.

Munck, Thomas.

1990. *Seventeenth-Century Europe: State, Conflict and the Social Order in Europe, 1598–1700*. Macmillan History of Europe. London: Macmillan.

Naphy, William G.

1994. *Calvin and the Consolidation of the Genevan Reformation*. Manchester: Manchester University Press.

Nicholls, David.

1980. "Social Change and Early Protestantism in France: Normandy, 1520–62." *European Studies Review* 10:279–308.

——.

1983. "The Nature of Popular Heresy in France, 1520–1542." *Historical Journal* 26:261–275.

——.

1984a. "Religion and Peasant Movements in Normandy during the French Religious Wars." In *Religion and Rural Revolt: Papers Presented to the Fourth Interdisciplinary Workshop on Peasant Studies, University of British Columbia, 1982*, ed. Janos M. Bak and Gerhard Benecke, 104–122. Manchester: University of Manchester Press.

——.

1984b. "The Social History of the French Reformation: Ideology, Confession and Culture." *Social History* 9:25–43.

——.

1992. "France." In *The Early Reformation in Europe*, ed. Andrew Pettegree, 120–141. Cambridge: Cambridge University Press.

Nicolas, Jean, ed.

1985.   *Mouvements populaires et conscience sociale, XVIe–XIXe siècles: Actes du Colloque de Paris, 24–26 mai 1984.* Paris: Maloine.

Nierop, Henk F.K. van.

1978.   *Beeldenstorm en burgerlijk verzet in Amsterdam 1566–1567.* Nijmegen: SUN.

———.

1991.   "A Beggar's Banquet: The Compromise of the Nobility and the Politics of Inversion." *European History Quarterly* 21:419–443.

———.

1995.   "Similar Problems, Different Outcomes: The Revolt of the Netherlands and the Wars of Religion in France." In *A Miracle Mirrored: The Dutch Republic in European Perspective,* ed. Karel Davids and Jan Lucassen, 26–56. Cambridge: Cambridge University Press.

Nijenhuis, W.

1979.   "Variants within Dutch Calvinism in the Sixteenth Century." *Low Countries History Yearbook* 12:48–64.

Nischan, Bodo.

1994.   "Confessionalism and Absolutism: The Case of Brandenburg." In *Calvinism in Europe, 1540–1620,* ed. Andrew Pettegree, Alastair Duke, and Gillian Lewis, 181–204. Cambridge: Cambridge University Press.

Ozment, Steven E.

1975.   *The Reformation in the Cities: The Appeal of Protestantism to Sixteenth-Century Germany and Switzerland.* New Haven: Yale University Press.

Parker, G., and L.M. Smith, eds.

1978.   *The General Crisis of the Seventeenth Century.* London

Parker, Geoffrey.

1984.   *The Thirty Years' War.* London: Routledge.

———.

1985.   *The Dutch Revolt.* Rev. ed. Harmondsworth: Penguin.

———.

1988.   *The Military Revolution: Military Innovation and the Rise of the West, 1500–1800.* Cambridge: Cambridge University Press.

———.

1992.   "Success and Failure during the First Century of Reformation." *Past and Present* 136:43–82.

Pettegree, A.

1986.   *Foreign Protestant Communities in Sixteenth-Century London.* Oxford.

———, ed.

1992a.   *The Early Reformation in Europe.* Cambridge: Cambridge University Press.

——.

1992b.   *Emden and the Dutch Revolt: Exile and the Development of Reformed Protestantism.* Oxford: Clarendon Press.

——.

1994.   "Coming to Terms with Victory: The Upbuilding of a Calvinist Church in Holland, 1572–1590." In *Calvinism in Europe, 1540–1620,* ed. Alastair Duke, Gillian Lewis, and Andrew Pettegree, 160–180. Cambridge: Cambridge University Press.

Peyer, Hans Conrad.

1978.   *Verfassungsgeschichte der alten Schweiz.* Zürich: Schultheis Polygraphischer Verlag.

Poelhekke, J.J.

1973.   *Geen blijder maer in tachtigh jaer: Verspreide studiën over de Crisisperiode 1648–1651.* Zutphen: De Walburg Pers.

Polisensky, J.V.

1971.   *The Thirty Years' War.* Berkeley: University of California Press.

Prak, Maarten.

1991.   "Citizen Radicalism and Democracy in the Dutch Republic: The Patriot Movement of the 1780s." *Theory and Society* 20:73–102.

Price, J. L.

1994.   *Holland and the Dutch Republic in the Seventeenth Century: The Politics of Particularism.* Oxford: Clarendon Press.

Rabb, T.K.

1975.   *The Struggle for Stability in Early Modern Europe.* Oxford: Oxford University Press.

Ranum, Orest.

1993.   *The Fronde: A French Revolution, 1648–1652.* Revolutions in the Modern World. New York: W.W. Norton.

Rebel, Hermann.

1983.   *Peasant Classes: The Bureaucratization of Property and Family Relations under Early Habsburg Absolutism, 1511–1636.* Princeton: Princeton University Press.

Reddy, William M.

1977.   "The Textile Trade and the Language of the Crowd at Rouen, 1751–1871." *Past and Present* 74:62–89.

Roberts, Michael.

1968.   *The Early Vasas: A History of Sweden, 1523–1611.* Cambridge: Cambridge University Press.

Robisheaux, Thomas.

1989.   *Rural Society and the Search for Order in Early Modern Germany.* Cambridge: Cambridge University Press.

Rokkan, Stein.

1975.   "Dimensions of State Formation and Nation-Building: A Possible Paradigm for Research on Variations within Europe." In *The Formation of National States in Western Europe,* ed. Charles Tilly, 562–600. Princeton: Princeton University Press.

Roorda, D.J.
1978.   *Partij en factie: De oproeren van 1672 in de steden van Holland en Zee-land, een krachmeting tussen partijen en factie.* Groningen: Wolters-Noordhoff.
Roper, Lyndal.
1987.   "'The Common Man,' 'the Common Good,' 'Common Women':
Gender and Meaning in the German Reformation Commune."
Social History 12:1–21.
Rosenberg, David Lee.
1978.   "Social Experience and Religious Choice: A Case Study: The
Protestant Weavers and Woolcombers of Amiens in the Sixteenth
Century." Ph.D. dissertation, Yale University.
Rowen, Herbert H., ed.
1972.   *The Low Countries in Early Modern Times: A Documentary History.*
Documentary History of Western Civilization. New York: Harper
and Row.
———.
1988.   *The Princes of Orange: The Stadholders in the Dutch Republic.* Cam-bridge Studies in Early Modern History. Cambridge: Cambridge
University Press.
Rublack, Hans-Christoph.
1987.   "Is There a 'New History' of the Urban Reformation?" In *Politics
and Society in Reformation Europe: Essays for Sir Geoffrey Elton on His
Sixty-fifth Birthday,* ed. E.I. Kouri and Tom Scott, 121–141.
London: Macmillan.
Rudé, George.
1964.   *The Crowd in History: A Survey of Popular Disturbances in France
and England, 1730–1848.* New York: Wiley.
———.
1980.   *Ideology and Popular Protest.* New York: Pantheon.
Russell, Conrad.
1987.   "The British Problem and the English Civil War." *History*
72:395–415.
———.
1988.   "The British Background to the Irish Rebellion of 1641." *Historical
Research* 61:166–182.
———.
1990.   *The Causes of the English Civil War.* The Ford Lectures, Oxford,
1987–1988. Oxford: Clarendon Press.
———.
1991.   *The Fall of the British Monarchies, 1637–42.* Oxford: Clarendon
Press.
Sabean, David.
1976.   "The Communal Basis of Pre-1800 Peasant Uprisings in Western
Europe." *Comparative Politics* 8:355–364.

Salmon, J.H.
  1975. *Society in Crisis: France in the Sixteenth Century.* New York: St. Martin's.

  ———.
  1979. "Peasant Revolt in Vivarais, 1575–1580." *French Historical Studies* 11:1–28.

Scarisbrick, J.J.
  1984. *The Reformation and the English People.* Oxford: Basil Blackwell.

Schepper, Hugo de.
  1980. "De burgerlijke Overheden en hun permanente kaders, 1480–1579." In *Algemene Geschiedenis der Nederlanden,* vol. 5, ed. D.P. Blok et al., 312–350. Haarlem: Fibula-Van Dishoeck.

  ———.
  1987. *Belgium Nostrum, 1500–1650: Over de integratie en desintgratie van het Nederland.* Antwerp: Orde Van de Prins.

Schilling, Heinz.
  1983. "The Reformation in the Hanseatic Cities." *Sixteenth-Century Journal* 14:443–456.

  ———.
  1988. "Between Territorial State and Urban Liberty: Lutheranism and Calvinism in the County of Lippe." In *The German People and the Reformation,* ed. R. Po-Chia Hsia, 263–283. Ithaca: Cornell University Press.

  ———.
  1991. *Civic Calvinism in Northwestern Germany and the Netherlands: Sixteenth to Nineteenth Centuries.* Sixteenth-Century Essays and Studies, vol. 17. Kirkville, Mo.: Sixteenth-Century Journal.

  ———.
  1992. "The Second Reformation: Problems and Issues." In *Religion, Political Culture, and the Emergence of Early Modern Society,* 247–301. Leiden: E.J. Brill.

Schulze, Winfried, ed.
  1983. *Aufstände, Revolten, Prozesse: Beiträge zu bäuerlichen Widerstandsbewegungen im frühneuzeitlichen Europa.* Stuttgart: Klett-Cotta.

  ———.
  1984. "Peasant Resistance in Sixteenth- and Seventeenth-Century Germany in a European Context." In *Religion, Politics and Social Protest,* ed. Kaspar von Greyerz, 161–198. London: George Allen and Unwin.

Scott, James C.
  1987. "Resistance without Protest and without Organization: Peasant Opposition to the Islamic Zakat and the Christian Tithe." *Comparative Studies in Society and History* 29:417–452.

  ———.
  1990. *Domination and the Arts of Resistance: Hidden Transcripts.* New Haven: Yale University Press.

Scott, Tom.
1979. "The Peasants' War: A Historiographical Review." *Historical Journal* 22:693–720, 953–974.

———.
1985. "Peasant Revolts in Early Modern Germany." *Historical Journal* 28:455–468.

———.
1986. *Freiburg and the Breisgau: Town-Country Relations in the Age of Reformation and Peasants' War*. Oxford: Clarendon Press.

———.
1989. *Thomas Müntzer: Theology and Revolution in the German Reformation*. New York: St. Martin's Press.

———.
1991. "The Common People in the German Reformation." *Historical Journal* 34:183–192.

Scott, Tom, and Bob Scribner, trans. and eds.
1991. *The German Peasants' War: A History in Documents*. Atlantic Highlands, N.J.: Humanities Press.

Scribner, Bob.
1994. "A Comparative Overview." In *The Reformation in National Context,* ed. Bob Scribner et al., 215–227. Cambridge: Cambridge University Press.

Scribner, R. W.
1986. *The German Reformation*. London: Macmillan.

———.
1987. *Popular Culture and Popular Movements in Reformation Germany*. London: Hambledon Press.

———.
1990. "Paradigms of Urban Reform: Gemeindereformation or Erastian Reformation?" In *Die dänische Reformation vor ihrem internationalen Hintergrund,* ed. Leif Grane and Kai Horby, 111–128. Göttingen: Vandenhoeck and Ruprecht.

Scribner, R. W., and Gerhard Benecke, eds.
1979. *The German Peasant War of 1525: New Viewpoints*. London: George Allen and Unwin.

Segui, Émile.
1933. *Une petite place protestant pendant les guerres de religion, 1562–1629: Faugères en Biterrois*. Nîmes: Larguier.

Spaans, Joke.
1989. *Haarlem na de Reformatie: Stedelijke cultuur en kerelijk leven, 1577–1620*. Hollandse Historische Reeks 11. 's-Gravenhage: Stichting Hollandse Historische Reeks.

Steen, Charlie R.
1985. *A Chronicle of Conflict: Tournai, 1559–1567*. Utrecht: HES.

Stevenson, David.
1973. *The Scottish Revolution 1637–1644: The Triumph of the Covenanters*. Newton Abbot: David and Charles.

———.
   1977.   *Revolution and Counter-Revolution in Scotland, 1644–1651.* London:
            Royal Historical Society.
Strauss, Gerald.
   1966.   *Nuremberg in the Sixteenth Century.* New York,
Strayer, Joseph R.
   1970.   *On the Medieval Origins of the Modern State.* Princeton: Princeton
            University Press.
Suter, Andreas.
   1995.   "Regionale politische Kulturen von Portest und Widerstand im
            Spätmittelalter und in der Frühen Neuzeit: Die schweizerische
            Eidgenossenschaft als Beispiel." *Geschichte und Gesellschaft*
            21:161–194.

———.
   1997.   *Der schweizerische Bauernkrieg von 1653: Politische Sozialgeschichte—
            Sozialgeschichte eines politischen Ereignisses.* Tübingen: Biblioteca
            Academica Verlag.
Sutherland, N. M.
   1980.   *The Huguenot Struggle for Recognition.* New Haven: Yale Univer-
            sity Press.
Tarrow, Sidney.
   1989.   *Struggle, Politics, and Reform: Collective action, Social Movements,
            and Cycles of Protest.* Western Societies Program, Occasional
            Papers, no. 21. Ithaca: Center for International Studies.

———.
   1994.   *Power in Movement: Social Movements, Collective Action and Politics.*
            Cambridge Studies in Comparative Politics. Cambridge:
            Cambridge University Press.
Te Brake, Wayne.
   1992.   "Provincial Histories and National Revolution in the Dutch
            Republic." In *The Dutch Republic in the Eighteenth Century: Decline,
            Enlightenment and Revolution,* ed. Margaret C. Jacob and Wijnand
            Mijnhardt, 60–90. Ithaca: Cornell University Press.
Te Brake, William H.
   1993.   *A Plague of Insurrection: Popular Politics and Peasant Revolt in Flan-
            ders, 1323–1328.* Middle Ages Series. Philadelphia: University of
            Pennsylvania Press.
Temple, William.
   1972.   *Observations upon the United Provinces of the Netherlands.* Ed.
            George Clark. Oxford: Clarendon Press.
Thompson, E. P.
   1971.   "The Moral Economy of the English Crowd in the Eighteenth
            Century." *Past and Present* 50:76–136.
Tilly, Charles.
   1978.   *From Mobilization to Revolution.* Reading, Mass.: Addison-Wesley.

———.
1981.   *As Sociology Meets History*. Studies in Social Discontinuity. New York: Academic Press.

———.
1985.   "Retrieving European Lives." In *Reliving the Past: The Worlds of Social History*, ed. Olivier Zunz, 11–52. Chapel Hill: University of North Carolina Press.

———.
1986.   *The Contentious French*. Cambridge, Mass.: Belknap Press.

———.
1990.   *Coercion, Capital, and European States, A.D. 990–1990*. Studies in Social Discontinuity. Oxford: Blackwell.

———.
1993.   *European Revolutions, 1492–1992*. The Making of Europe. Oxford: Blackwell.

———.
1995.   *Popular Contention in Great Britain, 1758–1834*. Cambridge, Mass.: Harvard University Press.

Tilly, Charles, and Wim Blockmans, eds.
1994.   *Cities and the Rise of States in Europe, A.D. 1000–1800*. Boulder: Westview.

Tracy, James D.
1985.   *A Financial Revolution in the Habsburg Netherlands: Renten en Renteniers in the County of Holland, 1515–1565*. Berkeley: University of California Press.

———.
1990.   *Holland under Habsburg Rule, 1506–1566: The Formation of a Body Politic*. Berkeley: University of California Press.

Trocmé, Etienne.
1976.   "Reflexions sur le separatisme rochelais, 1568–1628." *Bulletin de la Société de l'Histoire du Protestantisme Française* 122:203–210.

Trossbach, Werner.
1987.   *Soziale Bewegung und politische Erfahrung: Bäuerlicher Protest in hessischen Territorien 1648–1806*. Weingarten: Drumlin Verlag.

Underdown, David.
1971.   *Pride's Purge: Politics in the Puritan Revolution*. Oxford: Clarendon Press.

———.
1985.   *Revel, Riot and Rebellion: Popular Politics and Culture in England, 1603–1660*. Oxford: Oxford University Press.

———.
1996.   *A Freeborn People: Politics and the Nation in Seventeenth-Century England*. Oxford: Clarendon Press.

Urban, William L.
1991.   *Dithmarschen: A Medieval Peasant Republic*. Medieval Studies, vol. 7. Lewiston, N.Y.: Edwin Mellen Press.

Vann, James A.
   1986.   "New Directions for Study of the Old Reich." *Journal of Modern History* 58:S3–22.
Villari, Rosario.
   1993.   *The Revolt of Naples.* Trans. James Newell. Cambridge: Polity Press.
Vogler, Günter.
   1984.   "Religion, Confession and Peasant Resistance in the German Territories in the Sixteenth to Eighteenth Centuries." In *Religion and Rural Revolt: Papers Presented to the Fourth Interdisciplinary Workshop on Peasant Studies, University of British Columbia, 1982,* ed. Janos M. Bak and Gerhard Benecke, 173–187. Manchester: Manchester University Press.
Vries, Jan de.
   1984.   *European Urbanization 1500–1800.* Cambridge, Mass.: Harvard University Press.
Walker, Mack.
   1971.   *German Home Towns: Community, State and General Estate 1648–1871.* Ithaca: Cornell University Press.
Wallerstein, Immanuel.
   1974.   *The Modern World-System.* Vol. 1. *Capitalist Agriculture and the Origins of the European World-Economy in the Sixteenth Century.* Studies in Social Discontinuity. New York: Academic Press.
———.
   1980.   *The Modern World-System.* Vol. 2. *Mercantilism and the Consolidation of the European World-Economy, 1600–1750.* Studies in Social Discontinuity. New York: Academic Press.
Wandel, Lee Palmer.
   1989.   "The Reform of Images: New Visualizations of the Christian Community at Zürich." *Archiv für Reformationsgeschichte* 80:105–124.
———.
   1992.   "Strubelhans and the Singing Monks." In *Krisenbewusstsein und Krisenbewältigung in der frühen Neuzeit: Festschrift für Hans-Christolph Rublack,* ed. Monika Hagenmaier and Sabine Holtz, 307–315. Frankfurt am Main: Peter Lang.
———.
   1995.   *Voracious Idols and Violent Hands: Iconoclasm in Reformation Zurich, Strasbourg, and Basel.* Cambridge: Cambridge University Press.
Weinstein, Donald.
   1970.   *Savonarola and Florence: Prophecy and Patriotism in the Renaissance.* Princeton: Princeton University Press.
Westrich, S. A.
   1972.   *The Ormée of Bordeaux.* Baltimore: Johns Hopkins University Press.
Whiting, Robert.
   1989.   *The Blind Devotion of the People: Popular Religion and the English Reformation.* Cambridge: Cambridge University Press.

Wick, Markus René.
 1982. "Der 'Glarnerhandel': Strukturgeschichte und konflictsoziologis-
        che Hypothesen zum Glarner Konfessionsgegensatz." Ph.D.
        dissertation, Universität Bern. *Jahrbuch des Historischen Vereins
        Glarus* 69:49–240.
Woltjer, J. J.
 1962. *Friesland in hervormingstijd.* Leiden: Universitaire Pers.

————.
 1979. "De Vredemakers." In *De Unie van Utrecht: Wording en werking
        van een verbond en een verbondsacte,* ed. S. Groenveld and H. L. Ph.
        Leeuwenberg, 56–87. The Hague: Martinus Nijhoff.

————.
 1986. "De religieuse situatie in de eerste jaren van de Republiek." *In Ket-
        ters en papen onder Filips II.* Utrecht: Rijksmuseum het Catherijne-
        Convent.

————.
 1994. "Geweld tijdens de godsdienstoorlogen in Frankrijk en in de Ned-
        erlanden: Een vergelijking." *Trajecta. Tijdschrift voor de geschiedenis
        van het katholiek leven in de Nederlanden* 3:281–296.
Wuthnow, Robert.
 1989. *Communities of Discourse: Ideology and Social Structure in the Refor-
        mation, the Enlightenment, and European Socialism.* Cambridge,
        Mass.: Harvard University Press.
Zagorin, Perez.
 1982. *Rebels and Rulers 1500–1660: Society, States and Early Modern Revolu-
        tion.* Cambridge: Cambridge University Press.

Index

215

Designer: Barbara Jellow
Compositor: BookMatters
Text: 10/13 Galliard
Printer: Haddon Craftsmen
Binder: Haddon Craftsmen